연세국학 총서 107

1885 2015 연세대학교130주년 YONSEI 130th ANNIVERSARY

언더우드
내한 관련 자료집
1859-1885

박형우 편역

연세대학교 대학출판문화원

언더우드 내한 관련 자료집(1859~1885)

편 역 박형우
펴낸곳 연세대학교 대학출판문화원
주 소 서울시 서대문구 연세로 50
전 화 02) 2123-3380~2
팩 스 02) 2123-8673
e-mail: ysup@yonsei.ac.kr
http://press.yonsei.ac.kr
등 록 1955년 10월 13일 제9-60호
인 쇄 (주)동국문화

2015년 10월 30일 1판 1쇄
ISBN 978-89-6850-127-2 (93010)

값 30,000원

자료 호러스 G. 언더우드 사진. 미국 장로회 역사관 소장.

차 례

1-3. 조부모의 자녀들

2. 언더우드의 부모

2-1. 아버지 - 존 언더우드

2-2. 어머니 - 엘리자베스 그랜트 메어

2-3. 계모 - 캐롤라인 넌

3. 언더우드의 형제자매

3-1. 한나 E. 언더우드

3-2. 존 T. 언더우드

3-3. 프레데릭 W. 언더우드

4. 뉴브런즈윅신학교

5. 졸업 후 교육

제3부 선교사 임명과 내한

1. 선교사 지원

1-1. 선교사 지원 편지

1-2. 언더우드의 선교사 임명과 관련된 각종 추천서

2-2. 선교지에 도착한 언더우드

제4부 기타 자료

1. 화란개혁교회와 한국 선교

2. 미국 장로회 역사관 소장 자료

3. 기타

Contents

18281015 B. Critchett, *The Post-Office London Directory for 1829.* 30th Ed., London, p. 432. • 16

19130000 Howard J. Banker, *The Underwood Families of America. In Two Volumes,* Volume 2, 1913, p. 625. • 17

1-2. Grandmother - Mary Easton Waugh

17921015 *England & Wales, Non-Conformist and Non-Parochial Registers, 1567~1970,* (Birth, Mary Easton Waugh, Oct. 15th, 1792). • 18

17921115 *England & Wales, Non-Conformist and Non-Parochial Registers, 1567~1970,* (Baptism, Mary Easton Waugh, Nov. 15th, 1792). • 19

18510330 *1851 England Census,* (Mary Easton Underwood, Mar. 30th, 1851). • 21

18660000 *England & Wales, FreeBMD Death Index, 1837~1915,* (Mary E. Underwood, Oct-Nov-Dec 1866). • 22

1-3. Children of Grandparents

18180215 *England & Wales, Non-Conformist and Non-Parochial Registers, 1567~1970,* (Baptism, Mary Neill Underwood, Feb. 15th, 1818). • 23

18190404 *England & Wales, Non-Conformist and Non-Parochial Registers, 1567~1970,* (Baptism, Thomas Underwood, Apr. 4th, 1819). • 25

18470819 *London, England, Marriages and Banns, 1754~1921,* (Marriage, Thomas Underwood, Aug. 19th, 1847). • 27

18211014 *England & Wales, Non-Conformist and Non-Parochial Registers, 1567~1970,* (Baptism, Margaret Coventry Underwood, Oct. 14th, 1821). • 28

18231017 *England & Wales, Non-Conformist and Non-Parochial Registers, 1567~1970,* (Baptism, George Underwood, Oct. 17th, 1823). • 29

18250718 *England & Wales, Non-Conformist and Non-Parochial Registers, 1567~1970,* (Baptism, Jean Underwood, July 18th, 1825). • 30

18270703 *England & Wales, Non-Conformist and Non-Parochial Registers, 1567~1970,* (Baptism, John Underwood, July 3rd, 1827). • 31

18290718 *England & Wales, Non-Conformist and Non-Parochial Registers, 1567~1970,* (Baptism, Catherine Coventry Underwood, July 18th, 1829). • 32

2. Parents

2-1. Father - John Underwood

2-2. Mother - Elizabeth Grant Mair

2-3. Step-mother - Caroline Nunn

18510330 *1851 England Census,* (Caroline Nunn, Mar. 30th, 1851). • 72

18730303 *New York, Passenger Lists, 1820~1957,* (Caroline Underwood, Mar. 3rd, 1873). • 73

18740320 *New Jersey, Deaths and Burials Index, 1798~1971,* (Caroline Underwood, Mar. 20th, 1874). • 75

3. Brothers & Sisters

3-1. Hannah E. Underwood

18560000 *England & Wales, FreeBMD Birth Index, 1837~1915,* (Hannah E. Underwood, Apr-May-Jun 1856). • 77

18710402 *1871 England Census,* (Hannah Elizabeth Underwood, Apr. 2nd, 1871). • 79

18750523 *New York, Passenger Lists, 1820~1957.* (H. Underwood, May 23rd, 1875). • 80

18981012 *New York, Marriage Index, 1866~1937.* (Hannah Underwood, Oct. 12th, 1898). • 81

19100415 *1910 United States Federal Census,* (Clarence Stephens, Apr. 15th, 1910). • 83

19300429 *1930 United States Federal Census,* (Clarence Stephens, Apr. 29th, 1930). • 85

19311206 Clarence Stephens, Obituary, *The New York Times,* (Clarence Stephens, Dec 7th, 1931). • 86

3-2. John T. Underwood

18570000 *England & Wales, FreeBMD Birth Index, 1837~1915,* (John T. Underwood, Apr-May-Jun 1857). • 88

18820000 *Trow's New York City Directory. Vol. XCVI. For the Year Ending May 1, 1883,* p. 1658. • 89

18840000 *Trow's New York City Directory. Vol. XCVIII. For the Year Ending May 1, 1885,* p. 1781. • 90

2 PART Educational Backgrounds

4. New Brunswick Theological Seminary

5. Postgraduate Study

2-2. Underwood at the Field

PART 4 Miscellaneous Materials

1. Dutch Reformed Church and Korea Mission

2. Presbyterian Historical Society, Philadelphia, Pennsylvania

3. Etc

• 간행사

2015년인 올해는 언더우드 선교사가 우리나라에 온 지 130주년이 되는 해이다. 이 땅에 근대교육의 씨를 뿌리고 잘 가꾸고 키워 오늘의 연세대학교가 되도록 한 열정이 이미 130년 전에 있었던 것이다.

연세대학교가 근대를 거쳐 현대에 이르기까지 우리 민족의 삶과 함께 걸어온 최고의 교육기관이 될 수 있었던 것은 언더우드 선교사의 기독교 정신과 우리의 국학정신이 한데 어울러졌기에 가능했던 일이다.

언더우드는 기독교 복음 전파와 성경 번역 등의 선교활동은 물론이고 교육 · 의료 · 출판 등의 한국 근대화에까지 깊은 영향을 끼쳤다. 그의 대학 설립과 근대 교육의 시작은 단순한 신학적이고 선교적인 차원의 활동을 넘어 선 우리나라를 깊이 이해하고 사랑하는 진정에서 우러난 고매한 헌신이었다. 언더우드는 외국의 문화와 정신을 그대로 옮겨놓는 일차원적 선교를 수행한 선교사가 아니라 이 땅의 정신과 문화와 삶을 올바르게 살려내려고 평생을 노력했던 선구자였다. 연세대학교 초기부터 국학이 강조되고 커 나갈 수 있었던 바탕에는 언더우드의 이런 사상과 신념이 있었기 때문이다.

언더우드 선교사의 신학적 사상과 고매한 정신을 바탕으로 연세대학교는 일제하의 민족과 문화 연구의 산실 역할을 하였고, 광복 후 연세대학교에 우리나라 최초의 국학연구기관인 동방학연구소를 세웠으며, 이후 확대 개편하여 현재의 국학연구원을 설립하게 되었다. 연세대학교 국학연구원이 동아시아의 역사, 문학, 철학 등의 연구를 선도하고 교내외 국학 연구 진흥에 이바지함은 물론, 세계 속의 우리 국학을 위해 노력하는 것 역시 언더우드의 사상적 전통을 계승한 것이라 할 것이다.

언더우드의 내한과 그의 선교적 헌신과 국학에 대한 사랑은 늘 있는 단순한 행사나, 속 빈 화려한 퍼레이드, 시끌벅적한 일회성 이벤트가 아니었다. 그는 이 땅에 교육기관을 세웠고 인재를 양성했으며 그 인재들이 이 나라 이 민족을 이끌어가기를 바랐다. 특정 종교나 가치, 관념에 얽매이지 않아야 한다는 것을 스스로 다짐했으며, 밖에서 온 그들보다 여기에 살고 있는 우리들이 더 행복해야 한다는 참된 바른 삶의 모습을 사랑과 나눔을 통해 직접 보여주었다.

연세대학교가 좁은 가치에 골몰하고 작은 의식에 사로잡힌 지식을 추구하는 편협한 교육기관이 아닌 진정한 의미의 '큰 학문'을 하는 '대학'이 될 수 있었던 것도 모두 이런 언더우드의 정신에 바탕을 뒀기 때문이다. 이번에 국학연구원에서 간행하는 언더우드 내한 관련 자료집을 통해 언더우드의 그런 삶의 자세와 의미를 더 정확히 그리고 더 명확히 알 수 있게 될 것이다.

국학연구원에서는 2005년에 언더우드 내한 120주년을 맞아 언더우드가 이 땅에 온 1885년부터 1922년까지의 저술과 관련 자료들을 집대성하여 『언더우드 자료집』(Ⅰ~Ⅴ권)을 간행한 바 있다. 이런 노력에 이어 내한 130주년이 되는 올해 언더우드가 이 땅에 오기 전인 1885년까지의 삶을 정리한 자료집을 간행하게 되었다.

이 자료집에는 언더우드가 어떤 마음과 어떤 각오로 선교와 삶을 준비하고 노력했는지를 생생하게 알 수 있는 귀중한 자료들을 담고 있다. 언더우드의 가계와 정황, 그가 공부했던 학교들, 선교사에 지원하게 된 동기와 사정, 이 땅에 오기까지의 과정 등은 물론 미국 장로회의 역사와 미국의 한국 선교 상황에 대해서도 직접 알 수 있는 1차 자료들이 수록되어 있다.

이번 자료집을 출간하기 위해 많은 분들이 애를 쓰셨다. 저자인 의과대학 박형우 교수의 노고와 열정이 없었다면 이 자료집은 빛을 볼 수 없었을 것이다. 또한 신과대학 최재건 교수의 헌신적 협력이 있었기에 본서가 이렇게 될 수 있었다. 아울러 출판을 흔쾌히 허락해 주신 연세대학교 출판부와 간행을 지원해주신 언더우드 기념사업회에도 감사의 말씀을 드린다.

마지막으로 이 자료집을 통해 언더우드 선교사의 정신을 이어받고 그의 노고를 되새기는 모든 분들께도 감사를 드린다. 이분들 모두가 언더우드의 후계자이자 이 땅의 자손들이며 사랑과 평화의 가치를 널리 퍼뜨리는 소중한 분들임이 틀림없다.

2015년 10월

국학연구원장 도현철

축 사

저는 박형우 박사에게 진심으로 축하를 드리고 싶습니다.

그는 다양한 자료들을 발굴하였으며, 인상적이고 매혹적으로 언더우드 가문의 역사를 엮어 내었습니다. 저는 어려서 들었던 우리 조상들에 관해, 보다 깊이와 의미를 주는 많은 사실들을 알게 되었습니다. 박 박사는 이 일에 많은 시간을 할애했고, 우리 언더우드 가문 자신들 보다 훨씬 더 우리 가문에 대해 많이 공부했다는 점이 부끄러울 뿐입니다. 다시 한 번 광범위하고 걸출한 성과를 낸 것에 대해 축하를 드리는 바입니다.

2015년 10월 10일 원한석

Congratulations.

I would like to extend my deepest congratulation to Dr. Park, Hyoung-woo.

The volume of information from such diverse sources that he has unearthed and then woven into a mosaic of the Underwood family in both impressive and fascinating. I learned many details about my ancestors that added depth and color to stories I heard as a child. It is humbling to see that Dr. Park has dedicated so much time and learned so much about our family, far more than we know ourselves. Again, congratulations on a comprehensive and outstanding achievement.

October 10th, 2015 Peter Underwood

머리말

미국 북장로회에서 파송한 첫 목회 선교사인 언더우드의 내한 130주년을 맞이하여, 그가 내한하기까지의 자료를 담은 책을 내게 되어 무척 기쁩니다. 이미 언더우드에 관한 연구 혹은 학위 논문이 다수 있고, 5권의 자료집이 발간되었음에도 그가 어떻게 내한하게 되었는지에 관해서는 거의 연구가 없었다고 해도 과언이 아닐 것입니다. 언더우드 자신이 선교사 내한 25주년을 회상했던 글과, 부인 호튼이 저술한 *Underwood of Korea*가 계속 반복 인용되어 왔을 뿐이기 때문입니다. 이러한 사정은 비단 언더우드에 국한된 것은 아닐 것입니다. 새로운 자료의 발굴 등을 통해서가 아니라 2차 사료나 기존 논문의 재인용들을 통해 역사가 기술되고 있는 현상이 생각보다 광범위한 것 같습니다.

편자는 2000년대 초부터 언더우드와 절친했던 선교사 중의 한 명인 에비슨에 대한 자료를 수집하여 정리해 왔습니다. 이 과정에서 2002년 에비슨 자료집 제1권의 보고서를 연세대학교 의과대학에 제출한 바 있습니다. 하지만 비용 문제로 아직 출판하지는 못했습니다(다행히 조만간 출판될 예정입니다).

주로 초창기 선교사들에 관한 여러 자료를 수집하고 정리하는 과정 중에 언더우드의 선교사 지원 편지를 포함한 다수의 자료를 확보하였고, 그 활용 방안을 고심하였습니다. 현실적으로 의과대학 교수가 언더우드에 대한 자료집을 출판하겠다고 선뜻 나서기도 쉬운 일은 아니었습니다. 결국 2014년 11월 경 연세대학교 국학연구원 도현철 원장께 언더우드의 내한에 관한 발표회 개최와 자료집 발간을 건의했고, 이것이 받아 들여져 이 자료집이 나오게 된 것입니다. 도현철 원장께 진심으로 감사드립니다. 또한 이렇게 자료집 발간을 건의하게 된 데에는 평소

최재건 교수님이 해주신 많은 귀한 말씀의 힘도 컸다고 생각합니다.

막상 자료집 출판이 결정되자 보다 구체적인 자료의 확보에 온 힘을 쏟았습니다. 언더우드 집안과 관련에서는 영국의 다양한 자료들을 찾았고, 교육과 관련해서는 뉴욕대학교, 뉴브런즈윅 신학교 등과 관련된 자료를 찾았습니다. 이 과정에서 현재 옥스퍼드대학교에서 의학사로 박사학위 논문의 최종 심사를 기다리고 있는 드류대학교의 김신권 목사의 도움을 크게 받았습니다. 재정적, 시간적 제약으로 편저자 혼자 해결할 수 없는 일에 큰 도움을 받았고, 함께 언더우드가 다녔던 학교, 교회, 그리고 한국으로 이장되기 전에 매장되어 있던 묘지 등을 함께 둘러보았습니다. 다행이 이 책의 교정이 진행되는 중에 언더우드가 한국으로 오기 전에 시무했던 폼프턴 교회를 방문했고, 그 사진을 이 책에 실을 수 있게 되었습니다.

아직 잘 알려져 있지 않은 자료들을 이 책에 담은 기쁨도 큽니다. 하지만 미국과 캐나다에서 자료를 수집하는 중간 중간에 거의 혼자 내용의 교정을 볼 수밖에 없었기에 오자나 틀린 부분이 있디라도 여리분들의 넓은 이헤를 부탁드립니다.

저는 이 책에서 여러 자료를 모아 번역한 가장 기본적인 일을 했다고 생각합니다. 부디 이 책에 담긴 자료들이 저와는 전혀 다른 배경을 가진 분들에 의해 재해석되어 기존에 나와 있는 5권의 언더우드 전집과 함께 언더우드를 보다 정확하게 이해하는 바탕이 되었으면 하는 바람입니다.

마지막으로 언더우드 가문으로 연세대학교 재단이사로서 학교 발전에 큰 역할을 하시는 피터 언더우드 님이 축사를 보내주신 데 대해 깊은 감사를 드립니다.

참고로 이 책의 출판을 준비하면서 아래의 논문을 발표했음을 알려드립니다.

《박형우, 「미국 북장로회 선교사 호러스 G. 언더우드의 내한에 관한 연구」, 『동방학지』 170집, 2015, 52~83쪽.》

박형우 씀

2015. 10. 12.

Preface

Celebrating 130 years of Rev. Horace G. Underwood's coming to Korea, I am thrilled to publish a source book about the process of his coming as the very first clerical missionary by the Board of Foreign Missions, Presbyterian Church, U. S. A. Although several studies and source books were published about Rev. Underwood, it is not too much to say that none of these includes a details about his familial and educational backgrounds. Publications often and repeatedly used very limited referential quotes about Rev. Underwood, including his own writing, '*Reminiscences*', and a book written by his wife, Dr. Horton, '*Underwood of Korea*.' Citing of secondary sources and previous studies is extensively prominent in the study of early history of Christianity in Korea, and this phenomenon is not only limited to Rev. Underwood's case.

Since early 2000, I have collected and organized materials about one of Rev. Underwood's intimate friends, Dr. Oliver R. Avison. During the process, I have submitted the report 'Source book on Dr. Oliver R. Avison, Volume 1' to College of Medicine, Yonsei University in 2012, however, publication was delayed at the time. (Good news is, it will be published very soon)

While collecting materials regarding early missionaries, several data about Rev. Underwood, including his application letter, were found, and have thought for a long time about how to effectively utilize them. After a thoughtful thinking, around November of 2014, I carefully asked Prof. Hyeon Chul Do, Director of Institute of Korean Studies, regarding a Conference and publishing source book about Rev. Underwood. The idea was luckily accepted and resulted in publication. I would like to express my sincere gratitude to Prof. Do for making this possible, and also to Prof. Jae Keun Choi who has shared his wisdom words with me.

As the idea of publication became real, the next step was to focus on collecting more data. Regarding Rev. Underwood's family, most materials were collected from the United Kingdom and Educational data from New York University and New Brunswick Theological Seminary. During the process, I have had much support from Rev. Shin K. Kim from Drew University. My work would not have been possible to be completed without his help. We had an opportunity to visit Underwood' s former school, church, and his grave site together.

I have accomplished the very basic work of collecting data and translating them to the public. It is my hope to assist people with professional backgrounds in this field to utilize this data. It is an honour to be at this position to publish a rarely known facts about Rev. Underwood. As much as it excites me, however, since I have worked and proofread most of contents alone, there could be small rooms for error that I am not aware of and I hope that the readers could understand that.

Lastly, I'd like to express my deep appreciation to Mr. Peter Underwood who kindly send me a congratulation word to me as a family member of Rev. Horace G. Underwood.

I have published the following article while working on the book.

Hyoung W. Park, The Study on the Coming to Korea of Rev. Horace G. Underwood as a Clerical Missionary of Presbyterian Church, USA. The Journal of Korean Studies, 2015, (170), 52~83.

Hyoung Woo Park, M. D., Ph. D.
October 12th, 2015

• 일러두기

1. 이 책은 언더우드가 내한하기까지의 과정을 다루었고 제목에도 '1859~1885'라는 연도가 포함되어 있다. 하지만 집안 배경에는 언더우드가 출생하기 이전의 내용도 포함되어 있고, 교육 배경이나 기타 선교사로 파송되는 과정에서는 이해를 돕기 위해 1885년 이후에 것도 일부 수록하였다.
2. 호튼의 *Underwood of Korea*(1918)나 언더우드의 *Reminiscences*(1909)는 원문만을 수록하였다.
3. 영어 원문에는 출처를 가능한 한 표시하였다.
4. 다수의 자료에서는 영어 원문은 가능한 한 그대로 수록하였지만, 필요한 부분만 번역한 경우가 있다. 한글 번역만으로 이해가 잘 되지 않는 경우 영어 원문을 참고하기 바란다.
5. 번역은 가능한 한 원문에 충실하게 하였으며, 편지를 주고받은 사람의 입장을 살펴 경어체를 적용하였다.
6. 원문에서 철자가 해독되지 않는 부분은 빈칸에 밑줄을 그어 표시하였다.
7. 고유 명사는 가능한 한 원 발음을 살리도록 노력하였다.
8. 필요한 경우 각주를 달아 독자의 이해를 도왔다.

제1부

집안 배경

Part 1.
Familial Backgrounds

1.
언더우드의 조부모 (Grandparents)

언더우드 집안은 할아버지 토머스(Thomas Underwood, 1795~18??)까지 추적할 수 있다. 그는 10대 중반인 1810년경부터 런던에서 출판업(서적상)에 종사했으며, 1817년 2월 6일 미들섹스 주 웨스트민스터의 말러본(St. Marylebone, Westminster, Middlesex)에서 메리 이스턴 워(Mary Easton Waugh, 1792~1866)와 결혼하였다.

토머스는 메리와의 사이에서 메리 닐(Mary Neill Underwood, 1818~ ?), 토머스(Thomas Underwood, 1819~1900), 마가렛 코번트리(Margaret Coventry Underwood, 1821~35), 조지(George Underwood, 1823~ ?), 진(Jean Underwood, 1825~96), 존(John Underwood, 1827~81; 언더우드의 아버지) 및 캐서린 코번트리(Catherine Coventry Underwood, 1829~ ?) 등 5남 3녀를 두었던 것으로 파악된다.[1] 이들은 모두 외할아버지 알렉산더 워가 시무하던 웰즈 가(街)의 스코틀랜드 교회(Wells Street Scotch Church)에서 유아 세례를 받았다. 토머스는 1829년에서 1838년 사이에 사망하였다.[2]

할머니 메리는 1792년 10월 15일 영국 런던 말러본에서 출생했으며, 1866년 영국 미들섹스 주 런던 판크라스에서 사망하였다. 그녀의 증조할아버지인 애덤(Adam Waugh, ? ~ca. 1732)은 1670년 경 스코틀랜드 버윅 주 고든(Gordon, Berwick)에서 출생하여 1732년 경 사망했다. 할아버지인 토머스(Thomas Waugh)는 1706년 2월 24일 스코틀랜드 버윅 주 이스트 고든(East Gordon)에서 출생하여 1783년 7월 6일 그곳에서 사망했다.

---

1) 토머스 언더우드의 자녀에 대해서는 자료에 따라 상이한 점도 많이 있어 보다 정밀한 검토가 필요하다. 특히 알렉산더(Alexander Underwood, 1820년 출생 추정)에 대한 자료는 전혀 찾지 못하였다.

2) 토머스 언더우드는 「*Pigot and Co's Directory of London, 1839.*」에 들어 있지 않아, 1839년 이전에 사망한 것으로 추정된다.

자료 1-1 토머스 언더우드 (Thomas Underwood).

자료 1-2 알렉산더 워 (Alexander Waugh).

메리의 아버지 알렉산더(Alexander Waugh, 1754~1827)는 1754년 8월 16일 스코틀랜드 버윅 주 이스트 고든에서 빈농 집안의 막내로 출생했다. 그는 자신을 '전문 직업인'으로 키우려는 아버지의 뜻에 따라 1774년 에딘버러대학교를 졸업하고, 1777년에 아버딘대학교를 졸업했다. 알렉산더는 1779년 에딘버러의 장로회에서 목사 안수를 받은 후 뉴턴(Newton)의 교회에서 시무했다. 이후 여러 번에 걸쳐 런던 웰즈 가(街) 교회로부터 부임을 요청 받았다. 하지만 이를 거절한 바 있었던 알렉산더는 에딘버러 장로회의 허락으로 1782년 8월부터 런던 웰즈 가 교회에서 시무하기 시작했다. 런던에 정착한 알렉산더는 1786년 8월 10일 스코틀랜드 버윅 주 콜딩햄(Coldingham)에서 메리 닐(Mary Neill, 1760~1840)과 결혼하였다. 런던에서 활동을 시작한 알렉산더는 유명한 교회 설교자로 런던 기독교인들 중에 그 명성이 널리 알려졌다. 그는 해외 선교에도 관심을 쏟아 런던선교회(London Missionary Society)에 적극 참여하였고, 교파간 연합에 적극적으로 나서 국교인 성공회는 물론 장로회, 감리회, 침례회 및 회중교회 등이 연합하여 하나의 연합 선교회를 이루는데 힘을 쏟았다. 이러한 연합을 위해 알렉산더는 '기본 강령'을 기초한 것으로 알려져 있다. 알렉산더는 런던선교회 회원들의 적극적인 지지로 28년 동안 심사위원회 위원장으로 활동하였다. 그는 문서 선교 활동을 위해 대영성서공회에서도 적극적인 활동을 벌였다. 그는 1827년 12월 14일 런던에서 사망하였다.

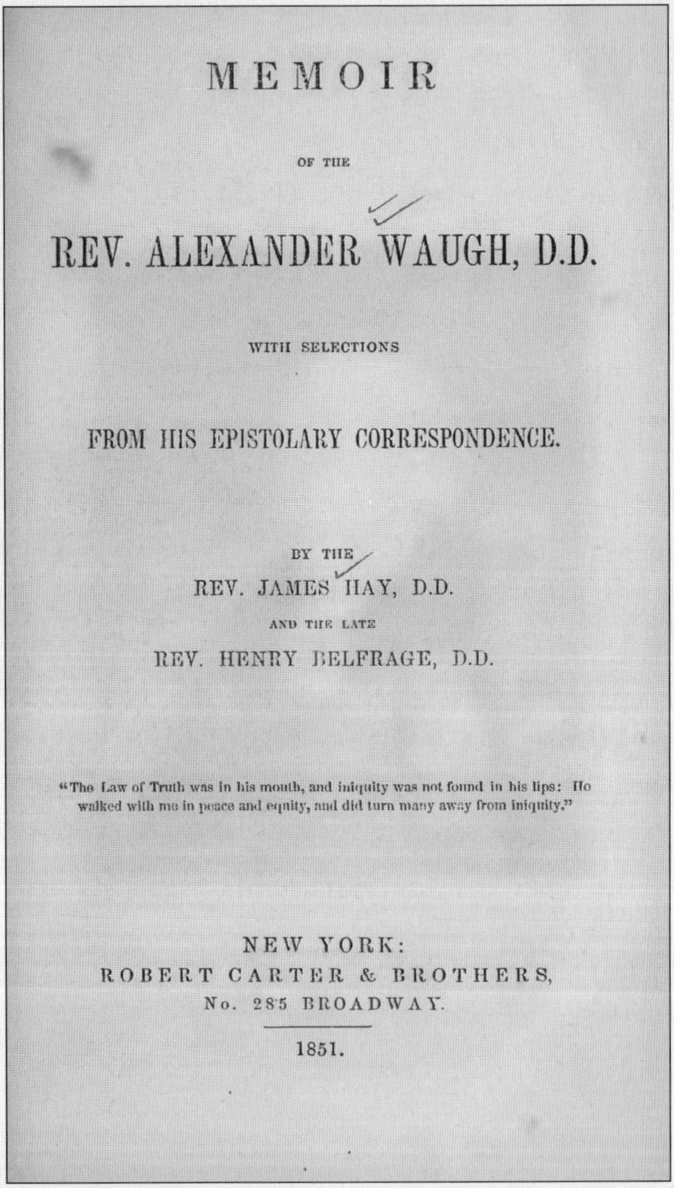

MEMOIR

OF THE

REV. ALEXANDER WAUGH, D.D.

WITH SELECTIONS

FROM HIS EPISTOLARY CORRESPONDENCE.

BY THE

REV. JAMES HAY, D.D.

AND THE LATE

REV. HENRY BELFRAGE, D.D.

"The Law of Truth was in his mouth, and iniquity was not found in his lips: He walked with me in peace and equity, and did turn many away from iniquity."

NEW YORK:

ROBERT CARTER & BROTHERS,

No. 285 BROADWAY.

1851.

자료 1-3 James Hay, *Memoir of the Rev. Alexander Waugh, D.D.* 3rd ed., Robert Carter & Bro., New York, 1851.

HOLDEN'S
ANNUAL
LONDON AND COUNTRY
DIRECTORY,
OF THE
United Kingdoms, and Wales,
IN THREE VOLUMES,
FOR THE YEAR 1811.

CONTENTS OF THE THREE BOOKS, AS STATED IN PAGE 4 AND 5.

FIRST VOLUME, LONDON PART.

Price 5 Guineas.

The present Edition has been struck off exclusively for
SUBSCRIBERS.

As will all future Editions of this Work be confined to Subscribers, prior to going to Press. The Proprietor, therefore, solicits Gentlemen to give their Orders to his Agents at the Time when they call round to take Names, &c. or send their Commands to the Office.

London:

Printed by W. Glendinning, Hatton Garden; J. Black, St. Martin's-le-Grand; and R. Wilks, Chancery Lane.

Published by W. HOLDEN, the only Proprietor, 122, Newgate Street.

THIS BOOK CONTAINS THE LONDON BUSINESS AND PRIVATE PARTS.
The Public Bodies of London are placed at the End of the 3rd Volume.

N.B.—The Proprietor begs Leave to observe, that he will be greatly convenienced by as early Knowledge as possible, in each Year, of Subscribers.

1811.

Underwood Robert, watchmaker, 3, Falcon-st. Aldersgate
Underwood S. the Gun, Shoreditch
Underwood Thomas, bookseller & stationer, 40, West Smithfield
Underwood Wm. boot & shoe maker, 37, Bread-st. Cheapside
Underwood Wm. woollen draper, &c. 20, Vere-st. Oxford-st.

자료 1-4 *Holden's Annual London and Country Directory, of the United Kingdoms, and Wales, in Three Volumes, for the Year 1811*. First Volume, London Part, London, 1811.

UNDER THE PATRONAGE OF
HIS MAJESTY's POSTMASTER-GENERAL.

THE
Post Office London Directory
For 1819.
BEING A LIST OF MORE THAN
18,000
Merchants, Traders, &c. of London, and Parts Adjacent;

LIST of the LORD MAYOR, and COURT of ALDERMEN.	NEWSPAPERS, with the Places and Days of Publication.
LIST of the BANKERS in LONDON.	LISTS of ARMY and NAVY AGENTS, DIRECTORS of the FIRE & INSURANCE OFFICES
LIST of 700 COUNTRY BANKERS, with the BANKERS they draw on in LONDON.	LISTS of the LONDON, WEST INDIA & EAST INDIA DOCK COMPANIES, FOREIGN MINISTERS, &c. &c.
LIST of PUBLIC NOTARIES.	
LIST of LONDON & COUNTRY	

General Information relating to the
POST OFFICE,
INCLUDING the LAST RATES of POSTAGE.
Regulations of the Twopenny Post-Office, &c. &c.

By CRITCHETT & WOODS.

THE TWENTIETH EDITION.

London: Printed by T. Maiden for the Proprietors,
And sold by J. Richardson, Royal Exchange; J. Asperne, Cornhill;
G. Cowie and Co. Poultry;
Black and Son, 9, York-Street, and 2, Tavistock-Street, Covent-Garden;
J. Walker; Sherwood, Neely & Co. & R. Fenner, Paternoster-Row;
Black, Kingsbury, Parbury, & Allen, Leadenhall-Street;
Simpkin and Marshall, Stationers'-Court;
T. Sotheran, 2, Little Tower-Street;
And by all the Booksellers and Stationers in the United Kingdom.
Price 3s. 6d. sewed, 4s. bound; or, with the Coach and Carriers' Guide, 5s. bound.

Underhill Thomas, *Publisher*, 11, Coleman-street
Underhell John, *Tanner*, Grange-road, Bermondsey
Underwood Thomas & George, *Booksellers*, 32, Fleet-street
Underwood H, *Cutler*, Corner of Russel-court, Drury-lane
H h 3

자료 1-5 Critchett & Woods, *The Post-Office London Directory for 1820*. 21st Ed., London.

1-1 할아버지 – 토머스 언더우드

Grandfather – Thomas Underwood

18110000

홀든의 1811년도 영국 및 웨일즈의 런던 및 지방 인명부, 제1권, 런던 지방, 런던, 1811년 발행.

언더우드, 토머스 서적상 및 출판업자
웨스트 스미스필드 40번지[3)]

***Holden's Annual London and Country Directory, of the United Kingdoms, and Wales, in Three Volumes, for the Year 1811*. First Volume, London Part, London, 1811.**

Underwood, Thomas Bookseller & Stationer
40, West Smithfield

3) 웨스트 스미스필드는 런던 중심 서북쪽 지역인 스미스필드의 주요 거리이다. 이 지역에는 특히 고대로부터 정육점이 번성했으며, 런던에서 유일하게 중세로부터 현재까지 도매시장이 남아 있는 곳이다.

18111015

크리쳇 및 우즈, 1812년도 우체국 목록. 제13판, 런던, 320쪽.[4)]

언더우드, 토머스	서적상
	웨스트 스미스필드 40번지

Critchett & Woods, *The Post-Office Annual Directory for 1812*. 13th Ed., London, p. 320.[5)]

Underwood, Thomas	Bookseller
	40, West Smithfield

---

4) 이 책은 1799년 창간된 이래 매년 발행되었다. 1813년 판의 경우 1812년 10월 중순까지 원고를 제출받아 출판되었으므로, 1812년 판은 1811년 10월 중순의 상황을 담고 있다고 볼 수 있다. 1808년판에는 토머스의 이름이 들어 있지 않다. 따라서 토머스는 1808년에서 1811년 사이에 출판업을 시작한 것으로 판단된다.

5) This directory was published annually since 1799. For the edition of 1813, deadline for the manuscript was middle of October, 1812. So the contents of the edition of 1812 reflect the conditions in October, 1811. The name of 'Thomas' was not listed in the edition of 1808. So it is assumed that Thomas opened his bookstore between 1808 and 1810.

18131015

크리첏 및 우즈, 1814년도 우체국 목록. 제15판, 런던, 332쪽.

언더우드, 토머스	서적상
	플리트 가 32번지 및 웨스트 스미스필드 40번지[6]

Critchett & Woods, *The Post-Office Annual Directory for 1814*. 15th Ed., London, p. 332.

Underwood, Thomas	Bookseller
	32, Fleet Street, and 40, West Smithfield[7]

6) 1816년 판에 서점의 주소가 플리트 가(街)로 되어 있는 것으로 보아 1813년 10월경에 서점을 이전하고 있었던 것으로 판단된다.
7) As the address of the bookstore was Fleet Street in the edition of 1816, it is assumed that the bookstore was moving during about October 1813.

18151015

크리쳇 및 우즈, 1816년도 우체국 런던 목록. 제17판, 런던, 342쪽.

언더우드, 토머스	서적상 플리트 가 32번지[8]

Critchett & Woods, *The Post-Office London Directory for 1816*. 17th Ed., London, p. 342.

Underwood, Thomas	Bookseller 32, Fleet Street[9]

8) 서점을 이전하였다. 플리트 가(街)는 1500년대부터 인쇄소가 들어오기 시작했으며, 1702년 런던 최초의 일간지가 이곳에서 발간된 이후 인쇄업의 중심이 되었다.

9) Bookstore had moved.

자료 1-6 Fleet Street (ca. 1890).

자료 1-7 토머스의 서점 자리. 현재의 플리트 가. 스타벅스 커피점 왼쪽 부분이 토머스가 서점을 열었던 플리트가 32번지이다. From Google Map.

18161015

크리첸 및 우즈, 1817년도 우체국 런던 목록. 제18판, 런던, 341쪽.

언더우드, 토머스	서적상 플리트 가 32번지

Critchett & Woods, *The Post-Office London Directory for 1817*. 18th Ed., London, p. 341.

Underwood, Thomas	Bookseller 32, Fleet Street

18170206

영국, 결혼 발췌, 1538~1973, (토머스 언더우드, 1817년 2월 6일).

결혼일　　: 1817년 2월 6일

결혼 장소　: 영국 미들섹스 주 말러본

배우자　　: 메리 이스턴 워

England, Select Marriages, 1538~1973, (Thomas Underwood, Feb. 6th, 1817).

Marriage Date　: Feb. 6th, 1817

Marriage Place　: Marylebone, Middlesex, England

Spouse　: Mary Easton Waugh

PHL Film Number　: 584230

18181015

크리쳇 및 우즈, 1819년도 우체국 런던 목록. 제20판, 런던, 353쪽.

언더우드 토머스 및 조지[10]	서적상 플리트 가 32번지

Critchett & Woods, *The Post-Office London Directory for 1819*. 20th Ed., London, p. 353.

Underwood Thomas & George[11]	Bookseller 32, Fleet Street

10) 조지가 합류하였다. 조지가 토머스의 형제인지 조카인지는 기록에 따라 다르다. 1817년 2월 토머스가 결혼한 후 1819년 10월 사이에 합류한 것으로 추정된다.

11) George Underwood had joined. The relation between George and Thomas is uncertain, whether brother or cousin. George joined between the marriage of Thomas in February and October, 1819.

18191015

크리쳇 및 우즈, 1820년도 우체국 런던 목록. 제21판, 런던, 364쪽.

언더우드, 토머스 및 조지	서적상 플리트 가 32번지

Critchett & Woods, *The Post-Office London Directory for 1820*. 21st Ed., London, p. 364.

Underwood, Thomas & George	Bookseller 32, Fleet Street

18250000

서적상, 피곳 회사의 런던 상업 목록, 1825~6, 48쪽.

언더우드 토머스 및 조지 플리트 가 32번지.

Bookseller, *Pigot and Co's Commercial Directory of London, 1825~6*, p. 48.

Underwood Ts. & Geo. 32 Fleet-st.

18281015

크리쳇, 1829년도 우체국 런던 목록. 제30판, 런던, 432쪽.

언더우드, 토머스 및 조지	서적상 플리트 가 32번지

B. Critchett, *The Post-Office London Directory for 1829*. 30th Ed., London, p. 432.

Underwood, Thos. & Geo.	Bookseller 32, Fleet Street

19130000

하워드 J. 뱅커, 미국의 언더우드 가문. 제2권, 1913, 625쪽.[12)]

존 언더우드는 토머스 언더우드의 아들이다. 토머스는 영국 런던의 플리트 가에서 형제인 조지와 함께 의학 및 다른 서적들을 출판했다.

Howard J. Banker, *The Underwood Families of America. In Two Volumes*, Volume 2, 1913, p. 625.[13)]

John Underwood was the son of Thomas Underwood who with his brother George Underwood, was a publisher of medical and other books having his place of business in Fleet Street, London, England.

12) 릴리어스의 저술 첫 부분에 인용된 문헌이다.
13) This book was cited in the book, *Underwood of Korea*, written by Lillias S. Underwood.

1-2 할머니 – 메리 이스턴 워
Grandmother – Mary Easton Waugh

17921015

영국 및 웨일즈, 비국교도 등록부, 1567~1970, (출생, 메리 이스턴 워, 1792년 10월 15일).

이 름 : 메리 이스턴 워
출생일 : 1792년 10월 15일
출생지 : 영국 미들섹스 주 말러본
아버지 : 알렉산더 워 목사
어머니 : 윌리엄 닐의 딸 메리
증 인 : 메리 앤 게일
존 볼튼, 외과의사

England & Wales, Non-Conformist and Non-Parochial Registers, 1567~1970, (Birth, Mary Easton Waugh, Oct. 15th, 1792).

Name : Mary Easton Waugh
Birth Date : Oct. 15th, 1792
Birth Place : St Marylebone, Middlesex, England
Father : Rev. Alex. Waugh
Mother : Mary daughter of William Neill
Witnesses : Mary Ann Gale
John Bolton, Surgeon
Piece Title : Piece 4660: Dr Williams' Library Registry, Birth Certificates, 1792~1805

17921115

영국 및 웨일즈, 비국교도 등록부, 1567~1970, (세례, 메리 이스턴 워, 1792년 11월 15일).

이 름	: 메리 이스턴 워	성 별	: 여자
아버지	: 알렉산더 워	어머니	: 메리
세례일	: 1792년 11월 15일		
세례 장소	: 영국 런던 웰즈 가(街)	교 파	: 스코틀랜드 교회

말러본 교구의 웰스 가(街) 회중에서 복음 전도 목사로 시무 중인 알렉산더 워와 그의 아내 메리의 딸인 메리 이스턴이 (1792년) 11월 15일 세례를 받았음을 증명함 – 알렉산더 워, 목사.

England & Wales, Non-Conformist and Non-Parochial Registers, 1567~1970, (Baptism, Mary Easton Waugh, Nov. 15th, 1792).

Name	: Mary Easton Waugh	Gender	: Female
Father	: Alexander Waugh	Mother	: Mary
Baptism Date	: Nov. 15th, 1792		
Baptism Place	: Wells Street, London, England		
Denomination	: Scotch Church		
Piece Title	: Piece 4205: Wells Street, Oxford Street (Scotch Church), 1753~1837		

That Mary Easton, the daughter of Alexander Waugh, Minister of the Gospel in the associate congregation in Well Street in the Parish of St. Mary le bone and Mary his wife, was baptised the fifteenth day of November in the year above written is attested by Al. Waugh, Min.

18510330

1851년 영국 인구주택총조사, (메리 이스턴 언더우드, 1851년 3월 30일).[14)]

마 을 : 켄티쉬 타운　　읍(邑) : 세인트 판크라스
카운티 : 미들섹스　　국 가 : 영국

등록 지구 : 판크라스　　등록 소지구 : 켄티쉬 타운
주 소 : 그래프턴 플레이스 4

나 이 : 58　　추정 출생연도 : 1793년
관 계 : 세대주　　상 태 : 과부
출생지 : 영국 미들섹스 주 말러본
지방 행정구 : 세인트판크라스　　직 업 : ________

세대원 (이름, 나이)

캐서린 코번트리 21
추정 출생연도 : 1830년　　관 계 : 딸
모친 이름 : 메리 이스턴 언더우드
출생지 : 영국 미들섹스 주 세인트 던튼

마리아 에일스 29
추정 출생연도 : 1822년　　관 계 : 하인
성 별 : 여성
출생지 : 영국 미들섹스 주 해머스미스

14) 영국의 1851년 총조사는 3월 30일 밤을 기준으로 작성되었다. 여행을 하거나 해외에 체류하고 있는 사람은 조사당일 숙박했던 곳에서 조사됐다. 이 조사에서는 거주지 주소, 세대주의 성(姓), 거주인의 이름과 세대주와의 관계, 결혼 여부, 만 나이, 성별, 직업, 출생지, 맹인, 귀머거리, 벙어리, 맹인, 혹은 지능 이상 여부 등을 조사했다.

1851 England Census, (Mary Easton Underwood, Mar. 30th, 1851).

Village of	: Kentish Town	Parish or Township of	: St. Pancras
County/Island	: Middlesex	Country	: England

Registration district	: Pancras	Sub-registration district	: Kentish Town

Road, Street, & c., and No. or Name of House : 4 Grafton Place

Age	: 58	Estimated Birth Year	: 1793
Relation	: Head	Condition	: Widower

Where born : Marylebone, Middlesex, England

Occupation : ____holder

Household Members (Name, Age)

Catherine Coventry 21

Estimated Birth Year	: 1830	Relation	: Daughter

Mother's name : Mary Easton Underwood

Where born : St Dunton, Middlesex, England

Maria Eyles 29

Estimated Birth Year	: 1822	Relation	: Servant

Gender : Female

Where born : Hammersmith, Middlesex, England

18660000

영국 및 웨일즈, 출생결혼사망 사망 색인, 1837~1915, (메리 E. 언더우드, 1866년 10~12월).

추정 출생년도	: 1793년		
등록년도	: 1866년	등록분기	: 10~12월
사망시 나이	: 73세		
등록 지구	: 판크라스	카운티	: 런던

England & Wales, FreeBMD Death Index, 1837~1915, (Mary E. Underwood, Oct-Nov-Dec 1866).

Estimated Birth Year	: 1793		
Registration Year	: 1866	Registration Quarter	: Oct-Nov-Dec
Age at Death	: 73		
Registration district	: Pancras	Inferred County	: London
Volume Number	: 1b	Page Number	: 115

1-3 조부모의 자녀들

Children of Grandparents

18180215

영국 및 웨일즈, 비국교도 등록부, 1567~1970, (세례, 메리 닐 언더우드, 1818년 2월 15일).

이 름	: 메리 닐 언더우드	성 별	: 여자
아버지	: 토머스 언더우드	어머니	: 메리 이스턴
세례일	: 1818년 2월 15일[15]		
세례 장소	: 영국 런던 세인트 말러본, 웰즈 가 스코틀랜드 교회		

세인트 던스턴-인-더-웨스트에서 서적상을 하고 있는 토머스 언더우드와 그의 아내 메리 이스턴의 딸인 메리 닐이 (1818년) 2월 15일 세례를 받았음을 증명함 – 알렉산더 워, 목사.

***England & Wales, Non-Conformist and Non-Parochial Registers, 1567~1970,* (Baptism, Mary Neill Underwood, Feb. 15th, 1818).**

Name	: Mary Neill Underwood	Gender	: Female
Father	: Thomas Underwood	Mother	: Mary Easton
Baptism Date	: Feb. 15th, 1818		
Baptism Place	: Wells Street Scotch Church, St. Marylebone, London, England		
FHL Film Number	: 0595438 (RG4 4205)		

15) 세례일을 2월 12일로 잘못 기록한 자료들도 있다.

That Mary-Neill, the daughter of Thomas Underwood, bookseller in the Parish of St. Dunstan in the West, & Mary Easton his wife, was baptised on the fifteenth day of February in the year above written is attested by Al. Waugh, Min.

18190404

영국 및 웨일즈, 비국교도 등록부, 1567~1970, (세례, 토머스 언더우드, 1819년 4월 4일).

이 름	: 토머스 언더우드	성 별	: 남자
아버지	: 토머스 언더우드	어머니	: 메리 이스턴
세례일	: 1819년 4월 4일		
세례 장소	: 영국 런던 웰즈 가		
교 파	: 스코틀랜드 교회		

세인트 던스턴-인-더-웨스트에서 서적상을 하고 있는 토머스 언더우드와 그의 아내 메리 이스턴의 아들인 토머스가 (1819년) 4월 4일 세례를 받았음을 증명함 – 알렉산더 워, 목사.

England & Wales, Non-Conformist and Non-Parochial Registers, 1567~1970, (Baptism, Thomas Underwood, Apr. 4th, 1819).

Name	: Thomas Underwood	Gender	: Male
Father	: Thomas Underwood	Mother	: Mary Easton
Baptism Date	: Apr. 4th, 1819		
Baptism Place	: Wells Street, London, England		
Denomination	: Scotch Church		
FHL Film Number	: Piece 4205: Wells Street, Oxford Street (Scotch Church), 1753~1837		

That Thomas, the son of Thomas Underwood, Bookseller in the Parish of St. Dunston in the West, and Mary Easton his wife, was baptised on the fourth day of April in the year above written is attested by Al. Waugh, Min.

18470819

영국, 런던, 결혼 및 결혼예고, 1754~1921, (결혼, 토머스 언더우드, 1847년 8월 19일).

1847년. 미들섹스 카운티 세인트 말러본 교구의 트리니티 교회 에서 결혼이 엄숙하게 거행됨.

결혼일 : 1847년 8월 19일
이름과 성 : 토머스 언더우드/ 이사벨라 워커
나 이 : 성년
상 태 : 미혼/ 미혼
직 업 : 치과의사/ –
결혼할 때 거주지 : 세인트 제임스, 웨스트민스터/ 트리니티 디스트릭트
아버지 이름과 성 : 토머스 언더우드/ 프랜시스 워커
아버지의 직업 : 출판업자 – 사망/ ______

본인 앞에서 인가 에 의해, 교회의 전례 및 의식에 따라 트리니티 지역교회 에서 결혼함.

해밀튼

이 결혼이 우리 사이	토머스 언더우드	우리가 참석한	토머스 워 및
			언더우드 메리 워
에 엄숙하게 진행됨,	이사벨라 워커	가운데,	앤 워커, 일리노어 워커

London, England, Marriages and Banns, 1754~1921, (Marriage, Thomas Underwood, Aug. 19th, 1847).

1847. Marriages solemnized at Trinity Church in the Parish of St. Marylebone in the County of Middlesex

When Married	: Aug. 19th, 1847
Name and Surname	: Thomas Underwood/ Isabella Walker
Age	: Full Age
Condition	: Bachelor/ Spinster
Rank of Profession	: Dentist/ -
Residences at the time of Marriage	: Parish of Saint James, Westminster/ Trinity District
Father's Name and Surname	: Thomas Underwood/ Francis Walker
Rank of Profession of Father	: Publisher - Deceased/ Gent____

Married in the District Church of Trinity according to the Rites and Ceremonies of the Established Church, by Licence or after _______ by me,

Hamilton

This Marriage was	Thomas Underwood	in the presence	Thos Waugh & Underwood Mary Waugh
solemnised between us,	Isabella Walker	of us,	Anne Walker, Eleanor Walker

18211014

영국 및 웨일즈, 비국교도 등록부, 1567~1970, (세례, 마가렛 코번트리 언더우드, 1821년 10월 14일).

이 름	: 마가렛 코번트리 언더우드	성 별	: 여자
아버지	: 토머스 언더우드	어머니	: 메리 이스턴
세례일	: 1821년 10월 14일	세례 장소	: 영국 런던 웰즈 가
교 파	: 스코틀랜드 교회		

세인트 던스턴-인-더-웨스트에서 서적상을 하고 있는 토머스 언더우드와 그의 아내 메리 이스턴의 아들인 토머스가 (1821년) 10월 14일 세례를 받았음을 증명함 – 알렉산더 워, 목사.

England & Wales, Non-Conformist and Non-Parochial Registers, 1567~1970, (Baptism, Margaret Coventry Underwood, Oct. 14th, 1821).

Name	: Margaret Coventry Underwood		
Gender	: Female		
Father	: Thomas Underwood	Mother	: Mary Easton
Baptism Date	: Oct. 14th, 1821		
Baptism Place	: Wells Street, London, England		
Denomination	: Scotch Church		
FHL Film Number	: Piece 4205: Wells Street, Oxford Street (Scotch Church), 1753~1837		

That Margaret Coventry, the Daughter of Thomas Underwood, Bookseller in the Parish of St. Dunston in the West, and Mary Easton his wife, was baptized on the fourteenth day of October in the year above written is attested by Al. Waugh, Min.

18231017

영국 및 웨일즈, 비국교도 등록부, 1567~1970, (세례, 조지 언더우드, 1823년 10월 17일).

이 름	: 조지 언더우드	성 별	: 남자
아버지	: 토머스 언더우드	어머니	: 메리 이스턴
세례일	: 1823년 10월 17일		
세례 장소	: 영국 런던 웰즈 가		
교 파	: 스코틀랜드 교회		

세인트 던스턴-인-더-웨스트에서 서적상을 하고 있는 토머스 언더우드와 그의 아내 메리 이스턴의 아들인 조지가 (1823년) 10월 17일 세례를 받았음을 증명함 – 알렉산더 워, 목사.

England & Wales, Non-Conformist and Non-Parochial Registers, 1567~1970, (Baptism, George Underwood, Oct. 17th, 1823).

Name	: George Underwood	Gender	: Male
Father	: Thomas Underwood	Mother	: Mary Easton
Baptism Date	: Oct. 17th, 1823		
Baptism Place	: Wells Street, London, England		
Denomination	: Scotch Church		
FHL Film Number	: Piece 4205: Wells Street, Oxford Street (Scotch Church), 1753~1837		

That George, the Son of Thomas Underwood, Bookseller in the Parish of St. Dunston in the West, and Mary Easton his wife, was baptized on the Seventeenth day of October in the year above written is attested by Al. Waugh, Min.

18250718

영국 및 웨일즈, 비국교도 등록부, 1567~1970, (세례, 진 언더우드, 1825년 7월 18일).

이 름	: 진 언더우드	성 별	: 여자
아버지	: 토머스 언더우드	어머니	: 메리 이스턴
세례일	: 1825년 7월 18일		
세례 장소	: 영국 런던 웰즈 가		
교 파	: 스코틀랜드 교회		

세인트 던스턴-인-더-웨스트에서 서적상을 하고 있는 토머스 언더우드와 그의 아내 메리 이스턴의 딸인 진이 (1825년) 7월 18일 세례를 받았음을 증명함 - 알렉산더 워, 목사.

England & Wales, Non-Conformist and Non-Parochial Registers, 1567~1970, (Baptism, Jean Underwood, July 18th, 1825).

Name	: Jean Underwood	Gender	: Female
Father	: Thomas Underwood	Mother	: Mary Easton
Baptism Date	: July 18th, 1825		
Baptism Place	: Wells Street, London, England		
Denomination	: Scotch Church		
FHL Film Number	: Piece 4205: Wells Street, Oxford Street (Scotch Church), 1753~1837		

That Jean, Daughter of Thomas Underwood, Bookseller in the Parish of St. Dunston in the West, and Mary Easton his wife, was baptized on the Eighteenth day of July in the year above written is attested by Al. Waugh, Min.

18270703

영국 및 웨일즈, 비국교도 등록부, 1567~1970, (세례, 존 언더우드, 1827년 7월 3일).

이 름	: 존 언더우드	성 별	: 남자
아버지	: 토머스 언더우드	어머니	: 메리 이스턴
세례일	: 1827년 7월 3일		
세례 장소	: 영국 런던 웰즈 가		
교 파	: 스코틀랜드 교회		

세인트 던스턴-인-더-웨스트에서 서적상을 하고 있는 토머스 언더우드와 그의 아내 메리 이스턴의 아들인 존이 (1827년) 7월 3일 세례를 받았음을 증명함 - 알렉산더 워, 목사.

England & Wales, Non-Conformist and Non-Parochial Registers, 1567~1970, (Baptism, John Underwood, July 3rd, 1827).

Name	: John Underwood	Gender	: Male
Father	: Thomas Underwood	Mother	: Mary Easton
Baptism Date	: July 3rd, 1827		
Baptism Place	: Wells Street, London, England		
Denomination	: Scotch Church		
FHL Film Number	: Piece 4205: Wells Street, Oxford Street (Scotch Church), 1753~1837		

That John, Son of Thomas Underwood, Bookseller in the Parish of St. Dunston in the West, and Mary Easton his wife, was baptised on the Third day of July in the year above written is attested by Al. Waugh, Min.

18290718

영국 및 웨일즈, 비국교도 등록부, 1567~1970, (세례, 캐서린 코번트리 언더우드, 1829년 7월 18일).

이 름	: 캐서린 코번트리 언더우드	성 별	: 여자
아버지	: 토머스 언더우드	어머니	: 메리 이스턴
세례일	: 1829년 7월 18일		
세례 장소	: 영국 런던 웰즈 가		
교 파	: 스코틀랜드 교회		

세인트 던스턴-인-더-웨스트에서 서적상을 하고 있는 토머스 언더우드와 그의 아내 메리 이스턴의 딸인 캐서린 코번트리가 (1829년) 7월 18일 세례를 받았음을 증명함 – 존 M. 렐런, 노회 서기.[16)]

England & Wales, Non-Conformist and Non-Parochial Registers, 1567~1970, (Baptism, Catherine Coventry Underwood, July 18th, 1829).

Name	: Catherine Coventry Underwood	Gender	: Male
Father	: Thomas Underwood	Mother	: Mary Easton
Baptism Date	: July 18th, 1829		
Baptism Place	: Wells Street, London, England		
Denomination	: Scotch Church		
FHL Film Number	: Piece 4205: Wells Street, Oxford Street (Scotch Church), 1753~1837		

16) 알렉산더 워는 1827년 12월 14일 사망했으므로 존 언더우드까지만 세례를 주었고, 막내 캐서린은 다른 목사가 세례를 주었다.

That Catherine Coventry, daughter of Thos Underwood, Bookseller in the Parish of St. Dunston in the West, and Mary Easton his wife, was baptized on the Eighteenth day of July in the year above written is attested by John M. Lellan, Session Clerk

2.
언더우드의 부모 (Parents)

언더우드의 아버지 존(John Underwood, 1727~1881)은 자신이 대단히 존경했던, 당시 영국의 유명한 물리학자 겸 화학자였던 마이클 패러데이(Michael Faraday, 1791~1867)의 학생으로 화학을 공부했다. 존은 1855년 7월 26일 런던 웨스트민스터의 말러본 교구에서 엘리자베스 그랜트 메어(Elizabeth Grant Mair, 1828~65)와 결혼했다.

존과 엘리자베스는 모두 3남 3녀를 두었다. 친척들은 생전의 엘리자베스에 대해 칭찬을 아끼지 않았는데, 그녀는 '화를 내거나, 아이들에게 큰 소리를 지른 일이 적이 없었다'고 한다. 그녀는 1865

자료 1-8 존 언더우드(John Underwood). Lillias H. Underwood, Underwood of Korea, Fleming H. Revell Co., 1918.

자료 1-9 호러스의 생모 엘리자베스(Elizabeth Grant Underwood). 연세대학교 박물관 제공.

년 낳은 막내 메리가 생후 2개월 만에 사망한 후, 자신도 사망했다.

존은 아내와 딸을 잃은 다음 해인 1866년 또 다른 충격적인 일을 겪었다. 동업자에게 사기를 당해 파산하고 말았던 것이다. 이런 곤란한 상황을 타개하기 위해 그는 새로운 곳에서 새로운 기회를 얻는 것이 나을 것이라고 생각하기 시작했음에 틀림없다.

자료 1-10 존 언더우드.

엘리자베스가 사망한 얼마 후 존은 캐롤라인 넌(Caroline Nunn, ca. 1830~74)과 재혼했다. 따라서 생모가 사망할 당시 나이가 9살에서 3살에 이르는 어린 5남매는 계모의 딸 앤(Ann Nunn, 1852~ ?)과 함께 성장했다. 넌은 1872년 존이 미국으로 건너간 후 아이들을 보살폈고, 1873년 학교를 다니던 한나를 제외한 나머지 아이들을 데리고 미국으로 이주했으며, 1874년 사망하였다.

자료 1-11 마이클 패러데이 (Michael Faraday).

캐롤라인은 전 남편 윌리엄과의 사이에 두 딸, 즉 레베카(Rebecca Nunn, 1851~1915)와 앤을 두었다. 앤은 넌이 미국으로 이주할 함께 건너 왔고, 레베카는 1884년 이주해 존 T.와 함께 살다가 1915년 사망하였다.

존과 넌 사이에는 자녀가 없었다.

2-1 아버지 – 존 언더우드

Father – John Underwood

18550726

영국, 런던, 결혼 및 결혼예고, 1754~1921, (결혼, 존 언더우드, 1855년 7월 26일).

1855년. 미들섹스 카운티 세인트 말러본 교구의 교구 교회 에서 결혼이 엄숙하게 거행됨.

결혼일	: 1855년 7월 26일
이름과 성	: 존 언더우드/ 엘리자베스 그랜트 메어
나 이	: 성년
상 태	: 미혼/ 미혼
직 업	: 문방구 도매업
결혼할 때 거주지	: 세인트 판크라스/ 세인트 말러본
아버지 이름과 성	: 토머스 언더우드/ 존 메어
아버지의 직업	: 출판업자/ 도매업

본인 앞에서 인가 에 의헤, 교회의 전례 및 의식에 따라 교구 교회 에서 결혼함.

디 NcAnally, 부목사

이 결혼이 우리 사이 에 엄숙하게 진행됨,	존 언더우드 엘리자베스 그랜드 메어	우리가 참석한 가운데,	호러스 그랜트 메리 이스턴 언더우드

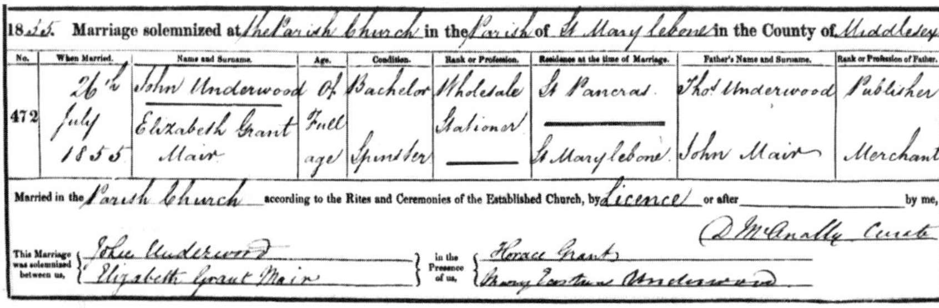

1855. Marriage solemnized at the Parish Church in the Parish of St Mary lebone in the County of Middlesex

No.	When Married.	Name and Surname.	Age.	Condition.	Rank or Profession.	Residence at the time of Marriage.	Father's Name and Surname.	Rank or Profession of Father.
472	26th July 1855	John Underwood Elizabeth Grant Mair	Of Full age	Bachelor Spinster	Wholesale Stationer —	St Pancras St Marylebone	Thos Underwood John Mair	Publisher Merchant

Married in the Parish Church according to the Rites and Ceremonies of the Established Church, by Licence or after ________ by me,
D McAnally Curate

This Marriage was solemnized between us, John Underwood, Elizabeth Grant Mair; in the Presence of us, Horace Grant, Mary Easton Underwood

자료 1-12 *London, England, Marriages and Banns, 1754~1921*, (Marriage, John Underwood, Jul. 26th, 1855).

London, England, Marriages and Banns, 1754~1921, (Marriage, John Underwood, Jul. 26th, 1855).

1855. Marriages solemnized at the Parish Church in the Parish of St. Marylebone in the County of Middlesex

When Married	: July 26th, 1855
Name and Surname	: John Underwood/ Elizabeth Grant Mair
Age	: Of Full Age
Condition	: Bachelor/ Spindler
Rank of Profession	: Wholesale Stationer/ -
Residences at the time of Marriage	: St. Pancras/ St. Marylebone
Father's Name and Surname	: Thomas Underwood/ John Mair
Rank of Profession of Father	: Publisher/ Merchant

Married in the Parish Church according to the Rites and Ceremonies of the Established Church, by Licence or after _______ by me,

D. NcAnally Curate

This Marriage was solemnised between us,	John Underwood Elizabeth Grant Mair	in the presence of us,	Horace Grant Mary Easton Underwood

18610407

1861년 영국 인구주택총조사, (존 언더우드, 1861년 4월 7일).[17)]

지방행정구 : 세인트 판크라스　　교 구 : 홀리 트리니티
읍(邑) : 켄티쉬 타운
선거구 : 말러본　　시(市) : 말러본
주(州) : 미들섹스　　국 가 : 영국

등록 지구 : 판크라스　　등록 소지구 : 켄티쉬 타운
주 소 : 아서 가(街) 5번지

나 이 : 34　　추정 출생연도 : 1827년
관 계 : 세대주　　배우자 이름 : 이 G. 언더우드
출생지 : 런던, 미들섹스, 영국
직 업 : 잉크 제조업자

세대원 (이름, 나이, 세대주와의 관계)

이 G. 언더우드　33　[부인]
　추정 출생연도 : 1828
　출생지 : 영국 미들섹스 주 런던
에이치 E. 언더우드　4　[딸]
　아버지 : 존 언더우드　어머니 : 이 G. 언더우드
　출생지 : 영국 서머셋 주 클리브돈
존 T. 언더우드　3　[아들]
　출생지 : 영국 미들섹스 주 말러본

17) 영국의 1861년 인구주택총조사는 4월 7일 밤을 기준으로 조사됐다. 여행을 하거나 해외에 체류하고 있는 사람은 그들이 총조사 당일에 숙박했던 곳에서 조사됐다. 이 조사에서는 거주지 주소, 거주인의 이름과 세대주와의 관계, 결혼 여부, 만 나이, 성별, 직업, 출생지, 맹인, 귀머거리 혹은 지능 이상 여부 등을 조사했다.

프레드 W. 언더우드	2	[아들]
출생지	: 영국 미들섹스 주 세인트 판크라스	
호러스 G. 언더우드	1	[아들]
출생지	: 영국 미들섹스 주 세인트 판크라스	
샬롯 매덤	25	[손님]
출생지	: 영국 미들섹스 주 햄스테드	

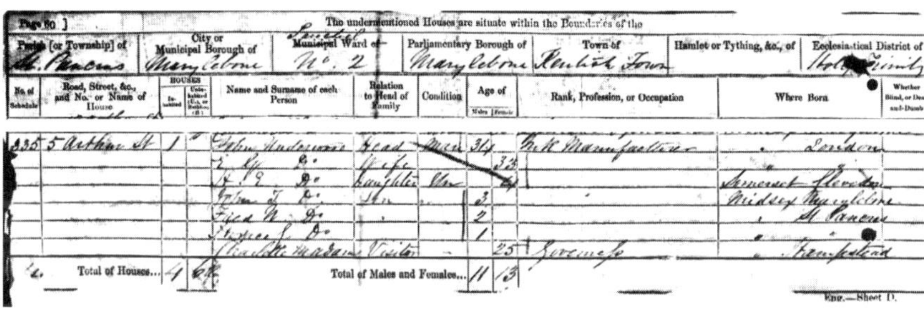

자료 1-13 *1861 England Census*, (John Underwood, Apr. 7th, 1861).

1861 England Census, (John Underwood, Apr. 7th, 1861).

Parish [or Township] of St. Pancras　　Ecclesiastical District of Holy Trinity

City or Municipal Borough of Marylebone

Parliamentary Borough of Marylebone　　Town of Kentish Town

Country/Island Middlesex　　Country England

Registration district : Pancras　　Sub-registration district : Kentish Town

Road, Street, & c., and No. or Name of House 5 Arthur St.

Age : 34　　Estimated Birth Year : 1827

Relation : Head　　Spouse's Name : E. G. Underwood

Where born : London, Middlesex, England

Rank, Profession, or Occupation : Ink Manufacturer

Household Members (Name, Age, Relation to Head)

E. G. Underwood 33 [Wife]

Estimated Birth Year : 1828

Where born : London, Middlesex, England

H. E. Underwood 4 [Daughter]

Father : John Underwood Mother : E. G. Underwood

Where born : Clevedon, Somerset, England

John T. Underwood 3 [Son]

Where born : Marylebone, Middlesex, England

Fred W. Underwood 2 [Son]

Where born : St. Pancras, Middlesex, England

Horace G. Underwood 1 [Son]

Where born : St. Pancras, Middlesex, England

Charlotte Madam 25 [Visitor]

Where born : Hampstead, Middlesex, England

18710402

1871년 영국 인구주택총조사, (존 언더우드, 1871년 4월 2일).[18]

지방행정구	: 혼지	교 구	: 세인트 마티어스
읍(邑)	: 하이게이트	주(州)	: 미들섹스
국 가	: 영국		

등록 지구	: 에드먼턴	등록 소지구	: 혼지
주 소	: 아치웨이 로드, 빅토리아 카티지 15호		

나 이	: 44	추정 출생연도	: 1827년
관 계	: 세대주	배우자 이름	: 캐롤라인 언더우드
출생지	: 런던, 영국	직 업	: 잉크 제조업자

세대원 (이름, 나이, 세대주와의 관계)

캐롤라인 언더우드		41	[부인]
추정 출생연도	: 1830	출생지	: 영국 에섹스 주 리틀
존 T. 언더우드		13	[아들]
출생지	: 영국 런던	직 업	: 학생
프레드 W. 언더우드		12	[아들]
출생지	: 영국 런던	직 업	: 학생
호러스 G. 언더우드		11	[아들]
출생지	: 영국 런던	직 업	: 학생
헬렌 M. 언더우드		8	[딸]

---

18) 영국의 1871년 인구주택총조사는 4월 2일 밤을 기준으로 조사됐다. 여행을 하거나 해외에 체류하고 있는 사람은 그들이 총조사 당일에 숙박했던 곳에서 조사됐다. 이 조사에서는 거주지 주소, 거주인의 이름, 출생지, 세대주와의 관계, 주택 소유 여부, 방의 개수, 각 개인의 만 나이, 성별, 결혼 여부, 직업, 맹인, 귀머거리 혹은 지능 이상 여부 등을 조사했다.

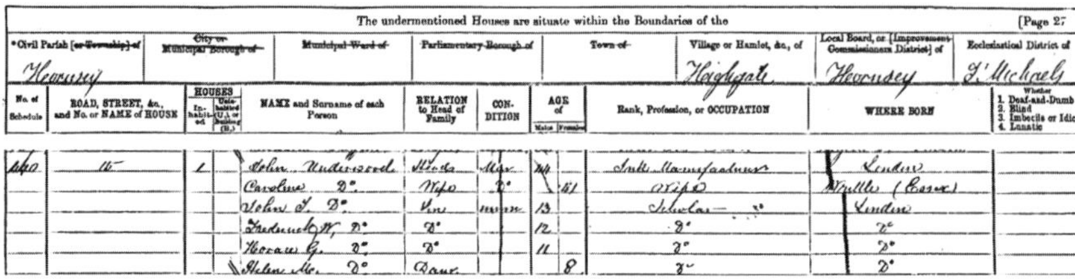
The undermentioned Houses are situate within the Boundaries of the [Page 27

Civil Parish [or Township] of	City or Municipal Borough of	Municipal Ward of	Parliamentary Borough of	Town of	Village or Hamlet, &c., of	Local Board, or [Improvement Commissioners District] of	Ecclesiastical District of
Hornsey					Highgate	Hornsey	S. Michaels

No. of Schedule	ROAD, STREET, &c., and No. or NAME of HOUSE	HOUSES In-habited	HOUSES Uninhabited (U.) or Building (B.)	NAME and Surname of each Person	RELATION to Head of Family	CONDITION	AGE of Males	AGE of Females	Rank, Profession, or OCCUPATION	WHERE BORN	Whether 1. Deaf-and-Dumb 2. Blind 3. Imbecile or Idiot 4. Lunatic
140	15	1		John Underwood	Head	Mar	44		Ink Manufacturer	London	
				Caroline Do.	Wife	Do.		41	Wife	Writtle (Essex)	
				John T. Do.	Son	unm	13		Scholar	London	
				Frederick W. Do.	Do.		12		Do.	Do.	
				Horace G. Do.	Do.		11		Do.	Do.	
				Helen M. Do.	Daur.			8	Do.	Do.	

자료 1-14 *1871 England Census*, (John Underwood, Apr. 2nd, 1871).

출생지 : 영국 런던 직 업 : 학생

1871 England Census, (John Underwood, Apr. 2nd, 1871).

Civil Parish of Hornsey Ecclesiastical Parish of St. Matthsas

Town of Highgate Country/Island Middlesex

Country England

Registration district : Edmonton Sub-registration district : Hornsey

Road, Street, & c., and No. or Name of House Archway Road, Victoria Cottages No. 15

Age : 44 Estimated Birth Year : 1827

Relation : Head Spouse's Name : Caroline Underwood

Where born : London, England Rank, Profession, or Occupation : Ink Manufacturer

Household Members (Name, Age, Relation to Head)

Caroline Underwood 41 [Wife]

Estimated Birth Year : 1830

Where born : Writtle, Essex, England

John T. Underwood 13 [Son]

Where born	: London, England	
Rank, Profession, or Occupation	: Scholar	
Fred W. Underwood	12	[Son]
Where born	: London, England	
Rank, Profession, or Occupation	: Scholar	
Horace G. Underwood	11	[Son]
Where born	: London, England	
Rank, Profession, or Occupation	: Scholar	
Helen M. Underwood	8	[Daughter]
Where born	: London, England	
Rank, Profession, or Occupation	: Scholar	

18741205

교인, 그로브개혁교회, 노스 버겐, 뉴저지, (존 언더우드, 1874년 12월 5일).

번호	이름	전 입[19]		전출		비고
		언제	어떻게	언제	어디로	
	언더우드, 존 T.	1874년 12월 5일	신앙 고백	1885년 11월 8일	라피엇스트리트 장로교회 (브루클린, 뉴욕)	
	언더우드, 프레데릭 W.	"	"	"	"	
	언더우드, 호러스 G.	"	"	"	"	한국 선교사
	언더우드, 헬렌 M.	"	"	"	"	
	부친 언더우드, 존 전 출	"	"			

Church Members, Grove Reformed Church, North Bergen, N. J., (John Underwood, Dec. 5th, 1874).

No.	Names	Received		Dismissed		Remarks
		When	How	When	Where to	
	Underwood, John T.	Dec. 5, 1874	Confession of Faith	Nov. 8. 1885	Lafayette Av Presb. Ch. Brooklyn, NY	

19) 언더우드 가족이 신앙고백을 할 당시 계모 캐롤라인은 이미 사망하였고, 큰 딸 한나는 아직 영국에 체류하고 있었다.

Underwood, Frederick W.	"	"	"	"	
Underwood, Horace G.	"	"	"	"	Missionary in Corea
Underwood, Helen M.	"	"	"	"	
F Underwood, John	"	"			
Dismissed					

자료 1-15 언더우드 집안이 다녔던 그로브 개혁교회 (1943년).

18800626

1880년 미국 연방 인구주택총조사, (존 언더우드, 1880년 6월 26일).[20)]

1880년 거주지 : 노스 버겐, 허드슨, 뉴저지 주

이 름	: 존 언더우드		
나 이	: 53세	추정 출생년도	: 1827년
출생지	: 영국	가장과의 관계	: 본인 (가장)
부친의 출생지	: 영국	모친의 출생지	: 영국
직 업	: 제조화학자		

세대원 (이름, 나이, 세대주와의 관계)

넌 언더우드[21)]	28세	[딸]	
추정 출생연도	: 1852	결혼 여부	: 독신
부친 이름	: 존 언더우드		
부친의 출생지	: 영국	모친의 출생지	: 영국
직 업	: 교사		
한나 언더우드	24	[딸]	
추정 출생연도	: 1856	관 계	: 딸
결혼 여부	: 독신	부친 이름	: 존 언더우드
부친의 출생지	: 영국	모친의 출생지	: 영국

20) 미국의 1880년 센서스는 제10차 센서스였으며, 6월 1일을 기준으로 했다. 이 조사에는 약 5천만 명에 대한 자료가 들어 있는데, 세대 거주자의 출생지, 직업, 건강 상태, 교육 정도 등을 알 수 있다. 1890년 센서스 자료가 불타 없어졌기에 1800년대 말 미국의 상황을 이해하는데 중요한 자료로 이용되고 있다. 1880년 센서스에서는 처음으로 세대주와의 관계를 알 수 있다. 또한 주, 카운티 및 다른 행정 구역, 거리(street) 및 번지, 센서스 시행 당시의 징병, 결혼 여부, 비고용 상태로 있었던 기간, 각 개인의 부모가 어느 주 혹은 군에서 출생했는가 하는 자료들이 포함되어 있다.

21) 1873년 후처 캐롤라인과 함께 미국으로 이주한 앤 넌으로 추정된다.

(존) 토머스 언더우드 23 [아들]
추정 출생연도 : 1857
결혼 여부 : 독신 부친 이름 : 존 언더우드
부친의 출생지 : 영국 모친의 출생지 : 영국
직 업 : 화학자

프레드 언더우드 23 [아들]
추정 출생연도 : 1857
결혼 여부 : 독신 부친 이름 : 존 언더우드
부친의 출생지 : 영국 모친의 출생지 : 영국
직 업 : 화학자

호러스 언더우드 20 [아들]
추정 출생연도 : 1860
결혼 여부 : 독신 부친 이름 : 존 언더우드
부친의 출생지 : 영국 모친의 출생지 : 영국
직 업 : 학생

헬렌 언더우드 18 [딸]
추정 출생연도 : 1862
결혼 여부 : 독신 부친 이름 : 존 언더우드
부친의 출생지 : 영국 모친의 출생지 : 영국

1880 United States Federal Census, (June 26th, 1880, John Underwood).

Home in 1880 : North Bergen, Hudson, New Jersey

Name : John Underwood
Age : 53 Estimated Birth Year : 1827
Birthplace : England

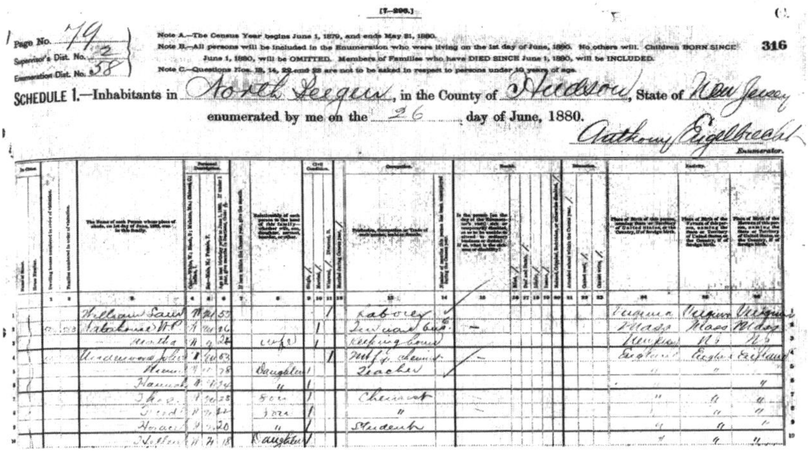

Page No. 79
Supervisor's Dist. No. 2
Enumeration Dist. No. 58

Note A.—The Census Year begins June 1, 1879, and ends May 31, 1880.
Note B.—All persons will be included in the Enumeration who were living on the 1st day of June, 1880. No others will. Children BORN SINCE June 1, 1880, will be OMITTED. Members of Families who have DIED SINCE June 1, 1880, will be INCLUDED.
Note C.—Questions Nos. 13, 14, 22 and 23 are not to be asked in respect to persons under 10 years of age.

316

SCHEDULE 1.—Inhabitants in North Bergen, in the County of Hudson, State of New Jersey, enumerated by me on the 26 day of June, 1880. Anthony Engelbrecht, Enumerator.

자료 1-16 *1880 United States Federal Census*, (June 26th, 1880, John Underwood).

Relation to Head of Household : Self (Head)

Father's birthplace: England Mother's birthplace : England

Occupation : Manufacturing Chemist

Household Members (Name. Age)

Nunn Underwood[22] 28

Estimated Birth Year	: 1852	Relation	: Daughter
Marital Status	: Single	Father's Name	: John Underwood
Father's Birthplace	: England	Mother's Birthplace	: England
Occupation	: Teacher		

Hannah Underwood 24

Estimated Birth Year	: 1856	Relation	: Daughter
Marital Status	: Single	Father's Name	: John Underwood
Father's Birthplace	: England	Mother's Birthplace	: England

22) It is assumed that Nunn Underwood was Ann Nunn who immigrated with Caroline in 1873.

(John) Thomas Underwood	23		
Estimated Birth Year	: 1857	Relation	: Son
Marital Status	: Single	Father's Name	: John Underwood
Father's Birthplace	: England	Mother's Birthplace	: England
Occupation	: Chemist		
Fred Underwood	23		
Estimated Birth Year	: 1857	Relation	: Son
Marital Status	: Single	Father's Name	: John Underwood
Father's Birthplace	: England	Mother's Birthplace	: England
Occupation	: Chemist		
Horace Underwood	20		
Estimated Birth Year	: 1860	Relation	: Son
Marital Status	: Single	Father's Name	: John Underwood
Father's Birthplace	: England	Mother's Birthplace	: England
Occupation	: Student		
Helen Underwood	18		
Estimated Birth Year	: 1862	Relation	: Daughter
Marital Status	: Single	Father's Name	: John Underwood
Father's Birthplace	: England	Mother's Birthplace	: England

18810607

뉴저지 주, 사망 및 매장 색인, 1798~1971년, (존 언더우드, 1881년 6월 7일).

이 름	: 존 언더우드		
출생일	: 1827년 경	출생지	: 영국
사망일	: 1881년 6월 7일	나 이	: 54년 3개월
사망지	: 뉴저지 주 허드슨 카운티 노스 버겐		
결혼 여부	: 사별		
주 거	: 뉴저지	모친 출생지	: 영국

New Jersey, Deaths and Burials Index, 1798~1971, (John Underwood, June 7th, 1881).

Name	: Jno Underwood		
Birth Date	: abt 1827	Birth Place	: England
Death Date	: 7 Jun 1881	Death Age	: 54 years 3 months
Death Place	: North Bergen, Hudson, New Jersey		
Marital Status	: Widowed		
Residence	: New Jersey	Mother Birth Place	: England
FHL Film Number	: 589829		

18810609

매장기록, 그로브교회 묘지, 노스 버겐, 뉴저지, (존 언더우드, 1881년 6월 9일).

언더우드, 존　　　　　　　　　　54세

1881년 6월 9일
181 구역

Burial Record, Grove Church Cemetery, North Bergen, N. J., (John Underwood, June 9th, 1881).

Underwood John　　　　　　　　　　54y

June 9 1881
L, 181

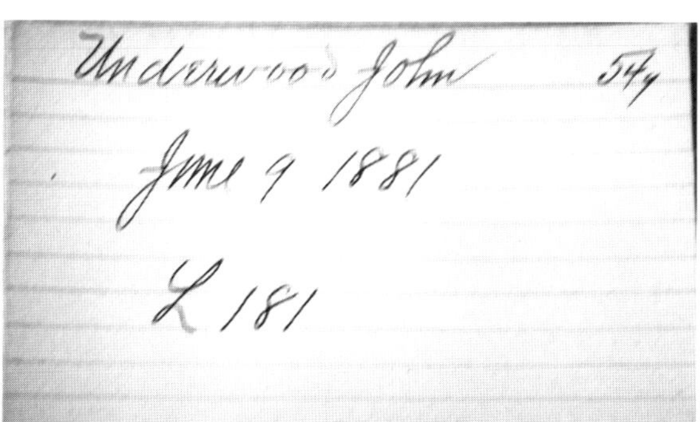

자료 1-17 *Burial Record, Grove Reformed Church, North Bergen, N. J., (John Underwood, June 9th, 1881).*

00000000

매장기록, 그로브교회 묘지, 노스 버겐, 뉴저지.

181 구역	서구역	
1881년 6월 9일	존 언더우드	54세
1891년 3월 25일	프레데릭 언더우드	33세
1916년 10월 15일	호러스 G. 언더우드 목사	57세
1938년 8월 5일	한나 E. 스티븐스	82세
1915년 6월 10일	레베카 C. 넌	65세
1926년 3월 6일	윌리엄 B. 언더우드	생후 2일

Burial Record, Grove Church Cemetery, North Bergen, N. J.

Lot. No. 181	West Half	
July 8, 1881	John Underwood	54 years
April 25, 1891	Frederick Underwood	33 years
October 15, 1916	Rev. Horace G. Underwood	57 years
August 5, 1938	Hannah E. Stephens	82 years
June 10, 1915	Rebecca C. Nunn	65 years
March 6, 1926	William B. Underwood	2 days

그로브교회 묘지, 노스 버겐, 뉴저지, (2015년, 박형우).

자료 1-18 Grove Church Cemetery. (2015년 3월 촬영). A. 묘지 입구. B. 181구역. 돌로 경계가 지워진 이 구역이 181구역 전체인지, 181구역 서구역인지 확실하지 않다. 또한 아버지 존의 묘비석도 찾을 수 없었다. 이곳에는 윗줄에 5개, 아랫줄에 2개의 묘지석이 있다. C~G 윗줄 맨 왼쪽의 묘비석(C)이 호러스의 것이며, 그 왼쪽(D)에 누나 한나의 묘비석이 있다. 그 다음 2개는 언더우드 집안과 관련이 없는 것이며, 아마 181구역 동구역의 묘비석일지도 모른다. 윗줄 맨 왼쪽의 묘비석(E)은 윌리엄(William B. Underwood)의 것이지만, 호러스와의 관계가 확실하지 않다. 아랫줄 왼쪽의 묘비석(F)은 이복누나 레베카 C. 넌의 것이며, 오른쪽의 묘비석(G)은 형 프레데릭의 것이다. 형 존 T.는 브루클린의 그린우드 묘지에 묻혔다.

그로브교회 묘지, 노스 버겐, 뉴저지, (1990년, 이광린).

자료 1-19 호러스의 묘비석. 이 사진은 이광린의 저서에 수록되어 있는 것이며, 최근의 사진 보다 글자가 훨씬 선명하다.

이광린, 초대 언더우드 선교사의 생애. 서울: 연세대학교 출판부, 서울 1990, 265~6쪽

"...... 대리석으로 구획이 짜여 있는데다가 '언더우드' 가문을 표시하는 'U'자가 그 위에 새겨져 있었다. 대리석 구획을 만드는 데에는 돈이 많이 들었을 것이므로 언더우드의 형으로 타이프라이터회사의 사장이었던 '존'이 돈을 냈을 것으로 생각되었다. 구획 안에 일곱 분이 묻혀 있었고 윗부분에 세 분, 아랫부분에 네 분이 묻혀 있었다.[23] 비석은 모두 쓰러져 있었고 다섯 분의 비문은 읽을 수 있었으나 두 분의 비문은 마멸되어 읽을 수 없었다. 관리인 말에 비석은 처음에 세워져 있었으나 근자에 와서 모두 쓰러졌다고 하였다.

윗부분 좌측 첫 번이 언더우드, 두 번째가 누이 '스테판' (Hannah E. Stephens),

23) 7개의 묘비석이 2015년과 다르게 배치되어 있는데, 이는 1999년 5월 20일 유해를 양화진 외국인묘지로 이장하는 과정에서 변경되었기 때문으로 생각된다.

세 번째가 동생 '윌리엄' (William B. Underwood)의 무덤이었다. 아랫부분 좌측의 비문은 마멸되어 읽을 수 없었고, 두 번째는 언더우드의 형 '프레드릭' (Frederick W. Underwood), 세 번째는 '난' (Rebecca C. Nuun), 네 번째의 비문 역시 읽을 수 없었다. 뒤에 한국에 돌아와 원일한 박사에게 물어 보았더니 아랫부분 첫 번째는 언더우드의 계모 '난' (Nunn), 세 번째는 계모의 동생, 네 번째는 아버지 '존' (John)일 것이라 하였다.[24)]

24) 저자는 '존'의 묘비석을 확인하지 못하였다. 또한 후처 '넌'은 언더우드 가족이 신앙을 고백하기 전에 사망했으므로 개혁교회 묘지에 묻혔을 명분이 적다. '레베카'는 계모의 동생이 아니라 딸, 즉 호러스의 이복 누나이다.

19130000

하워드 J. 뱅커, 미국의 언더우드 가문. 제2권, 1913, 625쪽.[25]

1231a. 뉴저지 주 뉴더햄의 존 언더우드, (영국 런던의 토머스의 아들) 출생. 1829년[26] 영국 런던; 결혼. 마드러러에서 존과 엘리자베스 (그랜트) 메어의 딸로 태어난 엘리자베스 그랜트 메어와 1855년 결혼하여 아래의 자녀들을 가짐:[27]

i. 한나 엘리자베스, 출생. 1856년; 결혼. 클래런스 스티븐스, 1명의 자녀를 가짐: 존 언더우드 스티븐스. 이 가족은 1912년 당시 매사추세츠 주 피츠필드에 거주하고 있음.

ii. 존 토머스, 출생. 1857년. (1231b를 볼 것.)

iii. 프레데릭 윌스, 출생. 1858년; 사망. 1892년[28] 뉴욕 블루클린.

iv. 호러스 그랜트, 출생. 1859년 7월 19일. (1231c를 볼 것.)

v. 헬렌 메리, 출생 1862년; 결혼. 조지 파웰 코나드, 4명의 자녀를 두었음: (i) 이디스 언더우드 코나드; (2) 프레데릭 언더우드 코나드; (3) 헬렌 이블린 코나드; (4) 릴리언 언더우드 코나드.

vi. 메리 이스턴, 출생. 1865년; 사망. 생후 2개월.

존은 실용 화학자가 되었으며, 사본을 만들 수 있는 필기용 및 인쇄용 잉크, 그리고 화학 안전용지를 발명했다. 그는 잉크, 특히 타자기용 잉크 제조업에 종사했다. 그의 부인과 막내 딸은 1865년 영국에서 사망했으며, 1872년 가족과 함께 미국으로 이주했다.[29] 그는 1882년 뉴저지 주 뉴더햄에서 사망했다.[30]

---

25) 릴리어스의 저술 첫 부분에 인용된 문헌이다.

26) 1827년생이다.

27) 다른 자료를 통해 확인하지 못하였다.

28) 1891년이다.

29) 이때 존은 혼자 미국으로 이주했고, 1873년 후처 캐롤라인이 한나를 제외한 나머지 가족들과 함께 미국으로 이주했다.

30) 1881년이다.

Howard J. Banker, *The Underwood Families of America. In Two Volumes*, Volume 2, 1913, pp. 625.[31)]

1231a. John Underwood of New Durham, N. J., (son of Thomas of London, England) b. in London, England, in 182932); m. in 1855 Elizabeth Grant Maire who was born in Madeira, a dau. of John and Elizabeth (Grant) Maire, and had children:[33)]

i. Hannah Elizabeth, b. in 1856; m. Clarence Stephens and has one child: John Underwood Stephens. The family lives (1912) in Pittsfield, Mass.

ii. John Thomas, b. in 1857. (See no. 1231b.)

iii. Frederick Wills, b. in 1858; d. in Brooklyn, N. Y., in 1892.[34)]

iv. Horace Grant, b. 19 July 1859. (See no. 1231c.)

v. Helen Mary, b. in 1862; m. George Powell Conard and has four children: (i) Edith Underwood Conard; (2) Frederick Underwood Conard; (3) Helen Evelyn Conard; (4) Lilian Underwood Conard.

vi. Mary Eastern, b. in 1865; d. aged two months.

John became a practical chemist and invented copyable writing and printing inks and chemical safety paper. He engaged in the manufacture of inks and especially typewriting ink. His wife and youngest child died in England in 1865 and he removed with his family to America in 1872.[35)] He d. in New Durham, N. J., in 1882.[36)]

31) Cited in "Underwood of Korea" by Lillias H. Underwood.
32) Born in 1827.
33) I couldn't confirm with other data.
34) Died in 1891.
35) John immigrated to America by himself, and rest members of his family except Hannah removed by his second wife to America in 1873.
36) 1881.

19180000

Lillias H. Underwood, *Underwood of Korea*. Fleming H. Revell Company, New York, 1918, pp. 15~19, pp. 21~23.[37]

Chapter I

Ancestry And Training

pp. 15~19

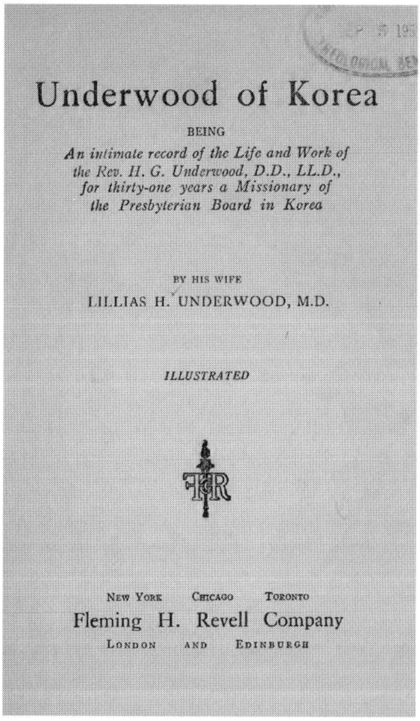

Underwood of Korea

BEING

An intimate record of the Life and Work of the Rev. H. G. Underwood, D.D., LL.D., for thirty-one years a Missionary of the Presbyterian Board in Korea

BY HIS WIFE

LILLIAS H. UNDERWOOD, M.D.

ILLUSTRATED

NEW YORK CHICAGO TORONTO

Fleming H. Revell Company

LONDON AND EDINBURGH

자료 1-20 Lillias H. Underwood, *Underwood of Korea*. Fleming H. Revell Company, New York, 1918.

In the second volume of the Book of the Underwood Families in America is found on page 625 the following: "John Underwood of New Durham, N. J., son of Thomas of London, England, bom in London, England, in 1829, married in 1855, Elisabeth Grant Maire." Six children were bom to this couple, of whom Horace Grant, born in London, July 19, 1859, was the fourth.

Thomas Underwood, the grandfather of Horace, was with his brother George a publisher of medical and other books, having his place of business in Fleet Street, London. They were both earnest Christian men, of English birth. The wife of Thomas was a daughter of Dr. Alexander Waugh, of Scotland, whose name even now is

37) 호러스 언더우드의 집안 및 그의 성격에 대해 유일하게 언급했던 부인 릴리어스의 저서 「Underwood of Korea」에서 해당 부분의 원문을 이곳에 실었다.

well known among Presbyterians in both England and Scotland. He was a man of much note and great influence, a powerful preacher and deeply interested in foreign missions. His character, his gifts and his whole attitude of mind are so strikingly like those of his great-grandson Horace Underwood, that it is worth while to note a few facts concerning him as set down in his biography.

Bom in 1754, he had graduated from the University of Edinburgh in 1770 and from the University of Aberdeen in 1777. He was licensed to preach at twenty-five, and had competing calls from London and Edinburgh, and became pastor of the Wells Street congregation, London. He was actively interested in a union of Episcopalians, Presbyterians, Baptists, Independents and Methodists which was formed for publishing a religious periodical for the spread of scripture truths. An appeal for missions had been made in 1794 through this paper, and in July of 1795 a meeting of some twenty members was held and a missionary society was formed. The committee who were to make plans for this society were twelve leading divines, including Dr. Waugh. The latter was individually the framer of the "fundamental principle" of the Society. This has been preserved in his own handwriting as follows: "As the union of God's people of various denominations in carrying on this great work is a most desirable object, so to prevent, if possible, any cause of future dissension it is declared to be a fundamental principle of this missionary society that our design is not to send Presbyterian, Independent, Episcopalian or any other form of church order and government, about which there may be a difference of opinion among serious persons, but the Glorious Gospel of the Blessed God to the heathen, and it shall be left to the minds of the persons whom God shall call into the fellowship of His Son from among them to assume for themselves such form of church government as to them shall appear most agreeable to the Word of God." This in 1795! Are we progressing? No wonder that the great-grand- son's ideal was unity!

To quote further from Dr. Waugh's biography: "On all occasions for thirty-three years. Dr. Waugh was uniformly the peace-maker in the society. For twenty-eight years he sat by the unanimous appointment of his brethren as chairrman of the examining committee of this London Missionary Society. He was deeply interested in the British and Foreign Bible Society from its beginning, in which he took part in 1804. For thirty-seven years he took an active interest in the Scottish Hospital, the Hibernian Society, the Irish Evangelical, the Religious Tract and Anti-Slavery Societies."

If there is anything in the theory of heredity, we have here in this great resemblance in the character and deeds of this man and those of his great-grandson a marked example. The broad-mindedness, the wide-reaching philanthropy, the love of unity, the charity, the qualities of leadership and organization, the intellectual gifts, all so similar, make one feel a bit creepy and we wonder whether Alexander wasn't pretty close to Horace, or at least whether the mantle of the one had not fallen upon the other.

John Underwood, the grandson of Dr. Waugh, and Horace's father, the manufacturing chemist, was both a scientist and inventor of rare intellectual gifts. He seems to have been a veritable genius, and one is tempted to turn aside to sketch that life so full of interest, accomplished benefits, sore trial, deep Christian experiences and victories of faith. His ardent, earnest Christianity evidenced in many evangelistic labors as well as in beautiful daily life, his constant looking for the coming of the Lord, his inventions which brought him a medal and words of high commendation from the Prince Consort himself in behalf of the Royal Society of Arts, were often recalled by his son with pardonable pride. He loved to tell how his father in his student days had an anonymous newspaper discussion with the famous Dr. Liebig of Germany on the potato disease, and how when he, John, had been admitted to be the victor and names were called for, the general surprise to find that John Underwood, aged twenty, student at Colchester, had been the successful contestant, only equalled his own astonishment to find that his opponent was the great! scientist whom he would not have presumed to oppose had he known his identity.

The energy, the versatility, the sunny, kindly, jovial nature, the wonderful indomitability and the scientific bias which, chanced they to be making inks, dictionaries or typewriters, founding missionary societies or schools and colleges, marked the character of Dr. Waugh and his grandsons and great-grandsons are extremely interesting to note.

Not only was Horace's father a remarkable instance of this but his brother John and his cousin Dr. Arthur Underwood were cast in much the same mold, though each had a different calling. The story of how John perfected his inks, typewriter supplies and typewriters, how he fought and outwitted the trusts, organized his companies, built tremendous factories, extended his sales to the limits of the known world, is too long to be told here, but it meant brains, courage, indefatigability, vision, concentration and scientific methods. The same broad, kindly, philanthropic spirit seen in Dr. Waugh, led his grandson generously to support the cause of Christ at home and abroad.

To return to Horace's father, John Underwood: his devout Christian character made a deep impression on all his children. He was a busy man, but he spent most of his Sunday afternoons with them when his mission school was done, and Horace always recalled those hours with great pleasure. Sunday was not a tiresome day for them; at church there were stools of varied height to suit short pendent legs, and everything was done to make church-going comfortable as well as interesting; of course the text and something about the sermon were required of the older ones when they returned home. Especially was Horace filled with his father's eager hope and longing for the return of the Lord. It was his constant thought and he never ceased to look and pray for that Glorious Appearing in his own time. This hope he passed on to the Koreans from the first days when he could teach them at all, and now probably the whole Korean church is one in looking and waiting for that day.

The wife and mother of this Underwood family must have been an extremely attractive personality. All the relatives have spoken of her in terms of unstinted praise and have repeatedly said that no one ever heard her raise her voice in anger or speak a single hasty or unkind word. But poor John Underwood was marked for trouble, and lost in one year, 1865, his sweet wife and her baby, and his beloved old mother. Not long after, financial difficulties due largely to the dishonesty of a partner, fell upon him, and he at length began to think it would be better to try his fortunes in a new country. A few years after his wife's death, left with five little children on his hands, he had married again.

pp. 21~23

The tie of affection between the Underwood children was always very strong from the earliest recollection of them all. Fred, who was reported to be more of a saint than the others, seemed to wield a great influence over them. Horace often told how this brother asked him to learn the 119th psalm as a favor, and how he, Horace, rebelling at the magnitude of the task, most positively and emphatically refused. "Think how you would feel if I should die and you had refused my last request," was the gentle but sad answer. Now Fred had weak lungs and took cod liver oil, so Horace's hard heart melted, as it always did when there was a plea for pity, and he forthwith tackled and learned the mighty psalm. But it was not strange for these children to learn Scripture. All three of the boys at least were obliged to memorize the whole book of Hebrews and other portions of the Bible so that they could go backward and forward and recite any verse or chapter called for by their father. A relative who saw much of them at the time, writes: "They were all lovely little children; we were very proud of them." Little Horace was very polite; would take off his hat and bow very low even when entering a shop, and then would frequently go out of the place forgetting the hat altogether. Horace's absent-minded ways were a joke in the family. He would seem to be in a brown study with, no doubt, great dreams in his child's brain. At one time when fhe family were in straitened circumstances and money was not too plentiful, Horace was given a five-dollar bill to make some purchases for the household at the grocery. Cheerfully he started forth but scarcely had he reached the shop when, to his horror, he discovered that he had unconsciously bitten off little by little one scrap after another of the precious bill like a piece of common paper, until only a small and useless fragment remained. This meant almost a tragedy at that time, but the very make-up of the boy's mind which caused it, made him capable in later days, of very remarkable concentration of thought upon any business which called for his attention.

On Sundays, when the father for any reason could not read with and amuse them, they often played church and on these occasions Horace was always by common consent, the preacher. Mounted on a stool or chair, he would lead the service in the regular way, and preach the sermon to the perfect satisfaction of both his audience and himself. As Fred had the reputation of being the saintliest and John was the oldest and most domineering, either one of them would have been more likely to take the leading part of preaching, had it not been that Horace was already beginning to develop some of those gifts which carried audiences away, when he stood in real pulpits in later years, or told Korea's story so winningly.

But, as I have said, financial misfortune dogged their poor father until, in 1872, he decided to go to America and start anew. The Boys had been in France only two years when they were sent for to follow him to the new country. Horace was then twelve, almost thirteen, and Fred fourteen years of age. One is greatly tempted to linger over these early years in America: the brave struggle under difficult circumstances in a new country; the slow but sure coming of success, earned by vigilance, energy, determination, brains and courage. Even in their most straitened circumstances they formed a circle of friends among the best people; associated themselves with the Dutch Reformed Church; took part in all the church work and became valued members of the little community. It is recorded in the book of Grove Church, that Mr. John Underwood the father, and his children John T., Frederick Wills, Horace Grant, and Helen Evelyn, joined that church on profession of faith December 5th, 1874. No doubt the difficulty and delay in getting letters from England at that time led their father to join as by profession, as he was a member of the church for many years in England.

2-2 어머니 – 엘리자베스 그랜트 메어

Mother – Elizabeth Grant Mair

17921027

영국, 출생 및 세례 발췌, 1538~1975, (존 메어, 1792년 10월 27일).[38]

출생일 : 1792년 10월 27일　　세례일 : 1792년 11월 13일

세례 장소 : 영국 런던 말러본 말러본로드 세인트매리교회

부 친 : 알렉산더 메어　　모 친 : 프랜시스 헬레나

England, Select Births and Christenings, 1538-1975, (John Mair, Oct. 27th, 1792).[39]

Birth Date : Oct. 27th, 1792　　Baptism Date : Nov. 13th, 1792

Baptism Place : Saint Mary - St Marylebone Road, St Marylebone, London, England

Father : Alexander Mair　　Mother : Frances Helena

FHL Film Number : 580906, 580907

38) 엘리자베스의 아버지, 즉 호러스의 외할아버지이다.

39) Father of Elizabeth, i. e. maternal grandfather of Horace G. Underwood.

18280211

영국, 출생 및 세례 발췌, 1538~1975, (엘리자베스 그랜트 메어, 1828년 2월 11일).

출생일	: 1828년 2월 11일	세례일	: 1828년 9월 28일
세례 장소	: 영국 런던 세인트 올레이브 하트 스트리트 교회		
아버지	: 존 메어	어머니	: 헬렌

England, Select Births and Christenings, 1538-1975, (Elizabeth Grant Mair, Feb. 11th, 1828).

Birth Date	: 11 Feb 1828	Baptism Date	: 28 Sep 1828
Baptism Place	: Saint Olave Hart Street, London, London, England		
Father	: John Mair	Mother	: Helen
FHL Film Number	: 557013		

18280928

영국, 런던, 출생 및 세례, 1813~1906, (세례, 엘리자베스 그랜트 메어, 1828년 9월 28일).

세례일	: 1828년 9월 28일		
아버지 이름	: 존 메어	어머니 이름	: 헬렌 메어
교구 혹은 구빈구연합	: 세인트 올레이브 하트 스트리트		
자치도시	: 런던 시	등록 유형	: 교구 등록

London, England, Births and Baptisms, 1813~1906, (Elizabeth Grant Mair, Sept. 28th, 1828).

Record Type	: Baptism	Baptism Date	: Sept. 28th, 1828
Father's Name	: John Mair	Mother's name	: Helen Mair
Parish or Poor Law Union	: St Olave Hart Street		
Borough	: City of London	Register Type	: Parish Registers

18510330

1851년 영국 인구주택총조사, (엘리자베스 그랜트 메어, 1851년 3월 30일).

지방 행정구 : 길포드 홀리 트리니티
카운티 : 서리 국 가 : 영국

등록 지구 : 길포드 등록 소지구 : 워킹

나 이 : 23 추정 출생연도 : 1828년
관 계 : 조수 직 업 : 독어 및 불어교사
출생지 : 영국 미들섹스 주 웨스트민스터

세내원 (이름, 나이)
덩컨 루이스 57
추정 출생연도 : 1794년 관 계 : 세대주
직 업 : 의사
엘리자베스 에이 루이스 50
추정 출생연도 : 1801년 관 계 : 아내
해리엇 골드스톤 29
관 계 : 처제 직 업 : 음악 및 미술교사
메리 소파 클로드 50
관 계 : 방문객

[이하 생략]

1851 England Census, (Elizabeth Grant Mair, Mar. 30th, 1851).

Civil parish : Guildford Holy Trinity

County/Island : Surrey   Country : England

Registration district : Guildford   Sub-registration distric : Woking

Age : 23   Estimated Birth Year : 1828

Relation : Assistant

Where born : Westminster, Middlesex, England

Occupation : Professor of German & French

Household Members (Name, Age)

Duncan Lewis 57

Estimated Birth Year : 1794   Relation : Head

Occupation : M. D., actually not practising

Elizabeth A Lewis 50

Estimated Birth Year : 1801   Relation : Wife

Harriet Goldstone 29

Relation : Sister-in-Law

Occupation : Professor of Music & Drawing

Mary Sopha Claude 50

Relation : Visitor

Anne Hoskins 20

Relation : Pupil

Annie Mary Dawson 16

Relation : Pupil

Harriot Dawson 14

Relation : Pupil

Catharine E Flintoff 17

Relation : Pupil

Annie Eliz Flintoff 13

Relation : Pupil

Catherine A Flintoff 12

Relation : Pupil

Adeline Flintoff 11

Relation : Pupil

Flora Catherine Flintoff 8

Relation : Pupil

Mary Flintoff 10

Relation : Pupil

Emma While 3

Relation : Pupil

Margaret Golling 30

Relation : Servant Occupation : Cook

Mary Enticknaf 25

Relation : Servant Occupation : Housemaid

Auda Clark 21

Relation : Servant Occupation : Parlor Maid

18650000

영국 및 웨일즈, 무료 출생결혼사망 사망 색인, 1837~1915, (엘리자베스 그랜트 언더우드, 1865년 4~6월).

이 름	: 엘리자베스 그랜트 언더우드
등록연도	: 1865년
등록분기	: 4~6월
등록지구	: 판크라스
카운티	: 런던

England & Wales, FreeBMD Death Index, 1837~1915, (Elizabeth Grant Underwood, Apr.~June, 1865).

Name	: Elizabeth Grant Underwood
Registration Year	: 1865
Registration Quarter	: Apr-May-Jun
Registration district	: Pancras
Inferred County	: London
Volume	: 1b
Page	: 122

2-3 계모 – 캐롤라인 넌

Step–mother – Caroline Nunn

18510330

1851년 영국 인구주택총조사, (캐롤라인 넌, 1851년 3월 30일).

군 구(郡區)	: 치덤	교구(敎區)	: 비교구교회
자치도시	: 맨체스터	카운티	: 랭커셔 주
국 가	: 영국		

등록 지구	: 맨체스터	등록 소지구	: 치덤
주 소	: 브로턴 뷰 5호		

나 이	: 23세	추정 출생연도	: 1828년
관 계	: 아내	배우자 이름	: 윌리엄 W. 넌
출생지	: 리틀, 에식스 주	직 업	: 외투 제작자

세대원 (이름, 나이)

윌리엄 W. 넌 26세

추정 출생연도 : 1826년 관 계 : 남편

출생지 : 힐리온스 브럼프스테드, 랭커셔 주

직 업 : 창고업

레베카 C. 넌 10/12세

추정 출생연도 : 1849년 관 계 : 딸

출생지 : 치덤, 랭커셔 주

도라 홀신 23세

추정 출생연도 : 1828년 관 계 : 하인

출생지 : 아일랜드

1851 England Census, (Caroline Nunn, Mar. 30th, 1851).

Township of	: Cheetham	Ecclesiastical District of	: Collegiate Church
Borough of	: Manchester	County/Island	: Lancashire
Country	: England		

Registration district : Manchester Sub-registration district : Cheetham

Road, Street, & c., and No. or Name of House : Broughton View No. 5

Age	: 23	Estimated Birth Year	: 1828
Relation	: Wife	Spouse's Name	: William W. Nunn
Where born	: Writtle Essex	Occupation	: Mantle Maker

Household Members (Name, Age)

William W. Nunn 26

Estimated Birth Year : 1826 Relation : Husband

Where born : Helions Bumpstead, Lancashire

Occupation : Salesman Warehouse

Rebecca C. Nunn 10/12

Estimated Birth Year : 1849 Relation : Daughter

Gender : Female Where born : Cheetham, Lancashire

Dora Holshin 23

Estimated Birth Year : 1828 Relation : Servant

Where born : Ireland

18730303

뉴욕, 승객 명단, 1820~1957년, (캐롤라인 언더우드, 1873년 3월 3일).

출발 항구 : 프랑스 르아브르 및 영국 런던
행선지 : 미합중국
도착 항구 : 뉴욕 항
선 명 : 덴마크 호

이름[40]	나이	성별	직업	국적	출생지
캐롤라인 언더우드	40	여성	아내	영국	영국
앤 넌[41]	19	〃	무직	〃	〃
J. 언더우드	16	남성	〃	〃	〃
프레드	15	〃	〃	〃	〃
에이치 G.	14	〃	〃	〃	〃
헬렌	10	여성	자녀	〃	〃

New York, Passenger Lists, 1820~1957, (Caroline Underwood, Mar. 3rd, 1873).

Port of Departure : Le Havre, France and London, England
Destination : United States of America
Port of Arrival : New York, New York
Ship Name : Denmark

---

40) 당시 한나는 베드포드에서 공부하고 있었으며, 1875년 미국으로 합류하였다.
41) 'Nunn'이란 성으로 보아 캐롤라인의 딸, 즉 레베카의 동생으로 추정된다.

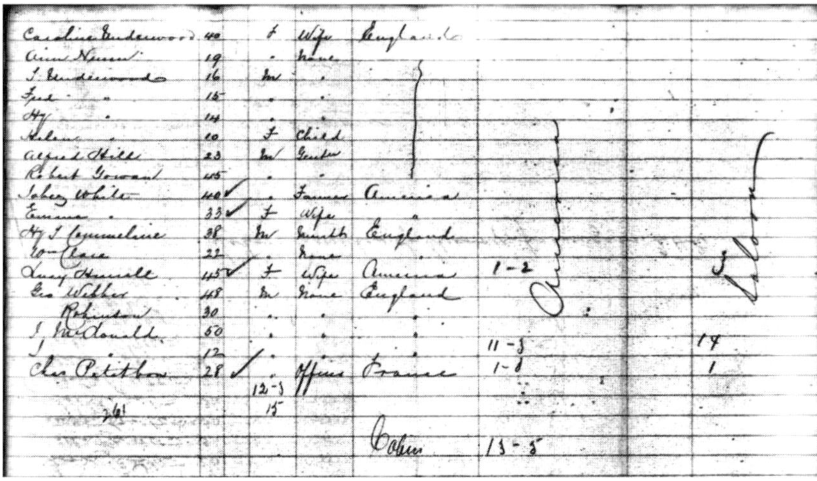

자료 1-21 *New York, Passenger Lists, 1820~1957*. (Caroline Underwood, Mar. 3rd, 1873).

Name[42)]	Age	Gender	Occupation	Ethnicity/ Nationality	Place of Origin
Caroline Underwood	40	Female	Wife	English	England
Ann Nunn[43)]	19	"	None	"	"
J. Underwood	16	Male	"	"	"
Fred.	15	"	"	"	"
H. G.	14	"	"	"	"
Helen	10	Female	Child	"	"

42) Hannah was studying at Bedford, and joined to her family in 1875.

43) It is assumed that 'Ann Nunn' is the daughter of Caroline, i. e. sister of Rebecca C. Nunn.

18740320

뉴저지, 사망 및 매장 색인, 1798~1971년, (캐롤라인 언더우드, 1874년 3월 20일).

이 름	: 캐롤라인 언더우드		
출생일	: 1829년 경	출생지	: 영국
사망일	: 1874년 3월 20일	나 이	: 45세
사망지	: 뉴저지 주 허드슨 카운티 노드 버겐		
결혼 여부	: 기혼	직 업	: __
주 거	: 뉴저지		

New Jersey, Deaths and Burials Index, 1798~1971, (Caroline Underwood, Mar. 20th, 1874).

Name	: Caroline Underwood		
Birth Date	: abt 1829	Birth Place	: England
Death Date	: Mar. 20th, 1881	Death Age	: 45 years
Death Place	: North Bergen, Hudson, New Jersey		
Marital Status	: Married	Occupation	: U
FHL Film Number	: 584597		

3.
언더우드의 형제자매 (Brothers & Sisters)

존과 엘리자베스는 모두 3남 3녀를 두었는데, 한나(Hannah Elizabeth, 1856~1938. 7. 31, Mrs. Hannah Underwood Stephens), 존(John Thomas, 1857. 4. 12~1937. 7. 2), 프레데릭(Frederick Wills, 1858~1891. 3), 호러스(Horace Grant, 1859. 7. 19~1916. 10. 12), 헬렌(Helen Mary, 1862. 5. 16~1942. 7. 24, Mrs. Helen Underwood Conard), 그리고 메리(Mary Easton, 1865~1865)의 순서였다. 호러스는 3남으로 4번째였다.

1865년 생모가 사망한 후 아버지 존은 캐롤라인 넌(Caroline Nunn, ca. 1830~74)과 재혼했다. 존과 넌 사이에는 자녀가 없었다. 캐롤라인은 전 남편 윌리엄과의 사이에 두 딸, 즉 레베카와 앤을 두었다.

3-1 한나 E. 언더우드

Hannah E. Underwood

18560000

영국 및 웨일즈, 출생결혼사망 출생 색인, 1837~1915년, (한나 E. 언더우드, 1856년 4월~6월).

이 름	: 한나 엘리자베스 언더우드
등록 연도	: 1856년
등록 분기	: 2사분기 (4월~6월)
등록 지구	: 베드민스터
해당 카운티	: 서머셋

***England & Wales, FreeBMD Birth Index, 1837~1915*, (Hannah E. Underwood, Apr-May-Jun 1856).**

Name	: Hannah Elizabeth Underwood		
Registration Year	: 1856		
Registration Quarter	: Apr-May-Jun		
Registration district	: Bedminster		
Inferred County	: Somerset		
Volume	: 5c	Page	: 812

18710402

1871년 영국 인구주택총조사, (한나 엘리자베스 언더우드, 1871년 4월 2일).

지방 행정구 : 세인트 폴　　　시 자치구 : 베드포드
시 지구 : 웨스턴 워드　　　국회의원 선거구 : 베드포드
읍 : 베드포드　　　교　구 : 세인트 폴

등록 지구 : 베드포드
등록 소지구 : 베드포드 및 카딩톤

나　이 : 14　　　추정 출생연도 : 1857
관　계 : 하숙인　　　직　업 : 학 생
출생지 : 브리스톨, 서머셋 주, 영국

세대원 (이름, 나이)

해리엇 바커　31
관　계 : 세대주　　　직　업 : 여교장
로라 엘리자베스 바커　28
관　계 : 의붓딸　　　직　업 : 교사
커트루드 바커　22
관　계 : 의붓딸　　　직　업 : 교사
헨리 마틴 바커　19
관　계 : 의붓아들
직　업 : 학생, 성 바르톨로메오 병원
이디스 엘리자베스 루이스　8
관　계 : 딸　　　직　업 : 학생
헬렌 이반 쉬워드　7
관　계 : 하숙인　　　직　업 : 학생

1871 England Census, (Hannah Elizabeth Underwood, Apr. 2nd, 1871).

Civil parish	: St. Paul	Municipal Borough of	: Bedford
Municipal Ward of	: Western Ward	Parliamentary Borough of	: Bedford
Town of	: Bedford	Ecclesiastical District of	: St. Paul

Registration district : Bedford
Sub-registration district : Bedford and Cardington

Age	: 14	Estimated Birth Year	: 1857
Relation	: Boarder	Occupation	: Scholar
Where born	: Bristol, Somerset, England		

Household Members (Name, Age)

Harriet Barker 31
Relation : Head Occupation : School Mistress

Laura Elizabeth Barker 28
Relation : Stepdaughter Occupation : Teacher

Gertrude Barker 22
Relation : Stepdaughter Occupation : Teacher

Henry Martyn Barker 19
Relation : Stepson
Occupation : Student, St. Bartholomew's Hospital

Edith Elizabeth Louise 8
Relation : Daughter Occupation : Scholar

Helen Evan Sheward 7
Relation : Boarder Occupation : Scholar

18750523

뉴욕, 승객 명단, 1820~1957년, (에이치 언더우드, 1875년 5월 23일).

출발 항구　: 영국 런던
행선지　: 미합중국
도착 항구　: 뉴욕 항
선　명　: 캐나다 호

이름	나이	성별	직업	국적	출생지
에이치 언더우드	18	여성	–	영국	영국

New York, Passenger Lists, 1820~1957. (H. Underwood, May 23rd, 1875).

Port of Departure　: London, England
Destination　: United States of America
Port of Arrival　: New York, New York
Ship Name　: Canada

Name	Age	Gender	Occupation	Ethnicity/ Nationality	Place of Origin
H. Underwood	18	Female	–	English	England

18981012

뉴욕 결혼 색인, 1866~1937년, (한나 언더우드, 1898년 10월 12일).

이 름	: 한나 언더우드
결혼일	: 1898년 10월 12일
결혼 장소	: 킹즈, 뉴욕, 미국
배우자	: 클래런스 스티븐스

New York, Marriage Index, 1866~1937, (Hannah Underwood, Oct. 12th, 1898).

Name	: Hannah Underwood
Date of Marriage	: Oct. 12th, 1898
Place of Marriage	: Kings, New York, USA
Spouse	: Clarence Stephens
Certificate Number	: 5139

19100415

1910년 미국 연방 인구주택총조사, (클래런스 스티븐스, 1910년 4월 15일).

1910년 거주지 : 피츠필드 시 제2구역, 버크셔 카운티, 매사추세츠 주

이 름	: 클래런스 스티븐스	나 이	: 63세
가장과의 관계	: 가장	출생지	: 뉴욕
부친 출생지	: 뉴욕	모친 출생지	: 뉴욕
현 결혼의 햇수	: 10년	배우자 이름	: 한나 E. 스티븐스
직 업	: 광산 기술자/ 광산/ 개인 소유		
주택 소유	: 소유	농장 혹은 주택	: 농장

세대원 (이름, 나이)

한나 이 스티븐스 53세

이민 온 해	: 1875년		
부친 출생지	: 영국	모친 출생지	: 영국
출산 아이 수	: 1명	생존 아이 수	: 1명

존 U. 스티븐스 9세 [아들]

부친 출생지 : 뉴욕

1910 United States Federal Census, (Clarence Stephens, Apr. 15th, 1910).

Home in 1910 : Pittsfield Ward 2, Berkshire, Massachusetts

Name	: Clarence Stephens	Age	: 63
Relation to Head of House	: Head	Birthplace	: New York
Father's birthplace	: New York	Mother's birthplace	: New York
No. of Years of Present Marriage	: 10	Spouse's Name	: Hannah E. Stephens
Occupation	: Mining Engineer/ Mines/ Working on own account		
Home owned	: Own	Farm or House	: Farm

Household Members

Name	Age		
Hannah E. Stephens	53		
Year of immigration	: 1875		
Father's birthplace	: England	Mother's birthplace	: England
No. of Children Born	: 1	No. of Children Living	: 1
John U. Stephens	9	[Son]	
Birthplace	: New York		

19300429

1930년 미국 연방 인구주택총조사, (클래런스 스티븐스, 1930년 4월 29일).

1930년 거주지 : 피츠필드 시 제1구역, 버크셔 카운티, 매사추세츠 주

이 름	: 클래런스 스티븐스	나 이	: 83세
가장과의 관계	: 가장	출생지	: 뉴욕
부친 출생지	: 뉴욕	모친 출생지	: 뉴욕
결혼 당시 나이	: 48세	배우자 이름	: 한나 이 스티븐스
직 업	: 은퇴	학 력	: 없음
주택 소유	: 소유	농장 혹은 주택	: 농장
주택 가격	: 50,000 달러	라디오	: 소유

세대원

이 름	나 이		
한나 이 스티븐스	71세		
이민 온 해	: 1885년[44]		
부친 출생지	: 영국	모친 출생지	: 영국
출산 아이 수	: 1명	생존 아이 수	: 1명
존 U. 스티븐스	9세	[아들]	

44) 1875년이 잘못 기재된 것이다.

1930 United States Federal Census, (Clarence Stephens, Apr. 29th, 1930).

Home in 1930	: Pittsfield Ward 1, Berkshire, Massachusetts		
Name	: Clarence Stephens	Age	: 63
Relation to Head of House	: Head	Birthplace	: New York
Father's birthplace	: New York	Mother's birthplace	: New York
No. of Years of Present Marriage	: 10		
Spouse's Name	: Hannah E. Stephens		
Occupation	: Mining Engineer/ Mines/ Working on own account		
Home owned	: Own	Farm or House	: Farm

Household Members

Name	Age		
Hannah E. Stephens	53		
Year of immigration	: 1885[45)]		
Father's birthplace	: England	Mother's birthplace	: England
No. of Children Born	: 1	No. of Children Living	: 1
John U. Stephens 9	[Son]		
Birthplace	: New York		

45) 1875 is correct.

19311206

클래런스 스티븐스, 부고, *The New York Times*, (클래런스 스티븐스, 1931년 12월 7일).

클래런스 스티븐스.
The New York Times 특보.

피츠필드, 매사추세츠 주, 12월 6일. 은퇴한 광산기술자 클래런스 스티븐스 씨가 어제 노스 가 874번지 자택에서 85세로 별세했다. 스티븐스 씨는 뉴욕 블루클린에서 출생했으며, 컬럼비아 대학교와 콜로라도 광산학교를 졸업했다. 그는 1904년 피츠필드로 오기 전에 덴버에서 살았다. 유족으로는 블루클린의 한나 E. 언더우드였던 부인과 1명의 아들, 즉 뉴욕 샌드 레이크의 존 언더우드 스티븐스 목사, 그리고 피츠필드에 거주하는 형제 멜빈이 있다.

Clarence Stephens, Obituary, *The New York Times*, (Clarence Stephens, Dec 7th, 1931).

Clarence Stephens.
Special to The New York Times.

Pittsfield, Mass., Dec. 6. Clarence Stephens. a retired mining engineer, died yesterday at his home, 874 North Street. in his eighty-fifth year. Mr. Stephens was born at Brooklyn. N. Y., and was graduated from Columbia University and the Colorado School of Mines. He lived in Denver before coming to Pittsfield in 1904. The survivors are his widow, the former Hannah E. Underwood of Brooklyn; one son, the Rev. John Underwood Stephens of Sand Lake. N. Y., and one brother, Melvin of Pittsfield.

클래런스 스티븐스

뉴욕 블루클린 5번가 500번지 그린우드 묘지. [3852번 구역, 18 소구역]

클래런스 스티븐스
1847년 2월 15일 출생
1931년 12월 3일 사망

멜빈 스티븐스
1844년 10월 4일 출생
1932년 10월 19일 사망

자료 1-22 뉴욕 블루클린의 그린우드 묘지에 위치한 클래런스 스티븐스의 묘비석. 형 멜빈과 합장되어 있으며, 부인 한나는 그로브교회 묘지에 안장되었다.

3-2 존 T. 언더우드

John T. Underwood

18570000

영국 및 웨일즈, 출생결혼사망 출생 색인, 1837~1915년, (존 T. 언더우드, 1857년 4월~6월).

이 름	: 존 T. 언더우드
등록 연도	: 1857년
등록 분기	: 2사분기 (4월~6월)
등록 지구	: 판크라스
해당 카운티	: 런던

***England & Wales, FreeBMD Birth Index, 1837~1915*, (John T. Underwood, Apr-May-Jun 1857).**

Name	: John T. Underwood		
Registration Year	: 1857		
Registration Quarter	: Apr-May-Jun		
Registration district	: Pancras		
Inferred County	: London		
Volume	: 1b	Page	: 17

18820000

1883년 5월 1일 끝나는 연도의 트로우 뉴욕 시 인명부, 제96권, 1658쪽.[46)]

언더우드 존 T.	화학약품,	비지 가(街) 30번지 자택 뉴저지
언더우드 존 앤드 컴퍼니	화학약품,	비지 가(街) 30번지

Trow's New York City Directory. Vol. XCVI. For the Year Ending May 1, 1883, p. 1658.[47)]

Underwood, John T.	chemicals,	30 Vesey, h N. J.
Underwood J. & Co.	chemicals	30 Vesey

46) 이 책은 1882년에 발행되었다. '1882년 5월 1일에 끝나는 명부'에는 언더우드의 이름이 담겨 있지 않은 것으로 보아 존 T. 언더우드는 1882년 경 브루클린에서 사업을 시작한 것으로 판단된다. 아버지 존이 타계한 이듬해이다. 하지만 1882년 6월 발행된 '1883년도 브루클린의 명부'에는 들어 있지 않으며, 1885년 6월 발행된 '1886년도 브루클린 명부'에 처음 나타난다. *Brooklyn Directory for the year ending May 1883*.

47) This directory was published in 1882. It is assumed that John stared his business about 1882 at Brooklyn after death of his father in 1881, because his name was not listed in the *Brooklyn Directory for the year ending May 1883*.

18840000

1885년 5월 1일 끝나는 연도의 트로우 뉴욕 시 인명부, 제98권, 1781쪽.[48)]

언더우드 프레데릭 W.	화학약품,	비지 가(街) 30번지 자택 뉴더햄, 뉴저지
언더우드 존 T.	화학약품,	비지 가(街) 30번지 자택 뉴더햄, 뉴저지
언더우드 존 앤드 컴퍼니	화학약품,	비지 가(街) 30번지

Trow's New York City Directory. Vol. XCVIII. For the Year Ending May 1, 1885, p. 1781.[49)]

Underwood, Frederick W.	chemicals,	30 Vesey h New Durham, N. J.
Underwood, John T.	chemist,	30 Vesey, h New Durham, N. J.
Underwood J. & Co.	chemist	30 Vesey

48) 프레데릭이 합류했는데, '1884년 5월 1일에 끝나는 명부'를 확인하지 못해 1883년인지 1884년인지 확실하지 않다.

49) Frederick had joined. But it is not certain that whether he joined in 1883 or 1884, because the Author couldn't check the *Trow's New York City Directory. Vol. XCVII. For the Year Ending May 1, 1884*.

18850000

1886년 5월 1일 끝나는 연도의 트로우 뉴욕 시 인명부, 제99권, 1948쪽.

언더우드, 프레데릭 W.	화학자,	비지 가(街) 30번지 자택 브룩클린[50)]
언더우드 존 앤드 컴퍼니	화학자, 복사, 필사 및 인쇄 잉크, 타자기 및 서예용 리본 및 먹지와 관련된 언더우드 특허 제조업, 비지 가(街) 30번지	
언더우드, 존 T.	화학자,	비지 가(街) 30번지 자택 브루클린

Trow's New York City Directory. Vol. XCIX. For the Year Ending May 1, 1886, p. 1948.

Underwood, Fred. W.	chemicals,	30 Vesey h B'klyn[51)]
Underwood John & Co.	chemists, manufacturers of Underwood's patent copying, writing and printing inks, typewriter and caligraph ribbons and carbon papers, 30 Vesey street	
Underwood, John T.	chemist,	30 Vesey, h B'klyn

---

50) 존과 프레데릭이 블루클린으로 이사했는데, 1885년 11월 뉴더햄의 그로브 개혁교회에서 전출한 사실과 일치하며, 이때 라파예트교회로 적을 옮겼다.

51) The address of John and Frederick was chaged to Brooklyn, and coincided with the fact that they transferred from Grove Reformed Church, New Durham to Lafayette Church, Brooklyn in November, 1885.

18850615

1886년 5월 1일 끝나는 연도의 레인 브루클린 인명부, 1073쪽.[52)]

프레데릭 W. 언더우드	화학자,	그랜드 가(街) 75번지 및 비지 가(街) 30번지, 뉴욕
	자택 – 세인트 제임스 플레이스 99번지	
존 T. 언더우드	화학자,	그랜드 가(街) 75번지 및 비지 가(街) 30번지, 뉴욕
	자택 – 세인트 제임스 플레이스 99번지	
언더우드 존 T 앤드 컴퍼니	화학자,	그랜드 가(街) 75번지 및 비지 가(街) 30번지, 뉴욕

Lain's Brooklyn Directory for the Year Ending May 1, 1886, p. 1073.[53)]

Underwood, Frederick W.	chemist,	75 Grand av & 30 Vesey N Y h 99 St. James' pl.
Underwood, .John T.	chemist,	75 Grand av & 30 Vesey N Y h 99 St. James' pl.
Underwood .John T & Co.	chemists,	75 Grand av & 30 Vesey N Y

52) 이 책의 서문이 1885년 6월 15일 쓰여 졌다.
53) Preface of this book was written in June 15th, 1885.

18860000

1887년 5월 1일 끝나는 연도의 트로우 뉴욕 시 인명부, 제100권, 1989쪽.

프레데릭 W. 언더우드	화학자, 비지 가(街) 30번지 자택 - 브루클린 세인트 제임스 플레이스 99번지
언더우드 존 앤드 컴퍼니	화학자, 복사, 필사 및 인쇄 잉크, 타자기 및 서예용 리본 및 먹지와 관련된 언더우드 특허 제조업, 비지 가(街) 30번지
존 T. 언더우드	화학자, 비지 가(街) 30번지 자택 - 브루클린 세인트 제임스 플레이스 99번지

Trow's New York City Directory. Vol. C. For the Year Ending May 1, 1887, p. 1989.

Underwood, Frederick W.	chemist, 30 Vesey, h. St. James' pl. B''klyn
Underwood John & Co.	chemists, manufacturers of Underwood's patent copying, writing and printing inks, typewriter and caligraph ribbons and carbon papers, 30 Vesey street
Underwood, John T.	chemist, 30 Vesey, h 99 St. James' pl. B'klyn

자료 1-23 존이 사업을 처음 시작했던 뉴욕 블루클린 비지 가 30번지. From Google Map.

18870000

1888년 5월 1일 끝나는 연도의 트로우 뉴욕 시 인명부, 제101권, 2001쪽.

프레데릭 W. 언더우드	잉크, 비지 가(街) 30번지 자택 – 브루클린 세인트 제임스 플레이스 99번지
언더우드 존 앤드 컴퍼니	화학약품, 복사, 필사 및 인쇄 잉크, 타자기 및 서예용 리본 및 먹지와 관련된 언더우드 특허 제조업, 비지 가 30번지
존 T. 언더우드	잉크, 비지 가 30번지 자택 – 브루클린 그랜드 가 175번지

Trow's New York City Directory. Vol. CI. For the Year Ending May 1, 1888, p. 2001.

Underwood, Frederick W.	ink,	30 Vesey,	h. 99 St. James' pl. B''klyn
Underwood John & Co.	chemists,	manufacturers of Underwood's patent copying, writing and printing inks, typewriter and caligraph ribbons and carbon papers, 30 Vesey street	
Underwood, John T.	ink,	30 Vesey,	h 175 Grand av. B'klyn

18890000

1890년 5월 1일 끝나는 연도의 트로우 뉴욕 시 인명부, 2016쪽.

프레데릭 W. 언더우드	화학자, 비지 가(街) 30번지 자택 – 브루클린 세인트 제임스 플레이스 99번지
언더우드 존 앤드 컴퍼니	화학약품, 복사, 필사 및 인쇄 잉크, 타자기 및 서예용 리본 및 먹지와 관련된 언더우드 특허 제조업, 비지 가 30번지
존 T. 언더우드	화학자, 비지 가 30번지 자택 – 브루클린 세인트 제임스 플레이스 99번지[54]

Trow's New York City Directory. For the Year Ending May 1, 1890, p. 2016.

Underwood, Frederick W.	ink,	30 Vesey, h. 99 St. James' pl. B''klyn
Underwood John & Co.	chemists,	manufacturers of Underwood's patent copying, writing and printing inks, typewriter and caligraph ribbons and carbon papers, 30 Vesey street
Underwood, John T.	ink,	30 Vesey, h 99 St. James' pl. B''klyn[55]

54) 주소가 다시 변경되었다.
55) The home address was changed.

18910000

1892년 5월 1일 끝나는 연도의 트로우 뉴욕 시 인명부, 1390쪽.[56)]

언더우드 존 앤드 컴퍼니	화학약품, 복사, 필사 및 인쇄 잉크, 타자기 및 서예용 리본 및 먹지와 관련된 언더우드 특허 제조업, 비지 가 30번지
존 T. 언더우드	화학자, 비지 가 30번지 자택 – 브루클린 세인트 제임스 플레이스 99번지

Trow's New York City Directory. For the Year Ending May 1, 1892, p. 1390.[57)]

Underwood John & Co.	chemists, manufacturers of Underwood's patent copying, writing and printing inks, typewriter and caligraph ribbons and carbon papers, 30 Vesey street
Underwood, John T.	ink, 30 Vesey, h 99 St. James' pl. B''klyn

56) 프레데렉이 빠진 것은 그가 1891년 사망했기 때문이다.
57) Frederick was omitted due to his death in March, 1891.

18920216

1892년 뉴욕주 인구주택총조사, (존 T. 언더우드, 1892년 2월 16일).

1892년 2월 15일 뉴욕 주, 킹즈 카운티에서 블루클린 시의 제7 구(區)의 248 선거구에 살고 있는 거주자를 조사한 것임.

이 름	성 별	나 이	출생지	시민 여부	직 업
존 T. 언더우드	남	34	영국	시민	분석화학자
한나 언더우드	여	35	"	"	주 부
레베카 넌	여	39	"	"	재 가
릴리 언더우드	여	39	"	"	
호러스 언더우드 주니어	남	33	"	"	성직자
호러스 H. 언더우드	남	2	한국	"	재 가

New York, State Census, 1892, (John T. Underwood, Feb. 16th, 1892).

Enumeration of the Inhabitants living in the 248 Election District of the Seventh Ward of the City of Brooklyn, in the County of Kings, State of, N. Y., on Feb. 16, 1892.

Name	Male or Female	Age	In What Country Born	Citizen or Alien	Occupation
John T. Underwood	M	34	England	C	Analytical Chemist
Hannah Underwood	F	35	"	"	Housewife
Rebecca Nun	F	39	"	"	Home
Lillie Underwood	F	39	"	"	
Horace Underwood Jr.	M	33	"	"	Clergyman
Horace H. Underwood	M	2	Corea	"	Home

18920000

1893년 7월 1일 끝나는 1892년도의 뉴욕 시 인명부, 1444쪽.

언더우드 존 앤드 컴패니	화학약품, 복사, 필사 및 인쇄 잉크, 타자기 및 서예용 리본 및 먹지와 관련된 언더우드 특허 제조업, 비지 가 30번지
___ 존 T.	화학자, 비지 가 30번지　　자택 – 브루클린

The New York City Directory for the Year 1892, Ending July 1, 1893, p. 1444.

Underwood John & Co.	chemists, manufacturers of Underwood's patent copying, writing and printing inks, typewriter and caligraph ribbons and carbon papers, 30 Vesey.
___ John T.	Chemist, 30 Vesey, h B"klyn

18930000

1894년 5월 1일 끝나는 연도의 레인 브루클린 인명부, 1305쪽.

언더우드 존 앤드 컴패니　　타자기 판매
그랜드 가 143번지 및 비지 가 30번지, 뉴욕

언더우드의
타지기 판매, 서예 용품 판매.
리본 및 카본지.
존 언더우드 앤드 컴패니,
독점 생산.
비지가 30번지, 뉴욕
브루클린 그랜드 가 143, 145, 147 및 149번지
라살 가 163번지, 시카고

***Lain's Brooklyn Directory for the Year Ending May 1st, 1894,* p. 1305.**

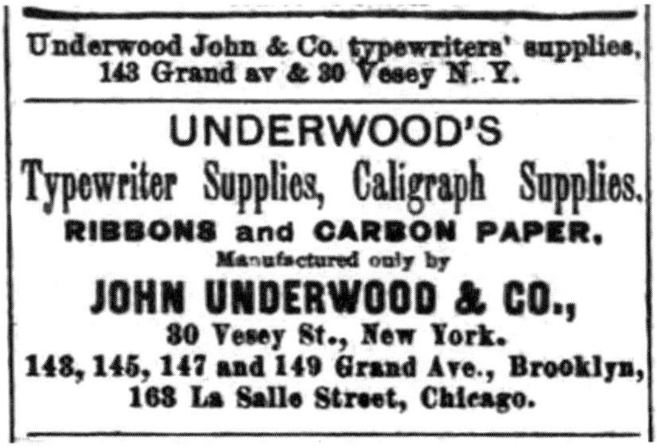

Underwood John & Co. typewriters' supplies,
143 Grand av & 30 Vesey N. Y.

UNDERWOOD'S
Typewriter Supplies, Caligraph Supplies.
RIBBONS and CARBON PAPER.
Manufactured only by
JOHN UNDERWOOD & CO.,
30 Vesey St., New York.
143, 145, 147 and 149 Grand Ave., Brooklyn,
163 La Salle Street, Chicago.

자료 1-24 「브루클린 인명부」에 실린 광고.

18930000

1894년 7월 1일 끝나는 연도의 트로우 뉴욕 시 인명부, 제107판, 1422쪽.

언더우드 존 앤드 컴패니	비지 가 30번지, 타자기 판매 및 잉크
존 T. 언더우드	판매, 비지 가 30번지 자택 - 브루클린 세인트 제임스 플레이스 99번지

Trow's New York City Directory. Vol. CVII. For the Year Ending July 1, 1894, p. 1422.

Underwood John & Co.	30 Vesey, typewriter supplies & inks.
___ John T.	supplies, 30 Vesey, h 99 St. James' pl. B''klyn

18990914

미국 여권 신청서, 1795-1925, (존 T. 언더우드, 1899년 9월 14일).

아메리카 합중국

주 뉴욕

카운티 뉴욕

나, 존 T. 언더우드 는 미국 태생 및 충실한 국민으로서, 워싱턴의 국무부에 18__ 년 ___ 월 ___ 일 __________ 에서 출생한 나 의 여권과 함께

나는 1857년 4월 12일 영국 런던 에서 출생했으며; 1873년 2월 20일 런던 에서 증기선 캐나다 호 에 승선하여 미국으로 이주했으며; 1873년부터 현재 까지 계속 26년 동안 뉴저지 주 허드슨 카운티 및 뉴욕 주 브루클린에서 거주했으며; 첨부한 귀화 증명서에서 보듯 1884년 11월 1일 뉴저지 주 허드슨 카운티 저지 시티 소재의 민사 법원에서 미국 시민으로 귀화했으며; 나는 그 증명서에 기술된 동일인이며; 나는 미국에 거주하는네, 주소는 뉴욕 주 뉴욕 시 브루클린 에서 거주하고 상업 에 종사하고 있으며; 나는 잠시 외국 여행을 할 예정이며; 몇 개월 내에 미국으로 돌아 와 거주하고 시민으로서 의무를 다 할 예정임을 엄숙히 선서합니다.

충성의 서약

더욱이, 나는 해외 및 국내의 모든 적에 대해 미국의 헌법을 유지하고 방어하며; 진실된 믿음과 충성을 지니고; 주저하지 않고 회피의 목적이 없이 자유의사로 이러한 의무를 받아들인다는 것을 맹세코 엄숙하게 선서합니다. 그러니 신이여 나를 도우소서

존 T. 언더우드

(신청자 서명)

1899년 9월 13일 내 앞에서 선서함

____

뉴욕 카운티 서기

신청자의 인상착의

나이	: 42 세	입	: 보통임
신장	: 5 피트, 8인치, Eng.	턱	: 둥그스름함
이마	: 높음	모발	: 갈색
눈	: 회색	피부색	: 흰색
코	: 뾰족함	얼굴	: 타원형

신원 증명

뉴욕 시, 9월 13일, 1899년

나는 위 존 T. 언더우드 를 개인적으로 알고 있으며, 귀화 증명서에 기술된 범위 안에서 동일인임을 알고 있고 진술서에 언급된 사실들이 내가 알고 믿는 한 틀림없다고 맹세합니다.

찰스 스트라우스

(증인의 주소) 브로드웨이 237번지, 뉴욕

지원자는 여권을 다음의 주소로 우송해 주기를 원합니다:

찰스 스트라우스
브로드웨이 237번지
뉴욕 시

U. S. Passport Application, 1795~1925, (John T. Underwood, June 28, 1899).

United States of America

State of New York

County of New York

I, John T. Underwood a Naturalized and Loyal Citizen of the United States, do hereby apply to the Department of State, at Washington for a passport for myself born at ______ on the ______ day of ______ 18___, and

I solemnly swear that I was born at London, England , in ______ on or about the 12th day of April , 1857; that I emigrated to the United States, sailing on board the S. S. Canada from London on or about the 20th day of February , 1873; that I resided 26 years, uninterruptedly, in the United States, from 1873 to date at Hudson County, N. J. & Brooklyn, N. Y.; that I was naturalized as a citizen of the United States before the ______ Court of Common Pleas at Jersey City, Hudson County, N. J. on the 1st day of the November 1884 as shown by the accompanying Certificate of Naturalization; that I am the Identical Person described in said Certificate; that I am domiciled in the United States, my permanent residence being at New York City, Borough of Brooklyn , in the State of New York where I follow the occupation of merchant ; that I am about to go abroad temporarily; and that I intend to return to the United States within a few months with the purpose of residing and performing the duties of citizenship therein.

Oath of Allegiance.

Further, I do solemnly swear that I will support and defend the Constitution of the United States against all enemies, foreign and domestic; that I will bear true faith and allegiance to the same; and that I take this obligation freely, without any mental reservation or purpose of evasion: So help me God,

John T. Underwood

Sworn to before me, this 13th day
of September , 1899

____

Notary Public,
N. Y. Co.

Description of Applicant

Age: 42 years Mouth; medium

Stature: 5 feet, 8 inched, Eng. | Chin: round

Forehead: High | Hair: grey

Eyes: Grey | Complexion: fair

Nose: sharp | Face: oval

Identification

New York City, September 13th , 1899

I Hereby Certify, that I know the above named John T. Underwood personally, and know him to be the identical person referred to in the within described Certificate of Naturalization, and that the facts stated in his affldavit are true to the best of my knowledge and belief.

Charles Strauss

Address of witness, 237 Broadway, N. Y.

Applicant desires passport sent to following address:

Charles Strauss
237 Broadway,
N. Y. City

19000609

1900년 미국 연방 인구주택총조사, (존 T. 언더우드, 1900년 6월 9일).

1900년 거주지 : 브루클린 제7구역, 킹 카운티, 뉴욕

이 름	: 존 T. 언더우드	나 이	: 42세
가장과의 관계	: 가장	출생지	: 영국
부친 출생지	: 영국	모친 출생지	: 영국
결혼 여부	: 독신	이민 연도	: 1873년
직 업	: 잉크 제조업		
주택 소유	: 임대	농장 혹은 주택	: 주택

세대원

이 름	나 이	가장과의 관계	
한나 E. 스티븐스	43세	[누나]	
이민 연도	: 1875년	결혼 연도	: 1899년
클래런스 스티븐스	53세	[매부]	
출생일	: 1846년 2월	출생지	: 뉴욕
부친 출생지	: 뉴욕	모친 출생지	: 뉴욕
직 업	: 파이프 제조업		
레베카 넌	46	[이복 누나]	
출생일	: 1854년 5월	출생지	: 영국
부친 출생지	: 영국	모친 출생지	: 영국
이민 연도	: 1884년	결혼 여부	: 독신
캐티 A. 케이시	19	[하인]	
출생일	: 1881년 3월	출생지	: 아일랜드
부친 출생지	: 아일랜드	모친 출생지	: 아일랜드
이민 연도	: 1898	결혼 여부	: 독신

메리 케이시	23	[하인]	
출생일	: 1877년 1월	출생지	: 아일랜드
부친 출생지	: 아일랜드	모친 출생지	: 아일랜드
결혼 여부	: 독신		

1900 United States Federal Census, (John T. Underwood, June 9th, 1900).

Home in 1900 : Brooklyn Ward 7, Kings, New York

Name	: John T. Underwood	Age	: 42
Relation to Head of House	: Head	Birthplace	: England
Father's birthplace	: England	Mother's birthplace	: England
Marital Status	: Single	Immigration Year	: 1873
Occupation	: Ink Mfr		
Home owned	: Rent	Farm or House	: House

Household Members

Name	Age	Relation to Head	
Hannah E. Stephens	43	[Sister]	
Immigration Year	: 1875		
Marriage Year	: 1899	Years Married	: 1
Clarence Stephens	53	[Son-in-law]	
Birth Date	: Feb. 1846	Birthplace	: New York
Father's birthplace	: New York	Mother's birthplace	: New York
Occupation	: Pipe Mfr		
Rebecca Nunn	46	[Step Sister]	
Birth Date	: May 1854	Birthplace	: England

Father's birthplace	: England	Mother's birthplace	: England
Immigration Year	: 1884	Marital Status	: Single
Katie A. Casey	19	[Servant]	
Birth Date	: Mar. 1881	Birthplace	: Ireland
Father's birthplace	: Ireland	Mother's birthplace	: Ireland
Immigration Year	: 1898	Marital Status	: Single
Mary Casey	23	[Servant]	
Birth Date	: Jan. 1877	Birthplace	: Ireland
Father's birthplace	: Ireland	Mother's birthplace	: Ireland
Marital Status	: Single		

19010424

뉴욕 결혼 색인, 1866~1937년, (존 언더우드, 1901년 4월 24일).

이 름	: 존 언더우드
결혼일	: 1901년 4월 24일
결혼 장소	: 킹즈, 뉴욕, 미국
배우자	: 그레이스 E. 브레이너드

New York, Marriage Index, 1866~1937, (John Underwood, Apr. 24th, 1901).

Name	: John Underwood
Date of Marriage	: Apr. 24th, 1901
Place of Marriage	: Kings, New York, USA
Spouse	: Grace E. Brainard
Certificate Number	: 2454

19050601

1905년 뉴욕주 인구주택총조사, (존 T. 언더우드, 1905년 6월 1일).

E1905년 6월 1일 뉴욕 주 킹즈 카운티 브루클린 제10선거구 a 블록, 제17선거 지역구에 살고 있는 거주민을 조사한 것임.

위싱턴 가(街).

이 름	: 존 T. 언더우드	나 이	: 45세
가장과의 관계	: 가장	시민 여부	: 시민
직 업	: 타자기 제조업	직업 분류	: 고용주

세대원

이 름	성 별	나 이	가장과의 관계
그레이스 B. 언더우드	여성	30세	[아내]
머빈 스티븐스	남성	60세	[아저씨][58]
그래디스 언더우드	여성	1세	[딸]
아크네스 퀸	여성	55세	[하인]
미국 체류 년수	: 15년		
시민 여부	: 외국인	태 생	: 아일랜드
메리 머피	여성	38세	[하인]
미국 체류 년수	: 10년		
시민 여부	: 외국인	태 생	: 아일랜드
케이트 켈리	여성	40세	[하인]
미국 체류 년수	: 10년		
시민 여부	: 외국인	태 생	: 아일랜드
거트루드 그로스	여성	37세	[하인]
존 머피	남성	30세	[하인]

58) 머빈은 존의 누나 한나의 남편 클래런스, 즉 매형의 형 멜빈(Melvin)인 것으로 추정된다.

New York, State Census, 1905, (John T. Underwood, June 1st, 1905).

Enumeration of the Inhabitants living in the 17 Election District, Block a, 10 Assembly District, Borough of Brooklyn, County of Kings, State of New York, on June 1, 1905.

Washington Ave.

Name	: John T. Underwood	Age	: 45
Relation to Head of House	: Head	Citizen or Alien	: Cit.
Occupation	: Typewriter Mfg	Class	: Emp.

Household Members

Name	Sex	Age	Relation to Head
Grace B. Underwood	F	30	[Wife]
Mervin Stephens	M	60	[Uncle][59]
Glades Underwood	F	1	[Daughter]
Agnes Quinn	F	55	[Servant]
Number of years in the US		: 15	
Citizen or Alien	: Al.	Nativity	: Cit. Ireland
Mary Murphy	F	38	[Servant]
Number of years in the US		: 10	
Citizen or Alien	: Al.	Nativity	: Cit. Ireland
Kate Kelly	F	40	[Servant]
Number of years in the US		: 10	
Citizen or Alien	: Al.	Nativity	: Cit. Ireland
Gertrude Gross	F	37	[Servant]
John Murphy	M	30	[Servant]

59) Mervin is presumed as 'Melvin', who is a brother of Clarence Stephens, husband of John's elder sister Hannah.

19370702

웹: 루츠웹 사망 색인, 1796~2010년, (존 토머스 언더우드, 1937년 7월 2일).

이 름 : 존 토머스 언더우드
출생일 : 1857년 경
사망 당시 나이 : 80세 2개월 20일
사망일 : 1937년 7월 2일
사망 장소 : 반스터블 카운티, 매서추세츠 주
마지막 거주지 : 위안노

Web: RootsWeb Death Index, 1796~2010, (John Thomas Underwood, July 2nd, 1937).

Name : John Thomas Underwood
Birth Date : abt 1857
Age at Death : 80y 2m 20d
Death Date : 2 Jul 1937
Death Place : Barnstable Co,, MA
Last Residence : Wianno

19370702

묘지 찾기 색인, 1600년대~현재, (존 T. 언더우드, 1937년 7월 2일).

이 름 : 존 토머스 언더우드
출생일 : 1857년 4월 12일
출생지 : 런던, 그레이터 런던, 영국
사망일 : 1937년 7월 2일
사망 장소 : 오스터빌, 반스터블 카운티, 매서추세츠 주, 미국
묘 지 : 그린우드 묘지
장례 장소 : 블루클린, 킹즈, 뉴욕, 미국
묘 역 : 3852번 구역, 18 소구역[60]
배우자 : 그레이스 E. 브레이너드 바튼 (1874~1968)
자 녀 : 글래디스 이블린 제임스 (1903~1975)

사업가. 영국 런던에서 출생하여 1873년 미국으로 이주했다. 그와 부친은 '언더우드 앤드 컴패니'를 설립했으며, 먹지 및 다른 용품 등 '레밍턴 앤드 손스'에서 생산하는 타자기 부품을 포함한 타자기 용품의 생산을 선도했다. 1894년 독일 출신의 발명가 프란츠 바그너는 타자수가 자신이 친 글자를 확인할 수 있도록 설계된 타자기를 개발했다. 1895년 언더우드는 바그너의 '전방 타자' 기계의 특허를 구입하여 개량했다. 후에 '언더우드'란 이름을 갖게 된 그의 새 회사는 빠르게 성장하여 1898년 매주 200대의 타자기를 생산했다. 1901년에는 '언더우드'는 5호 모델을 선 보였는데, 30년 이상의 기간에 수백만 대가 판매되었다. '언더우드' 제품에 적용된 새로운 기술로는 리본 선택기, 역행기 및 도표 작성 장치 등이었다. 1915년 언더우드는 전체 타자기 산업의 기준을 만들었으며, 레밍턴 회사를 젖치고 전 세계 최고의 타자기 회사가 되었다. 당시 '언더우드 컴패니'는 매일 약 500대의 타자기를 생산했으며, 모두 자신이 친 글자를 확인할 수 있도록 설계된 것이었다. 최신의 언더우드 타자기는 1939년 뉴욕 만국박람회에서 '미래 세계'를 대표

60) 매형 클래런스 스티븐스와 같은 구역이다.

하는 제품으로 선정되었다.

묘비석에 적힌 문구

나이는 자신의 통찰력을 흐리게 하거나
자신의 지성을 덮을 수 없다.
그는 자신이 살았던 것처럼 죽었다.
미래를 향해 눈을 뜨고, 영원히 젊게.

자료 1-24 브루클린의 그린우드 묘지의 입구와 존 T. 언더우드의 묘비석.

Find A Grave Index, 1600s-Current, (John T. Underwood, July 2nd, 1937).

Name	: John Thomas Underwood
Birth Date	: 12 Apr 1857
Birth Place	: London, Greater London, England
Death Date	: 2 Jul 1937
Death Place	: Osterville, Barnstable County, Massachusetts, USA
Cemetery	: Green-Wood Cemetery
Burial or Cremation Place	: Brooklyn, Kings County (Brooklyn), New York, USA
Plot	: Section 18, Lot 3852
Spouse	: Grace E. Brainard Barton (1874~1968)
Children	: Gladys Evelyn James (1903~1975)

Businessman. Born in London, England, he emigrated to the United States in 1873. He and his father established Underwood & Company, pioneering the manufacture of typewriter supplies, including carbon paper and other accessories to support the typewriters being manufactured by Remington & Sons. In 1894, Franz Wagner, a German born inventor, developed a typewriter design that finally made the print fully visible to the operator as it was being typed. In 1895 Underwood bought the patent to Wagner's 'front-stroke' machine and improved upon it before deciding to manufacture the design. His new company, which later became Underwood, grew rapidly, and was producing 200 typewriters per week by 1898. In 1901, Underwood introduced its No. 5 model, which was sold in the millions over 30 years of production. Some of the new features Underwood included were a ribbon selector, a back spacer, and a tabular. By 1915, Underwood had created the standard for the entire typewriter industry and the company replaced the Remington as the number one typewriter manufacture in the world. At the time, the Underwood Company was producing some 500 machines a day, all of which had the visible print design. A state-of-the-art Underwood typewriter was featured in the 1939 New York World's Fair to represent the 'World of Tomorrow.'

Passages on the Tombstone

Age Could not Cloud
His Vision or Close His
Mind. He Died as He Had
Lived. Eyes Open to the
Future, Eternally Young

자료 1-25 존 T. 언더우드.

존 언더우드 앤드 컴패니 (John Underwood & Co.)

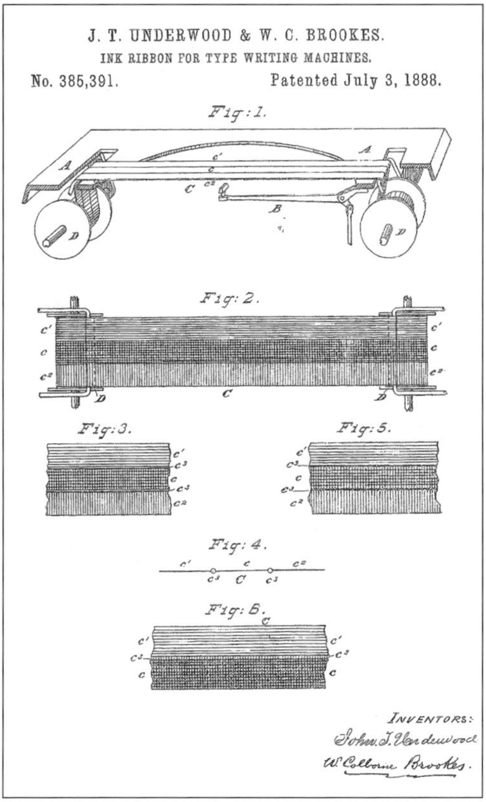

자료 1-26 존 T. 언더우드의 특허 관련 자료.

자료 1-27 타자기용 잉크.

자료 1-28 타자기 광고.

자료 1-29 언더우드 타자기.

19130000

하워드 J. 뱅커, 미국의 언더우드 가문. 제2권, 1913, 625쪽.

1231b. 뉴욕 블루클린의 존 토머스 언더우드, (1231a 존의 아들) 출생. 1857년 영국; 결혼. 그레이스 브레이너드, 1명의 자녀.

i. 글래디스 이블린, 출생.

존 T. 언더우드는 아버지의 사업을 이어 받아 타자기용 잉크의 제조 및 보급업에 종사했다. 지금은 잘 알려진 언더우드 타자기를 제조하고 있는데, 코네티컷 주 하트포드에 큰 공장을 갖고 있으며, 전 세계에 대리점을 갖고 있다. 그는 뉴욕의 블루클린에 거주하고 있으며, 뉴욕 시에 본사를 갖고 있다.

Howard J. Banker, *The Underwood Families of America. In Two Volumes*, Volume 2, 1913, pp. 625.

1231b. John Thomas Underwood of Brooklyn, N. Y., (son of John 1231a) b. in England in 1 857; m. Grace Brainard and has one child

i. Gladys Evelyn, b. .

John T. Underwood continued the business of his father in the manufacture of typewriter inks and supplies and now manufactures the well known Underwood typewriters for which he has a large factory located at Hartford, Conn., with agencies all over the world. He resides in Brooklyn, N. Y., and has his main office in New York City.

3-3 프레데릭 W. 언더우드

Frederick W. Underwood

18580000

영국 및 웨일즈, 출생결혼사망 출생 색인, 1837~1915년, (프레데릭 윌스 언더우드, 1858년 4월~6월).

이 름	: 프레데릭 윌스 언더우드
등록 연도	: 1858년
등록 분기	: 2사분기 (4월~6월)
등록 지구	: 판크라스
해당 카운티	: 런던

England & Wales, FreeBMD Birth Index, 1837~1915, (Frederick Wills Underwood, Apr-May-Jun 1858).

Name	: Frederick Wills Underwood		
Registration Year	: 1858		
Registration Quarter	: Apr-May-Jun		
Registration district	: Pancras		
Inferred County	: London		
Volume	: 1b	Page	: 124

3-4 호러스 G. 언더우드

Horace G. Underwood

18590000

영국 및 웨일즈, 출생결혼사망 출생 색인, 1837~1915, (호러스 그랜트 언더우드, 1859년 7~9월).

이　름	: 호러스 그랜트 언더우드
등록 연도	: 1859년
등록 분기	: 3사분기 (7월~9월)
등록 지구	: 판크라스
해당 카운티	: 런던

***England & Wales, FreeBMD Birth Index, 1837~1915*, (Horace Grand Underwood, Jul-Aug-Sept 1859).**

Name	: Horace Grand Underwood		
Registration Year	: 1859		
Registration Quarter	: Jul-Aug-Sep		
Registration district	: Pancras		
Inferred County	: London		
Volume	: 1b	Page	: 159

3-5 헬렌 M. 언더우드
Helen M. Underwood

18620000

영국 및 웨일즈, 출생결혼사망 출생 색인, 1837~1915, (헬렌 메리 언더우드, 1862년 4~6월).

이 름 : 헬렌 메리 언더우드
등록 연도 : 1862년
등록 분기 : 2사분기 (4월~6월)
등록 지구 : 판크라스
해당 카운티 : 런던

***England & Wales, FreeBMD Birth Index, 1837~1915*, (Helen Mary Underwood, Apr-May-Jun 1862).**

Name : Helen Mary Underwood
Registration Year : 1862
Registration Quarter : Apr-May-Jun
Registration district : Pancras
Inferred County : London
Volume : 1b Page : 171

18881010

뉴욕 결혼 색인, 1866~1937년, (헬렌 언더우드, 1888년 10월 10일).

이　름	: 헬렌 언더우드
결혼일	: 1888년 10월 10일
결혼 장소	: 킹즈, 뉴욕, 미국
배우자	: 조지 P. 코나드

New York, Marriage Index, 1866~1937, (Helen Underwood, Oct. 10th, 1888).

Name	: Helen Underwood
Date of Marriage	: Oct. 10th, 1888
Place of Marriage	: Kings, New York, USA
Spouse	: George P. Conard
Certificate Number	: 3766

19370724

묘지 찾기 색인, 1600년대~현재, (헬렌 메리 코나드, 1942년 7월 24일).

이 름	: 헬렌 메리 코나드
출생일	: 1862년 5월 16일
출생지	: 영국
사망일	: 1942년 7월 24일
사망 장소	: 렘센버그, 서픽 카운티, 뉴욕 주, 미국
묘 지	: 렘센버그 묘지
장례 장소	: 렘센버그, 서픽 카운티, 뉴욕 주, 미국
배우자	: 조지 파웰 코나드 (1864~1939)
자 녀	: 이블린 고스넬 (1896~1979)

자료 1-30 헬렌 메리 코나드의 묘비석.

***Find A Grave Index, 1600s-Current*, (Helen Mary Conard, July 24th, 1942).**

Name	: Helen Mary Conard
Birth Date	: May 16th, 1862
Birth Place	: England
Death Date	: July 24th, 1942
Death Place	: Remsenburg, Suffolk County, New York, USA
Cemetery	: Remsenburg Cemetery
Burial or Cremation Place	: Remsenburg, Suffolk County, New York, USA
Spouse	: George Powell Conard (1864~1939)
Children	: Evelyn Gosnell (1896~1979)

3-6 메리 E. 언더우드

Mary E. Underwood

18650000

영국 및 웨일즈, 출생결혼사망 출생 색인, 1837~1915, (메리 이스턴 언더우드, 1865년 4~6월).

이 름	: 메리 이스턴 언더우드
등록 연도	: 1865년
등록 분기	: 2사분기(4월~6월)
등록 지구	: 판크라스
해당 카운티	: 런던

England & Wales, FreeBMD Birth Index, 1837~1915, (Mary Easton Underwood, Apr-May-Jun 1865).

Name	: Mary Easton Underwood		
Registration Year	: 1865		
Registration Quarter	: Apr-May-Jun		
Registration district	: Pancras		
Inferred County	: London		
Volume	: 1b	Page	: 180

18650000

영국 및 웨일즈, 출생결혼사망 사망 색인, 1837~1915, (메리 이스턴 언더우드, 1865년 7~9월).

이 름	: 메리 이스턴 언더우드
등록 연도	: 1865년
등록 분기	: 3사분기 (7월~9월)
등록 지구	: 판크라스
해당 카운티	: 런던

England & Wales, FreeBMD Death Index, 1837~1915, (Mary Easton Underwood, Jul-Aug-Sept 1865).

Name	: Mary Easton Underwood
Registration Year	: 1865
Registration Quarter	: Jul-Aug-Sep
Registration district	: Pancras
Inferred County	: London
Volume	: 1b
Page	: 102

3-7 레베카 C. 넌

Rebecca C. Nunn

18500000

영국 및 웨일즈, 출생결혼사망 출생 색인, 1837~1915년, (레베카 캐롤라인 넌, 1850년 4월~6월).

이 름	: 레베카 캐롤라인 넌
등록 연도	: 1850년
등록 분기	: 2사분기 (4월~6월)
등록 지구	: 맨체스터
등록 카운티	: 랭커셔 주

England & Wales, FreeBMD Birth Index, 1837~1915, (Rebecca Caroline Nunn, Apr-May-Jun 1850).

Name	: Rebecca Caroline Nunn		
Registration Year	: 1850		
Registration Quarter	: Apr-May-Jun		
Registration District	: Manchester		
Inferred County	: Lancashire		
Volume	: 20	Page	: 612

18610407

1861년 영국 인구주택총조사, (레베카 C. 넌, 1861년 4월 7일).

지방행정구	: 뎃퍼드 세인트 폴		
교 구	: 햇챔 세인트 제임스	읍(邑)	: 뎃퍼드
카운티	: 서 리	국 가	: 영국
등록 지구	: 그리니치	등록 소지구	: 세인트 폴 뎃퍼드
나 이	: 10세	관 계	: 학생 (단체)
출생지	: 맨체스터, 랑커셔 주, 영국		

세대원 (이름, 나이, 세대주와의 관계)

메리 세퍼드	46세	[교상]
엘리자베스 로이드	48세	[Officer – _____cess]
윌리엄 에이브럼스	25세	[부교장]

레베카를 포함한 학생 명단은 생략함.

1861 England Census, (Rececca C. Nunn, Apr. 7th, 1861).

Civil Parish of Deptford St. Paul

Ecclesiastical District of Hatcham St. James

Town of Deptford

County/Island Surrey Country England

Registration district : Greenwich Sub-registration district : St. Paul Deptford

Age	: 10	Relation	: Scholar (Institutional)
Where born	: Manchester, Lancashire, England		

Household Members (Name, Age, Relation to Head)

Mary Shephard	46	[Officer - Matron]
Elizabeth Lloyd	48	[Officer - _____cess]
William Abrams	25	[Officer - Assistant Master]

Lists of Scholars were omitted.

18710402

1871년 영국 인구주택총조사, (레베카 C. 넌, 1871년 4월 2일).

지방행정구 : 켄징턴 세인트 메리 애벗
교　구 : 온슬로우 스퀘어 세인트 폴
주(州) : 런던　　국　가 : 영국

등록 지구 : 켄징턴　　등록 소지구 : 브럼프턴
주　소 : 플럼 로드 106번지

나　이 : 20세　　추정 출생연도 : 1851년
관　계 : 조수 (종업원)
출생지 : 맨체스터, 랑커셔 주, 영국
직　업 : 모직물 상인 조수

세대원 (이름, 나이, 세대주와의 관계)
조지 A. 쉽라이트　48　[세대주]
직　업 : 포목상

이하 생략함.

1871 England Census, (Rebecca C. Nunn, Apr. 2nd, 1871).

Civil Parish of Kensington St Mary Abbott
Ecclesiastical Parish of Onslow Square St. Paul
Country/Island London　　Country England

Registration distric : Kensington Sub-registration district : Brompton

Road, Street, & c., and No. or Name of House 106 Fulham Road

Age : 20 Estimated Birth Year : 1851

Relation : Assistant (Employee)

Where born : Manchester, Lancashire, England

Rank, Profession, or Occupation : Linendraper's assistant

Household Members (Name, Age, Relation to Head)

George A. Shipwright 48 [Head]

Rank, Profession, or Occupation : Draper

Omitted Below.

제2부

교육 배경

Part 2.
Educational Backgrounds

1.

미국 이주 이전의 교육 (Education before Immigrating to America)

자료 2-1 불로뉴 쉬르 메르. 루브르호텔에서 바라 본 마흐귀에 교(橋) 및 어시장.

동업자에게 사기를 당해 파산하여 생활이 어려웠음에도 아버지 존은 아이들에게 교육을 시켰는데, 구체적으로 호러스는 집 근처의 콕스공립학교(Cox's Collegiate Institute)에서 초등 교육을 받

았다.[61]

1871년 4월 총조사 당시, 형 존 T., 프레데릭, 호러스 및 헬렌은 모두 학교에 다니고 있었던 것으로 기록되어 있다.[62] 그런데 당시 형 프레데릭과 호러스는 이미 1869년에 프랑스 불로뉴 쉬르 메르(Boulogne-sur-Mer)의 가톨릭에서 운영하는 기숙학교(Ecole Dié)로 유학을 떠난 상태였다.[63] 따라서 존 T.와 헬렌은 런던에서 인근 학교에 다니고 있었다.

불로뉴 쉬르 메르는 영국과 가장 가까운 프랑스 북부의 항구 도시로서 런던과 그리 멀리 떨어진 곳은 아니었다. 하지만 존이 경제적으로 어려운 상황에서 아들 둘을 외국으로, 그것도 가톨릭 계열의 학교로 유학을 보낸 이유는 확실하지 않다.

---

61) 이 학교에 대해 알려주는 자료는 찾지 못하였다. 교사의 이름이 'Cox'이었을 것으로 추정될 뿐이다. 당시 영국에는 여교사 한 사람이 어린이들을 위해 개설, 운영하던 자택 개방 학교(自宅 開放 學校, dame school)가 많았다. 이 학교는 대개 선생님 집을 학교로 사용했으며, 어린이들은 신약 성서를 교재로 삼아 알파벳과 읽기를 배웠다. *Personal Record of Horace Grant Underwood*, (Nov. 3rd, 1914), Presbyterian Historical Society.

62) 1871년 영국 인구주택총조사, (존 언더우드, 1871년 4월 2일). →41쪽을 볼 것.

63) 당시 영국에서 발행되던 「가톨릭 안내서」에는 프랑스의 몇몇 기숙학교에 대한 광고가 실려 있다. 불로뉴 쉬르 메르의 학교도 소개되어 있으나 언더우드가 다녔던 학교에 대해 알려주는 자료는 찾지 못하였다. 이 학교에서 가르치던 교사의 이름이 'Die'이었던 것으로 알려져 있다.

2.
해스브룩학원 (Hasbrouck Institute)

언더우드의 아버지 존은 어려서부터 목사 및 선교사가 되고 싶다는 언더우드가 다른 형들과 달리 자신의 사업을 물려받게 하고 싶지 않았다. 그래서 미국으로 이주한 후 저지 시티(Jersey City)에 있던 해스브룩학원(Hasbrouck Institute)에 호러스를 입학시켰다.

이 학원은 저지 시티의 젊은이들이 미국의 주요 대학에 진학하고, 사회 활동을 준비할 수 있도록 열었던 사립학교였다. 교장 워싱턴 해스브룩(Washington Hasbrouck)은 이미 뉴욕 주 소거티스(Saugerties)에서 사립학교를 세워 운영했던 경험이 있었다. 1856년 개교 당시, 이 학원은 웨인 가(街) 근처의 머서 가(街) 53-55에 위치한 작은 건물에서 시작하였다.

자료 2-2 해스브룩학원. 언더우드가 졸업한 후 다른 곳으로 이전한 학원의 모습이다(1900년대 초).

그의 노력으로 이 학교는 저지 시티의 명문 학교로 발전했다. 언더우드가 다녔던 당시 이 학교는 설비나 교육 방식 등 모든 면에서 저지 시티 최고의 학교였던 것으로 알려져 있다. 하지만 그 학제나 교과 내용 등은 알려져 있지 않다.[64] 이 학교의 많은 졸업생들이 저지 시티의 주요 직책을 맡아 활동했다.

교장 워싱턴 해스브룩은 1876년 트렌턴(Trenton)에 위치한 뉴저지 주 사범학교(지금의 뉴저지 대학)의 교장으로 부임했다.

언더우드가 졸업한 후 이 학교는 크게 확장되었으며, 1880년 여자부를 병설하였다. 저지 시티가 크게 확장되면서 1893년 9월 학교는 해리슨 가(街)와 만나는 크리센트 가(街) 모퉁이로 이전했는데 당시 학생 수는 305명이었다. 하지만 저지 시티가 공립교육에 일대 변혁을 일으키기 위해 공립학교의 건물 확장을 추진하면서 저지 시티 교육위원회가 해스브룩학원을 사들이면서 이 학교는 문을 닫게 되었다. 학교 건물은 1920년 해체되었다.

64) 언더우드 보다 늦게 해스브룩학원에서 수학했던 프랭클린은 3년 과정을 다녔다고 한다. "His early education was obtained in the schools of Monsey and Jersey City, and for three years attended the Hasbrouck Institute of the latter city." Franklin DeRonde Furman, M. E., *The Year Book of Stevens Institute of Technology*. The Trow Press, New York, 1906, p. 8.

18950000

알렉산더 맥린, 뉴저지 주 저지 시티의 역사: 초기 정착 및 발전. 저지 시티 인쇄소, 1895, 158~9쪽.

해스브룩학원

벤 보스트 군구(郡區)의 초기에 유일한 남학교는 현재 에리 가와 그로브 가 사이의 3가에 있었다. 이 학교는 군구 아래구역의 소년들이 통학하기에는 너무 멀었기 때문에, 유일한 대안은 저지 시티의 그랜드 가에 위치한 학교에 다니는 것이었다. 그 학교는 그로브 가와 뉴어크 가를 통해서만 갈 수 있었다. 군구 아래구역의 주민들에게 편의를 제공하기 위해, 코르넬리우스 밴 보스트는 배로우 근처의 머서 가 남쪽의 두 구역의 중심에 단층의 목조 건물을 건축하였다. 그곳에 남학교가 개교하였다. 그것은 유료 학교였으며, 25명의 학생을 수용하였다. 몇 년 후 많은 영향력 있는 시민들이 힘을 합쳐 뉴욕의 워싱턴 해스브룩에게 용커스의 학교를 그만두고 [저지 시티의] 소년들이 대학 입학을 준비하는 작은 학교의 책임을 맡아 주도록 요청했다. 첫 2년 동안 해스브룩 씨는 거의 혼자 강의를 담당했다. 웨인 가 개혁교회의 목사인 피 D. 밴 클리프 목사가 희랍어와 라틴어 교육을 도왔으나, 학교는 한 명의 교사가 지도하는 한 학급에 불과했다. 이 학교는 인기가 있었고 성공적이었다. 부모들의 소년들의 입학을 위해 개강 몇 주 전부터 [입학을] 지원해야 했다. 강단을 이용하고 좁혀 앉게 하여 40명의 학생을 수용할 수 있었다. 입학을 위한 열화 같은 성원과 비좁은 교실로 해스브룩은 1866년 그랜드 가 109번지에 위치한 문화회관 건물을 임대하였다. 당시 밴 보스트는 저지 시티에 있었으며, 거리는 모두 연결되어 있었다. 1866년 5월, 학원은 67명의 남학생으로 개교했다. 피터 해스브룩은 부교장이 되었으며, 새로운 반이 편성되었고 더 많은 교사가 필요해졌다. 학교는 규모 뿐 만이 아니라 사회적 명성도 커져 갔다.

1876년 워싱턴 해스브룩은 트랜턴에 위치한 주립사범학교의 교장으로 선출되었다. 형제 피터의 사망 및 다른 이유들로 인해 20년 동안 인기 있고 유익한 학교를 만드는데 헌신했던 그는 교장직을 수락했다. 당시 사범학교의 강사였던 헨리 C. 밀러와 찰스 C. 스티메츠는 해스브룩학원을 구입하여 더 광범위한 교육 사업을 위해 개조하였다. 1877년 호러스 C. 웨이트는 학원과 연관을 맺었고, 현재 경영자 중의 한 사람이며 부교장이다. 제임스 호프먼과 이 H. 클라크가 교사로 합류하며 모두 5명의 남교사가 근무하였다. 그들의 능력은 곧 분명해졌으며, 학교는 빠르게 발전했다. 1880년 밀러 씨가 사직했고, 교사의 수는 증가했다. 학교가 유명해지면서 많은 학부모들은 교장에게 여학생부를 개설하도록 요청했고, 결국 받아들여졌다. 학교가 발전하면서 문화회관 건물이 너무나도 비좁게 되었고, 인접 건물을 임대하였다. 그리고 음악 및 미술부가 추가되었고, 이 분야의 전문 교사들이 채용되었다. 1892년 건물에 비해 학교 규모가 너무 커졌다. 크레센트, 해리슨 및 커뮤티퍼 가에 있는 본넬 부동산을 구입하여 현재의 학원이 건축되었다. 이 학원은 현재 뉴저지 주에서 가장 크며 성공적인 사립학교이다. 이 학교는 주민들의 필요에 의해 성장하였다. 50년 전 25명의 학생을 수용하는 작은 학교는 이제 심화 교육에 필요한 모든 기재가 구비되고 약 500명의 학생이 재학하는 현대적 학교가 되었다. 이 학교에는 많은 교사가 있으며, 배출된 많은 사람들 중에는 현재 저지 시티에서 개업하고 있는 호프만 박사, 파슨스 박사 및 블랑샤드 박사 등이 있다. 헨리 프라이 교수는 해스브룩학원에 3년 동안 근무했고, 졸업생들의 기억에 다정하게 남아 있다. 여학생부의 첫 책임자인 캐리 S. 스토우 양, 후임 제니 C. 드레이크 양, 제3대 책임자인 플로렌스 파크 양은 노련하고 능력 있는 여성들이다. 빅토르 바이어 교수는 개설 이래 음악부의 책임자로 근무해 왔다. 스티메츠 씨는 아직 교장 직에 수행하고 있으며, 웨이트 씨는 부교장이다.

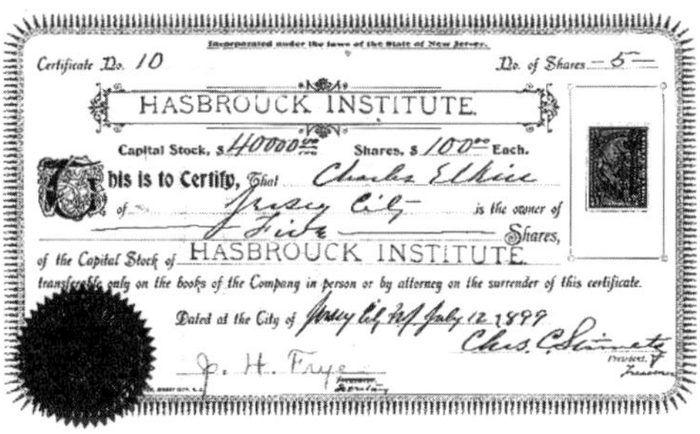
Incorporated under the laws of the State of New Jersey.
Certificate No. 10 No. of Shares — 5 —
HASBROUCK INSTITUTE
Capital Stock, $40000.00 Shares, $100.00 Each.
This is to Certify, That ... of Jersey City is the owner of Five Shares, of the Capital Stock of HASBROUCK INSTITUTE transferable only on the books of the Company in person or by attorney on the surrender of this certificate.
Dated at the City of Jersey City N.J. July 12 1899
Chas. C. Stimets President
J. H. Frye Secretary

자료 2-3 해스브룩학원과 관련된 자료 (1899). 프라이의 서명이 들어있다.

Alexander McLean, *History of Jersey City, N. J.: A Record of its Early Settlement and Corporate Progress*. Press of the Jersey City Printing Company, 1895, pp. 158~9.

Hasbrouck's Institute.

In the early days of Van Vorst township the only school for boys was in what is now Third Street, between Erie and Grove streets. It was a long distance for boys to go from the lower section of the township, and the only alternative was to go to the Grand Street school in Jersey City. That could only be reached by way of Grove Street and Newark Avenue. To afford school facilities convenient for residents of the lower section of the town, Cornelius Van Vorst built a one-story frame building in the centre of two lots on the south side of Mercer .Street, near Barrow. There a school for boys was opened. It was a pay school and accommodated twenty-five pupils. After a few years the teacher found a more lucrative field, and a number of influential citizens united in requesting Washington Hasbrouck, of Newburgh, N. Y., to abandon a school in Yonkers, and take charge of the little school to prepare boys there for college. During the first two years Mr. Hasbrouck taught almost alone. Rev, P. D. Van Cleef. the pastor of the Wayne Street Reformed Church, aided by giving instruction in Greek and Latin, but the school was practically for a single class under the direction of an individual teacher. It was popular and successful. Parents had to apply weeks before terms opened to secure admission for their boys. By utilizing the platform and crowding it had been possible to admit forty boys. The pressure for admittance, and the cramped quarters caused Mr. Hasbrouck to lease the Lyceum building at 109 Grand Street in 1866. Van Vorst was Jersey City then, and the street were all connected. In May, 1866, the Institute was opened with sixty-seven boys as pupils. Peter Hasbrouck became vice-principal, new lasses were formed and more teachers were required. The school grew in size and public esteem.

In 1876 Washington Hasbrouck was chosen principal of the State Normal School at Trenton. The death of his brother Peter and other causes moved him to accept, after having devoted twenty years to building up a popular and profitable school. Henry C. Miller and Charles C. Stimets, at that time instructors in the Normal School, purchased the institute and remodelled it for more extensive educational work. In 1877 Horace C. Wait became connected with the school, and is now one of the proprietors and vice-principal. James Hoffman and E. H. Clark were added to the faculty, making five male teachers. Their ability soon became manifest, and the school increased rapidly. In 1880 Mr. Miller withdrew, and the faculty was increased. The popularity of the school caused many parents to request the principal to add a girls' department, and it was done. The growth of the school had made the Lyceum building too small, and adjoining buildings were leased and connected with it. Schools of music and art were added in time, and special instructors were obtained for these branches. In 1892 the school had grown too large for the buildings. The Bonnell estate, on Crescent, Harrison and Communipaw avenues, was purchased, and there the present institute was erected. It is now the largest and most successful private school in the State. It has been a growth produced by the needs of the people. Half a century ago a small school that would accommodate twenty-five, it is now a modern school equipped with everything required for advanced education and attended by about five hundred students. It has a large corps of teachers, and has had many who have gone out from it, among whom are Doctors Hoffman, Parsons and Blanchard, now practising physicians in the city. Prof. Henry Frye, who is still in the faculty, has been there many years, and has a warm place in the memory of the alumni. Miss Carrie S. Stow, the first superintendent in the girls' department, Miss Jennie C. Drake, her successor, and Miss May Florence Park, the third in the position, have been women of skill and ability. Prof. Victor Baier has been superintendent of the school of music since it was opened. Mr. Stimets still remains in charge as principal, and Mr Wait as vice-principal.

3.
뉴욕대학교 (New York University)

해스브룩학원을 수학한 언더우드는 바로 대학교에 진학하지 않았다. 대신 자신이 다니던 그로브 개혁교회의 메이본 목사로부터 1877년 초부터 희랍어 개인지도를 받았고, 그해 6월 12일 뉴욕대학교의 입학이 허락되었다. 언더우드가 입학할 당시 뉴욕대학교(New York University, NYU)의 명칭은 'University of the City of New York'이었다.

뉴욕대학교는 1831년 다운타운 맨해튼의 그리니치 마을에 설립된 특정 종파가 없는 사립대학교로서 미국 사립 고등교육기관 중 가장 큰 학교의 하나이다. 언더우드는 20개 이상의 대학원, 대학 및 기관으로 이루어진 뉴욕대학교에서 가장 역사가 깊고 큰 문리대에 입학하였다.

자료 2-4 다운타운 맨해튼의 뉴욕대학교.

뉴욕대학교는 일종의 주식회사로 설립되었으므로 기관의 운영에 어떠한 종파가 우세해지는 것을 막았다. 하지만 개교 초기에는 뉴욕의 부유한 개신교 집안 자제가 많이 입학했다. 교과 과정은 고전 이외에도 실용학문을 중요시했기에 언어, 과학, 기술 및 농업 등을 가르쳤다. 학생은 특정 과목만을 등록할 수 있었다. 문리대는 언더우드가 졸업한 후인 1894년 브롱스로 이전했다.

1881년 뉴욕대학교를 졸업한 호러스는 뉴브런즈윅신학교에 입학하였고, 1884년 신학교 졸업과 함께 뉴욕대학교에서 석사 학위를 취득하였다. 언더우드는 1892년 명예 법학박사의 학위를 받은데 이어, 1912년에는 명예 신학박사의 학위를 받았다. 그의 아들 호러스 호튼도 1912년 문학사의 학위를 받음으로써 호러스 부자는 뉴욕대학교의 동문이 되었다.

자료 2-5 뉴욕대학교.

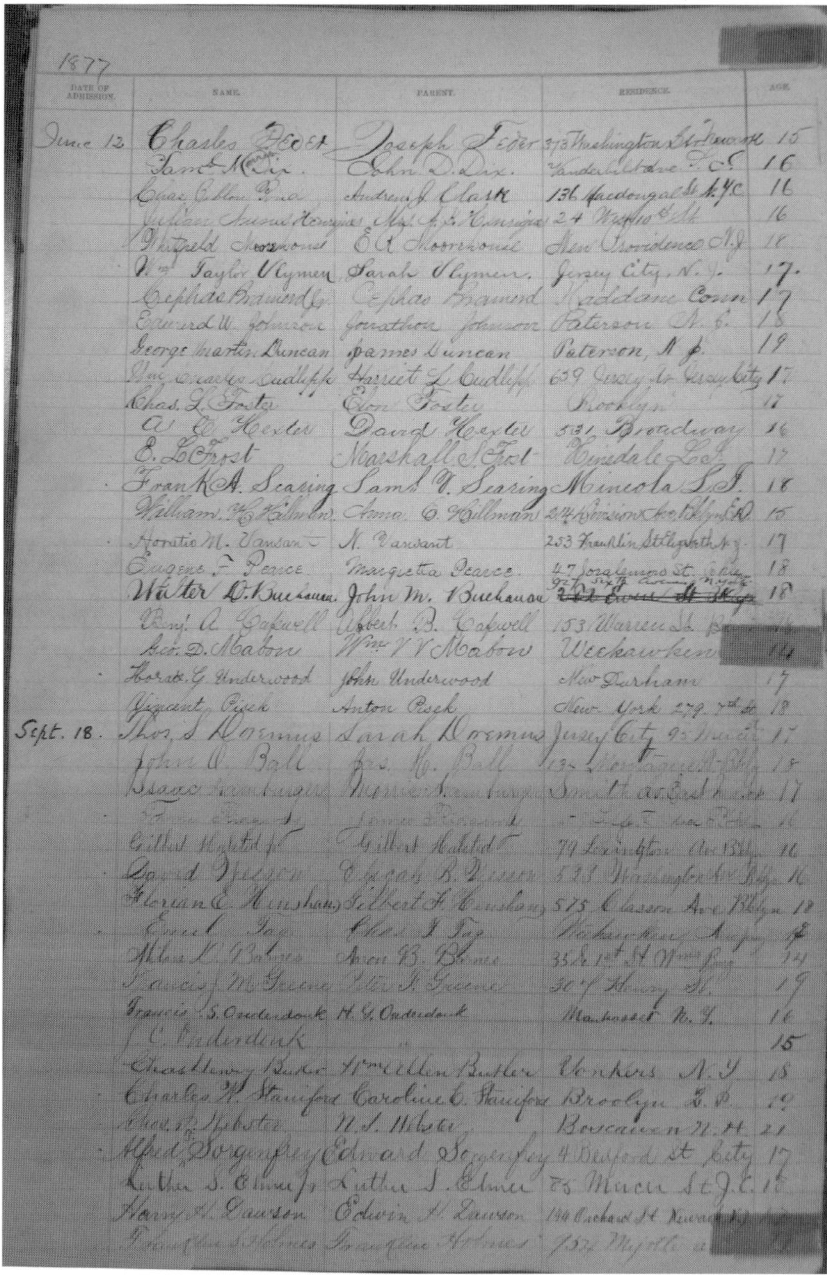

1877

DATE OF ADMISSION.	NAME.	PARENT.	RESIDENCE.	AGE.
June 12.	Charles Feder	Joseph Feder	373 Washington St. Newark	15
	Saml. M. Dix	John D. Dix	[illegible]	16
	Chas. [illegible] Clark	Andrew J. Clark	136 Macdougal St. N.Y.C.	16
	Julian [illegible]	[illegible]	24 W. [illegible] St.	16
	Whitfield Moorhouse	E. A. Moorhouse	New Providence N.J.	18
	Wm. Taylor Vlymen	Sarah Vlymen	Jersey City, N.J.	17
	Cephas Brainerd Jr.	Cephas Brainerd	Haddam Conn	17
	Edward W. Johnson	Jonathan Johnson	Paterson N.J.	18
	George Martin Duncan	James Duncan	Paterson, N.J.	19
	Wm. Charles Cudlipp	Harriet L. Cudlipp	639 Jersey Av. Jersey City	17
	Chas. L. Foster	Elon Foster	Brooklyn	17
	A. G. Hexter	David Hexter	531 Broadway	16
	E. L. Frost	Marshall S. Frost	Hinsdale [illegible]	17
	Frank A. Searing	Saml. V. Searing	Mineola L.I.	18
	William H. Hillman	Anna C. Hillman	[illegible]	15
	Horatio M. Vansant	N. Vansant	253 Franklin St. Elizabeth N.J.	17
	Eugene F. Pearce	Marguetta Pearce	47 Joralemon St. [illegible]	18
	Walter D. Buchanan	John M. Buchanan	92 [illegible] Sixth Avenue N. York	18
	Benj. A. Capwell	Albert B. Capwell	153 Warren St. [illegible]	[illegible]
	Geo. D. Mabon	Wm. V. V. Mabon	Weehawken	16
	Horace G. Underwood	John Underwood	New Durham	17
	Vincent Pisek	Anton Pisek	New York 279 7th St.	18
Sept. 18.	Thos. S. Doremus	Sarah Doremus	Jersey City [illegible]	17
	John O. Ball	Jas. H. Ball	[illegible]	18
	Isaac Hamburger	[illegible] Hamburger	Smith [illegible]	17
	[illegible]	[illegible]	[illegible]	[illegible]
	Gilbert Halsted Jr.	Gilbert Halsted	79 Lexington Av. Bklyn	16
	David Weeson	Elijah B. Weeson	523 Washington Av. Bklyn	16
	Florian E. Henshaw	Gilbert F. Henshaw	575 Classon Ave Bklyn	18
	Emil Tag	Chas. F. Tag	[illegible]	[illegible]
	Albert K. Barnes	Aaron B. Barnes	35 E. 1st St. [illegible]	14
	Francis J. McGreene	Peter J. Greene	30 ½ Henry St.	19
	Francis S. Onderdonk	H. G. Onderdonk	Manhasset N.Y.	16
	J. C. Onderdonk	"		15
	Chas. Henry Butler	Wm. Allen Butler	Yonkers N.Y.	18
	Charles H. Stanford	Caroline C. Stanford	Brooklyn E.D.	19
	Thos. P. Webster	N. S. Webster	Boscawen N.H.	21
	Alfred Sorgenfrey	Edward Sorgenfrey	4 Bedford St. City	17
	Luther S. Elmer Jr.	Luther S. Elmer	85 Mercer St. J.C.	18
	Harry H. Dawson	Edwin H. Dawson	149 Orchard St. Newark N.J.	[illegible]
	Franklin S. Holmes	Franklin Holmes	153 Myrtle a[illegible]	[illegible]

자료 2-6 *Class Merit Book*, *July 1835~June 1888*, Vol. 4, University of the City of New York.

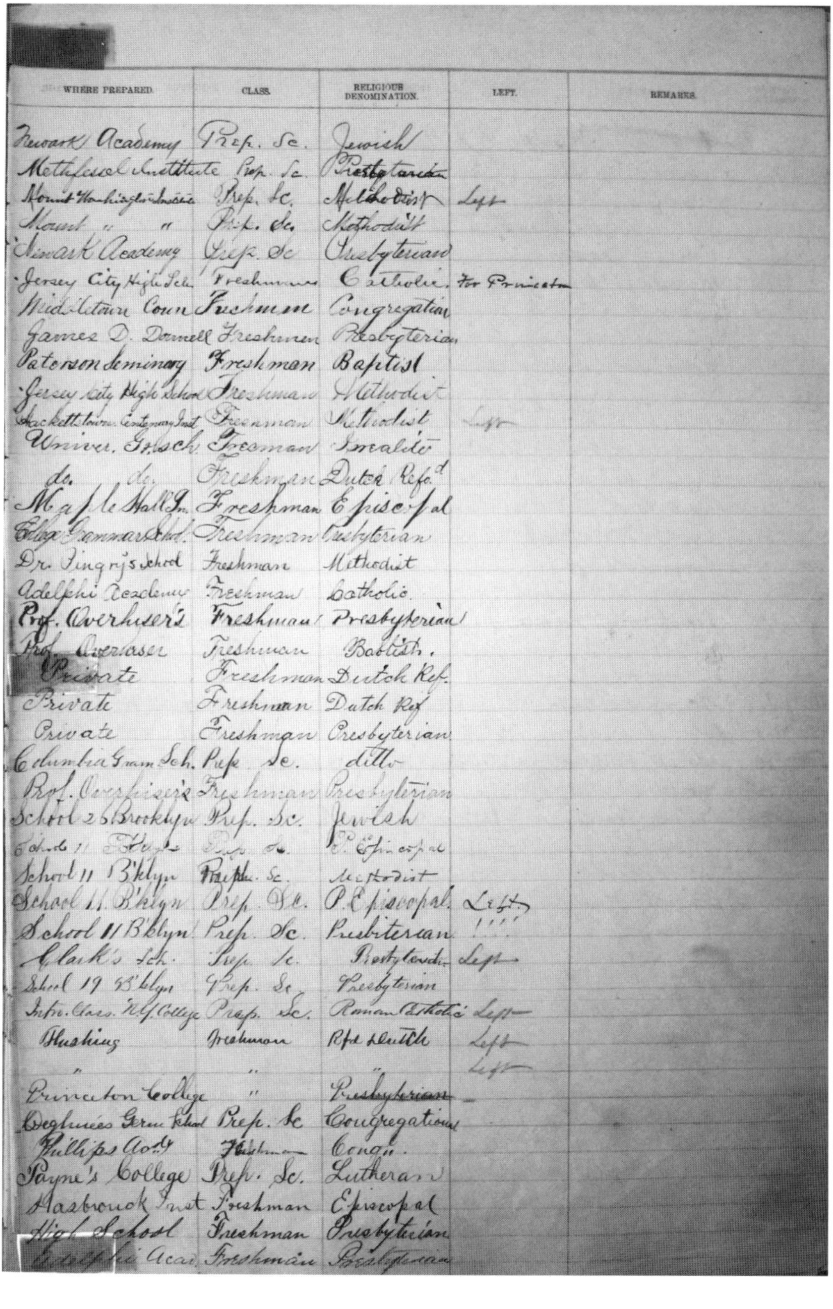

WHERE PREPARED.	CLASS.	RELIGIOUS DENOMINATION.	LEFT.	REMARKS.
Newark Academy	Prep. Sc.	Jewish		
Methfessel Institute	Prep. Sc.	Presbyterian		
Mount Washington Institute	Prep. Sc.	Methodist	Left	
Mount " "	Prep. Sc.	Methodist		
Newark Academy	Prep. Sc.	Presbyterian		
Jersey City High Sch.	Freshman	Catholic	For Princeton	
Middletown Conn	Freshman	Congregational		
James D. Donnell	Freshman	Presbyterian		
Paterson Seminary	Freshman	Baptist		
Jersey City High School	Freshman	Methodist		
Hackettstown Centenary Inst.	Freshman	Methodist	Left	
Univer. Gr. Sch.	Freshman	Israelite		
do. do.	Freshman	Dutch Ref.d		
Maple Hall In.	Freshman	Episcopal		
College Grammar School	Freshman	Presbyterian		
Dr. Pingry's School	Freshman	Methodist		
Adelphi Academy	Freshman	Catholic		
Prof. Overhiser's	Freshman	Presbyterian		
Prof. Overhiser	Freshman	Baptist		
Private	Freshman	Dutch Ref.		
Private	Freshman	Dutch Ref.		
Private	Freshman	Presbyterian		
Columbia Gram Sch.	Prep. Sc.	ditto		
Prof. Overhiser's	Freshman	Presbyterian		
School 26 Brooklyn	Prep. Sc.	Jewish		
School 11 B'klyn	Prep. Sc.	P. Episcopal		
School 11 B'klyn	Prep. Sc.	Methodist		
School 11 B'klyn	Prep. Sc.	P. Episcopal	Left	
School 11 B'klyn	Prep. Sc.	Presbyterian	"	
Clark's Sch.	Prep. Sc.	Presbyterian	Left	
School 19 B'klyn	Prep. Sc.	Presbyterian		
Intr. Class. N.Y. College	Prep. Sc.	Roman Catholic	Left	
Flushing	Freshman	Ref. Dutch	Left	
"	"		Left	
Princeton College	"	Presbyterian		
Deghuée's Gram School	Prep. Sc.	Congregational		
Phillips Acad.	Freshman	Congn.		
Payne's College	Prep. Sc.	Lutheran		
Hasbrouck Inst.	Freshman	Episcopal		
High School	Freshman	Presbyterian		
Adelphi Acad.	Freshman	Presbyterian		

18770612

학적부, 1835년 7월~1888년 6월, 제4권, 뉴욕대학교.

1877년

입학일	: 6월 12일
이 름	: 호러스 G. 언더우드
부 모	: 존 언더우드
거주지	: 뉴더햄
나 이	: 17세
입학 준비	: 사숙(私塾)
학 년	: 신입생
교 파	: 화란개혁교회

Class Merit Book, July 1835~June 1888, Vol. 4, University of the City of New York.

1877

Date of Admission	: June 12
Name	: Horace G. Underwood
Parent	: John Underwood
Residence	: New Durham
Age	: 17
Where Prepared	: Private
Class	: Freshman
Religious Denomination	: Dutch Ref.

18770600

뉴욕대학교 일람, 1876~77년. 1877년 6월, 뉴욕: 리처드 핸디, 프린터, 듀언 가 62 및 64번지.

대학교의 과(科)는 다음과 같다:

1. 문과.
2. 이과.

이 두 과의 수업료는 없음.

3. 의과.
4. 법과.

1. – 문과.
수업료 없음.

교수진.
하워드 크로스비, 신학박사, 법학박사
대학교 총장
이 A. 존슨, 법학박사
라틴어 및 문학 교수, 학장
존 W. 드레이퍼, 의학박사, 법학박사
화학 및 자연사 교수
벤저민 N. 마틴, 신학박사, 인문학박사
논리 지성 도덕철학 교수
리처드 H. 불, 문학석사
수학 겸임교수
헨리 M. 베어드, 철학박사
희랍어문학 교수

조지 W. 코클리, 법학박사
수학, 자연철학,[65] 및 천문학, 교수회 간사

헨리 드레이퍼, 의학박사
화학 및 자연사 겸임 교수

빈센조 보타, 철학박사
이탈리아어문학 교수

찰스 캐롤, 철학박사
프랑스, 독일어문학 교수

헨리 P. 모트
정치학 교수

루이스 F. 맨틸라, 문학석사
스페인어문학 교수 대우

디 N. 보타시
현대 희랍어문학 교수

입학 조건

뉴욕 주의 대학교 평의회는 아래의 조건을 추천하였으며, 교수회는 신입반에 입학하기 위한 필요조건으로 채택하였다.

수 학: 대수 (이차방정식까지), 평면 기하학.

라틴어: 카이사르의 갈리아전기(4권); 베르길리우스의 아이네이드(6권); 키케로의 연설(6선); 살루스티우스의 카틸리나; 살루스티우스의 유구르타, 혹은 베르길리우스의 목가; 아놀드의 라틴어 작문(12장)

희랍어: 크세노폰의 아나바시스(3권), 호머의 일리아드(1권) 및 운율학

기초 필수: 산술과 영문법; 지리, 미국 역사, 희랍 및 로마 고전

65) 자연철학은 지금의 자연과학, 특히 물리학을 의미한다.

교과 과정.

이 과에서는 다음과 같은 강의가 진행될 예정이다:

1학년.

제1삼분기.

루미스, 대수 (제13장까지)
보이시의 희랍어 작문 연습
리비우스
번역 연습
헤로도투스.
오비드의 파스티
아놀드의 라틴어 산문 작문

제2삼분기.

루미스, 대수
헤로도투스.
보이시의 희랍어 작문 연습 (속)
웨이틀리, 수사학
크세노폰의 비망록
영어 작문 및 번역 연습

제3삼분기.

루미스, 기하학
보이시의 희랍어 작문 연습 (종)
호러스의 시(詩)
호머의 오딧세이
아놀드의 라틴어 산문 작문 (속)

학급에는 다음과 같은 주제의 강의가 진행된다.

화학. 자연사. 지질학. 자연철학. 천문학. 영어 연극 및 서사시. 미국 문학. 문체와 작문. 수사학과 평론. 고전. 고대사. 희랍 고고학. 계시종교의 근거. 생리학. 지성철학.

희랍어와 라틴어 작문은 각 삼분기의 고전 학습과 연관되어 있다.

낭독 연습은 매일 아침 예배 시간에 기도 후에 총장의 비평이 있다: 2학년과 1학년은 엄선한 연설을, 4학년과 3학년은 독창적인 내용으로 연설한다.

문과 시간표.

1학년

	제1삼분기	제2삼분기	제3삼분기
제1교시	수 학	수 학	수 학
제2교시	희랍어	희랍어	희랍어
제3교시	라틴어	라틴어	라틴어

1학년, 2학년 및 3학년은 수업 시간 중에 수사학 교수에 의해 작문 및 연설 시험이 있다.

출석, 시험 등

대학교에 등록할 때 학생은 문과 혹은 이과를 선택할 수 있으며, 만일 원하면 학위를 받지 않는 조건으로 교수진의 허락에 따라 과목을 선택할 수 있다.

이 두 과에는 등록금이 없다. 대학교에서 수여하는 우등상은 두 과에 균등하게 주어지며, 졸업식에서 적절한 학위와 우등상이 수여된다.

문과와 이과에서, 입학시험은 1877년 6월 12일 화요일과 9월 18일 화요일에 치러지며, 이후 매년 9월 제1삼분기 개학 전 화요일에 치러진다.

각 과는 4년 과정이다.

다음 학년은 1877년 9월 19일 시작되며,

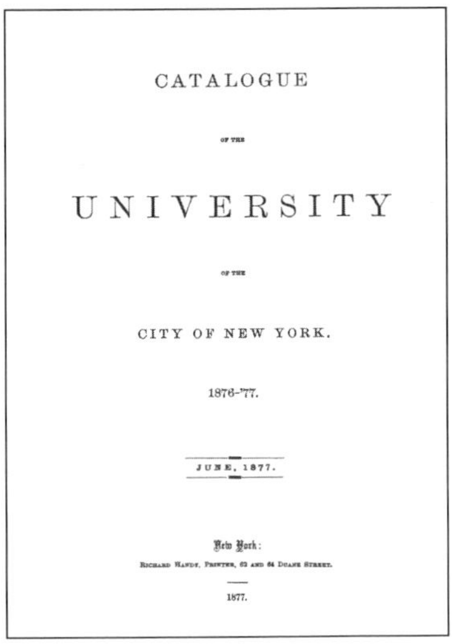
CATALOGUE

OF THE

UNIVERSITY

OF THE

CITY OF NEW YORK.

1876-'77.

JUNE, 1877.

New York:

RICHARD HANDY, PRINTER, 62 AND 64 DUANE STREET.

1877.

자료 2-7 *Catalogue of the University of the City of New York*, *1876~77*. June, 1877, New York: Richard Handy, Printer, 62 and 64 Duane Street.

3 삼분기로 구성된다. 제1삼분기는 개학일부터 성탄절 연휴까지 진행되며 1주일 동안의 휴식이 있다.

제2삼분기는 신년 바로 직후에 시작하며 4월 첫 월요일 시작되는 1주일 동안의 4월 방학까지 계속된다.

제3삼분기는 4월 두 번째 월요일에 시작하며, 졸업까지 계속된다. 다음 졸업식은 1877년 6월 14일 목요일에 거행될 예정이다.

법정 혹은 정부가 권장하는 공휴일, 학기 중의 성 금요일에는 학사 일정이 중지된다.

대학 출석 시간은 오전 10시부터 오후 1시 30분 혹은 2시이다.

약간의 예외가 있지만 시험은 학년이 끝날 때 치러지며, 구두 및 필기시험을 모두 본다.

다른 대학으로부터 입학하려는 자는 증명서와 성적 이외에, 들어가려는 학년에 자격이 되는지 시험을 보아야 한다. 4학년 제2삼분기가 시작된 이후에는 편입을 허락하지 않는다.

각 학생은 전기, 난방 및 부수적인 경비를 위해 매년 15달러를 납부해야 한다.

일반적인 규칙.

매일 아침 예배시간에 성경을 읽으며 기도를 드린다. 이때 총장 혹은 교수 1명이 집전하며, 학생들은 필히 출석해야 한다.

부모가 뉴욕에 거주하는 학생은 집에서 통학할 것을 권한다. 타 지방에서 온 학생은 훌륭한 가정에서 하숙할 수 있다.

건물을 손상시킨 학생은 교수회가 정한 벌칙을 받는 것 이외에, 필요한 수리에 드는 경비를 지불해야 한다.

습관적으로 나태하거나 학습에 태만하면 대학교의 규칙 및 정신을 위반한 것으로 간주될 것이며, 교수진이 적절하다고 결정한 벌칙을 받을 것이다.

자주 부도덕한 영향을 끼치는 학생은 대학교의 학생으로 허용되지 않을 것이다.

예배와 수업에 결석하거나 지각을 한 경우, 부모나 보호자로부터의 설명 혹은

자료 2-8 예배당

책임 교수에게 충분한 설명이 없는 한, 부모나 보호자에게 통고될 것이고 벌칙을 받을 것이다. 부모나 보호자의 요청이 없이 학생이 학기 중에 뉴욕을 떠나는 것을 허락하지 않는다.

허락 받지 않고는 어떠한 일을 위해 학생들이 모일 수 없다.

Catalogue of the University of the City of New York, 1876~77. June, 1877, New York: Richard Handy, Printer, 62 and 64 Duane Street.

Page 7

The Departments of the University are as Follows:

1. The Department of Arts.
2. The Department of Science.

In these two departments instruction is free.

3. The Department of Medicine.
4. The Department of Law.

Page 11

1. - The Department of Arts.

Instruction Free.

Faculty.

Howard Crosby, D. D., LL. D.,

Chancellor of the University.

E. A. Johnson, LL. D.,

Professor of the Latin Language and Literature, and President of the Faculty.

John W. Draper, M. D., LL. D.,

Professor of Chemistry and Natural History.

Benjamin N. Martin, D. D., L. H. D.,

Professor of Logic, and Intellectual and Moral Philosophy.

Richard H. Bull, A. M.,

Adjunct Professor of Mathematics.

Henry M. Baird, Ph. D.

Professor of the Greek Language and Literature.

George W. Coakley, LL. D.,

Professor of Mathematics, Natural Philosophy, and Astronomy, and Secretary of the Faculty.

Henry Draper, M. D.,

Adjunct Professor of Chemistry and Natural History.

Vincenzo Botta, Ph. D.,

Professor of the Italian Language and Literature,

Charles Carroll, Ph. D.,

Professor of the French and German Languages and Literatures.

Henry P. Mott

Professor of Political Science.

Luis F. Mantilla, A. M.

Acting Professor of the Spanish Language and Literature.

D. N. Botassi,

Professor of the Modern Greek Language and Literature.

Page 14

Terms of Admission.

The following were recommended by the University Convocation of the State of New York, and have been adopted by the Faculty as the requirements of admission to the Freshman Class:

In Mathematics: Algebra, to equations of the second degree, and Plane Geometry.

In Latin: Four books of Caesar's Commentaries; six books of Virgil's Aeneid; six select orations of Cicero; Sallust's Catiline; Sallust's Jugurthine War, or the Eclogues of Virgil; together with twelve chapters of Arnold's Latin Prose Composition.

In Greek: Three books of Xenophon's Anabasis; one book of Homer's Iliad, with Prosody.

Prerequisities: Thorough preparation in Arithmetic and English Grammar; a knowledge of Descriptive and Classical Geography, United States History, Greek and Roman Antiquities.

Course of Instruction.

In this Department, instruction will be given by the Professors as follows:

Freshman Class.

First Term.

Algebra, to Section XIII., Loomis.

Boise's Exercises in Greek Composition.

Livy.

Arnold's Latin Prose Composition.

Herodotus.

Ovid's Fasti.

Exercises in Translation.

Second Term.

Algebra, Loomis.

Herodotus.

Boise, continued.

Exercises in English Composition and Translation.

Rhetoric, Whately

Xenophon's Memorabilia.

Third Term.

Geometry, Loomis.

Boise, concluded.

Horace's Odes.

Homer's Odyssey.

Arnold, continued.

Page 16

Lectures are Delivered to the Classes on the Following Subjects.

Chemistry. Natural History. Geology. Natural Philosophy. Astronomy. The English Drama and Epic. American Literature. Style and Composition. Rhetoric and Criticism. Classical Literature. Ancient History. Greek Archaeology. Evidences of Revealed Religion. Physiology. Intellectual Philosophy.

Greek and Latin Composition is connected with the classical studies of each term.

Exercises in Declamation are criticised by the Chancellor every morning in the Chapel, after prayers: on these occasions, the Sophomores and Freshmen furnish selected speeches; the Seniors and Juniors, original orations.

Page 17

Scheme of Study in the Department of Arts.

Freshman Class.

	First Term	Second Term	Third Term
First Hour	Mathematics.	Mathematics.	Mathematics.
Second Hour	Greek.	Greek.	Greek.
Third Hour	Latin.	Latin.	Latin.

There are exercises In Composition and Declamation in the freshman, Sophomore and Junior Classes, during the hours with the Professor of Rhetoric.

Page 24

Attendance, Examinations, etc.

A student on matriculating in the University will have the option of entering the Department of Arts or the Department of Science, or, if he so desire, and have no academic degree in view, he may, with the permission of the Faculties, take selected studies in each.

In these two Departments, no tuition fees are charged. The academical honors of the University will be shared in equally by both Departments, suitable degrees being conferred in each, and parallel honors given in each, at the Public Commencement.

In the Department of Arts and in the Department of Science, examinations for admission will take place on Tuesday, the 12th of June, and on Tuesday, the 18th of September, 1877; and for ensuing years, on the Tuesday preceding the opening of the first term in September, in each year.

In each of these Departments the full course occupies four years.

The next Academic year begins on the 19th of September, 1877, and have three terms. The first begins on that day, extends to the Christmas holidays, and is followed by a recess of one week.

The second term begins immediately after the new year, and extends to the April vacation, which begins on the first Monday of April, and lasts one week.

The third term begins on the second Monday of April, and extends to Commencement. The next annual Commencement will take place on Thursday, the 14th of June, 1877.

There is also an intermission of College duties on such days as are made public holidays by law or government recommendation, and on Good-Friday when it occurs in term-time.

The hours of College attendance are from 10 A.M., to 1½ P.M., or 2 P.M.

The Class Examinations, with few exceptions, take place at the close of the academic year, and are both oral and written.

Applicants for admission from other colleges, in addition to the presentation of certificates of good character and class standing, are examined on their qualifications for the class they seek to join. No admission will be made to the Senior Class after the opening of the second term of the Senior year.

A charge of fifteen dollars per annum is made to each student for lighting and warming rooms and. incidental expenses.

General Regulations.

The Scriptures are read and prayer offered every morning in the Chapel, when the Chancellor or one of the Professors officiates, and the students are required to be present.

Students whose parents reside in the city are supposed to live in their own families. For those who come from a distance, board may be obtained in respectable private families.

Any student who shall injure or deface the building, in addition to such penalties as the Faculty shall see fit to inflict, will be subject to the expense occasioned by the necessary repairs.

Habitual indolence or inattention to study, will be regarded as an offence against the laws and spirit of the Institution, and will be made the subject of such discipline as the Faculty may deem expedient.

No student who frequents places of corrupting influence will be allowed to remain a member of the University.

Absences from the Chapel and recitation, or tardy attendance upon the same, unless explained by a note from the parent or guardian, or otherwise satisfactorily accounted for to the officiating professor, will be communicated to the parent or guardian, and will subject the student to discipline. No student will be permitted to leave the city during termtime unless a request to that effect is made by his parent or guardian.

No meeting of the students can be held in the University for the transaction of any kind of business, except by permission.

18780600

1877~8년도, 1학년, 학적부, 1853~1893년, 제2권.

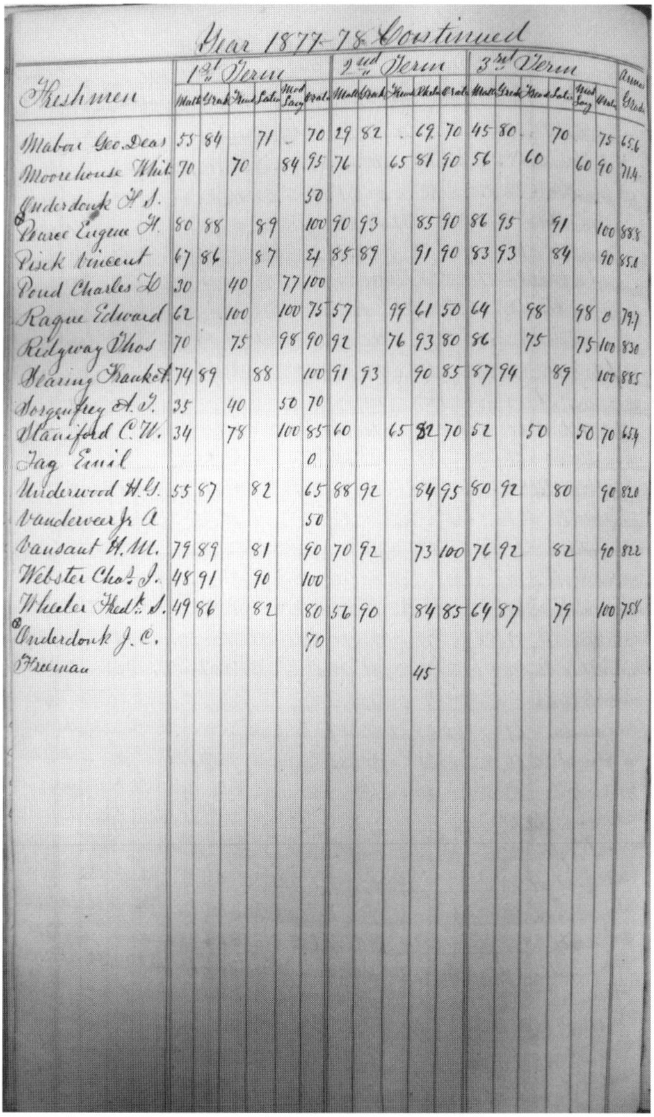

Year 1877-78 Continued

Freshmen	1st Term Math	Greek	French	Latin	Mod Lang	Orat	2nd Term Math	Greek	French	Phil	Orat	3rd Term Math	Greek	French	Latin	Mod Lang	Orat	Annual Grade
Mabon Geo. Deas	55	84		71	-	70	29	82	.	69	70	45	80	.	70		75	65.6
Moorehouse Whit	70		70		84	75	76		65	81	90	56		60		60	90	71.4
Underdonk H. S.						50												
Pearce Eugene H.	80	88		89		100	90	93		85	90	86	95		91		100	88.8
Pisek Vincent	67	86		87		84	85	89		91	90	83	93		84		90	85.8
Pond Charles L.	30		40		77	100												
Rague Edward	62		100		100	75	57		99	61	50	64		98		98	0	79.7
Ridgway Thos	70		75		98	90	92		76	93	80	86		75		75	100	83.0
Searing Frank et	74	89		88		100	91	93		90	85	87	94		89		100	88.5
Sorgenfrey A. G.	35		40		50	70												
Staniford C. W.	34		78		100	85	60		65	82	70	52		50		50	70	65.4
Tag Emil						0												
Underwood H. G.	55	87		82		65	88	92		84	95	80	92		80		90	82.0
Vanderveer Jr A						50												
Vansant H. M.	79	89		81		90	70	92		73	100	76	92		82		90	82.2
Webster Chas J.	48	91		90		100												
Wheeler Fred S.	49	86		82		80	56	90		84	85	64	87		79		100	75.8
Underdonk J. C.						70												
Freeman										45								

자료 2-9 *Year 1877~8*, *Freshmen*, *Matriculation Book*, *1853~1893*, Vol. 2.

1학년(1877~8년)

1학기	수학 55, 희랍어 87, 라틴어 82, 웅변 65.
2학기	수학 88, 희랍어 92, 수사학 84, 웅변 95.
3학기	수학 80, 희랍어 92, 라틴어 80, 웅변 90.

1학년 평균 성적 82.0

Year 1877~8, Freshmen, Matriculation Book, 1853~1893, Vol. 2.

Freshmen (1877~8)

First Term	Mathematics 55, Greek 87, Latin 82, Oratory 65.
Second Term	Mathematics 88, Greek 92, Rhetoric 84, Oratory 95.
Third Term	Mathematics 80, Greek 92, Latin 80, Oratory 90.

Annual Grade 82.0

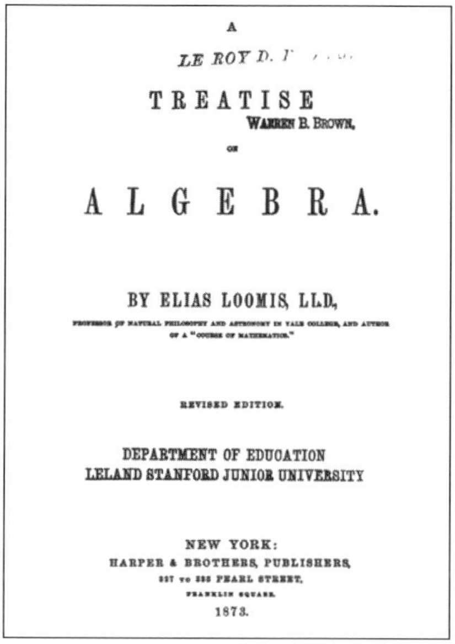
A

LE ROY D. F

TREATISE

WARREN B. BROWN,

ON

ALGEBRA.

BY ELIAS LOOMIS, LL.D.,

PROFESSOR OF NATURAL PHILOSOPHY AND ASTRONOMY IN YALE COLLEGE, AND AUTHOR OF A "COURSE OF MATHEMATICS."

REVISED EDITION.

DEPARTMENT OF EDUCATION
LELAND STANFORD JUNIOR UNIVERSITY

NEW YORK:
HARPER & BROTHERS, PUBLISHERS,
327 TO 335 PEARL STREET,
FRANKLIN SQUARE.
1873.

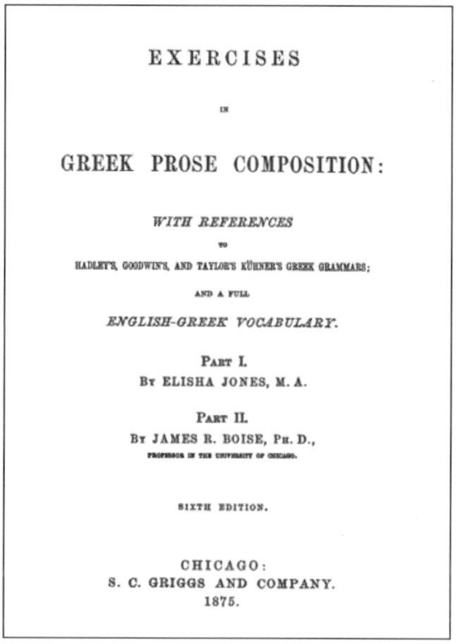
EXERCISES

IN

GREEK PROSE COMPOSITION:

WITH REFERENCES

TO

HADLEY'S, GOODWIN'S, AND TAYLOR'S KÜHNER'S GREEK GRAMMARS;

AND A FULL

ENGLISH-GREEK VOCABULARY.

PART I.
BY ELISHA JONES, M. A.

PART II.
BY JAMES R. BOISE, PH. D.,
PROFESSOR IN THE UNIVERSITY OF CHICAGO.

SIXTH EDITION.

CHICAGO:
S. C. GRIGGS AND COMPANY.
1875.

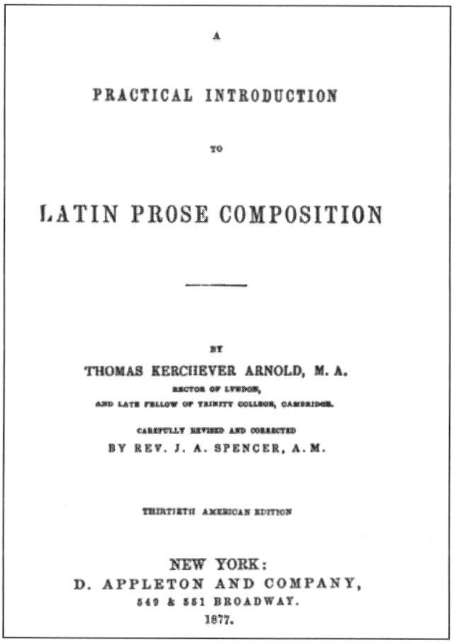
A

PRACTICAL INTRODUCTION

TO

LATIN PROSE COMPOSITION

BY

THOMAS KERCHEVER ARNOLD, M. A.
RECTOR OF LYNDON,
AND LATE FELLOW OF TRINITY COLLEGE, CAMBRIDGE.

CAREFULLY REVISED AND CORRECTED
BY REV. J. A. SPENCER, A. M.

THIRTIETH AMERICAN EDITION

NEW YORK:
D. APPLETON AND COMPANY,
549 & 551 BROADWAY.
1877.

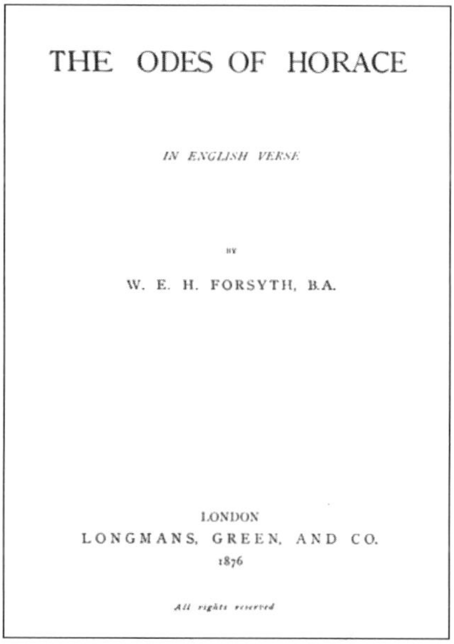
THE ODES OF HORACE

IN ENGLISH VERSE

BY

W. E. H. FORSYTH, B.A.

LONDON
LONGMANS, GREEN, AND CO.
1876

All rights reserved

자료 2-10 언더우드가 1학년 과정에서 사용했던 교과서. A. Elias Loomis, *A Treatise on Algebra*, Harper & Brothers, Publishers, 1873. B. Elisha Jones, James R. Boise, *Exercises in Greek Prose Composition*, S. C. Griggs and Company, 1875. C. Thomas K. Arnold, *A Practical Introduction to Latin Prose Composition*, D. Appleton and Company, 1877. D. W. E. H. Forsyth, *The Odes of Horace*, Longmans, Green, and Co., 1876.

18780600

뉴욕대학교 일람, 1877~78년. 1878년 6월, 뉴욕: 리처드 핸디, 프린터, 듀언 가 62 및 64번지.

문리대에는 다음과 같은 학생이 재학중이다.[66]

1학년[67]

이름	거주지
호러스 그랜트 언더우드	뉴더햄, 뉴저지 주

월터 덩컨 뷰캐넌
학급대표

교과 과정

2학년

제1삼분기.

드레이퍼, 화학	루미스, 기하학 및 삼각법
포셋, 정치 경제학	영어 작문 및 번역 연습

제2삼분기.

루미스, 삼각법 및 측량	독일어
데모스테니스와 아이스키네스	에우리피데스
희랍 문학 강의	드레이퍼, 화학
영어 작문 연습	

66) 모두 138명이며, 1학년은 52명이다.
67) 나머지 학생 명단은 영어 원문을 참고하시오.

제3삼분기.

루미스, 분석 기하학 및 미분학	키케로
스폴딩, 영문학사	

문과 시간표.

2학년

	제1삼분기	제2삼분기	제3삼분기
제1교시	화학	화학	분석 기하학, 미분학
제2교시	삼각법	삼각법	라틴어
제3교시	정치 경제학	희랍어	영문학

입학, 시험, 등

다음 학년은 1878년 9월 18일 시작되며, 3 삼분기로 구성된다. 제1삼분기는 개학일부터 성탄절 연휴까지 진행되며 1주일 동안의 휴식이 있다.

제2삼분기는 신년 바로 직후에 시작하며 4월 첫 월요일 시작되는 1주일 동안의 4월 방학까지 계속된다.

제3삼분기는 4월 두 번째 월요일에 시작하며, 졸업까지 계속된다. 다음 졸업식은 1878년 6월 20일 목요일에 거행될 예정이다.

Catalogue of the University of the City of New York, 1877~78. June, 1878, New York: Richard Handy, Printer, 62 and 64 Duane Street.

In The Departments of Arts and of Science are the Following Students.

Page 9

Freshman Class.

Name.	Home.
Herbert C. Alden	New York.
Benjamin Aycrigg, Jr.	Passaic, N. J.
John Oscar Ball	Brooklyn.
Milan D. Barnes	Brooklyn.
Cephas Brainerd, Jr.	Haddam, Conn.
Walter Duncan Buchanan	New York.
Charles Henry Butler	Yonkers
Benjamin Avery Capwell	Brooklyn.
Albert F. Cornelius	Freeport.
William Charles Cudlipp	Jersey City, N. J.
Harry Hollister Dawson	Newark, N. J.
F. W. Deitering	Hoboken
John Devins	Elizabeth, N. J.
Samuel M. Dix	Staten 1sland.
Robert P. Doremus	Jersey City. N. J.
George Martin Duncan	Paterson, N. J.
Luther Stewart Elmer	Jersey City
Arthur English	Fort Lee, N. J.
Charles Feder	Newark, N. J.

Cuyler Freemsn	Brooklyn
Edward Lawrence Frost	East Hinsdale.
Thomas John Campbell Grey	New York
Francis J. M. Greene	New York
Egbert Guernsey, Jr.	New York
Gilbert Halsted, Jr.	Brooklyn.
Isaac Hamburger	East New York.
George Hannum Hazen	Haddam, Conn.
Julian Nunes Henriques	New York.
Florian E. Henshaw	Brooklyn
Alexander Caufman Hexter	New York
William Henry Hillman	Brooklyn.
Franklin Sawyer Holmes	Brooklyn.
Edward Weed Johnson	Paterson, N. J.
George Deas Mabon	Weekawken, N. J.
Whitfield Moorehouse	N. Providence, N. J.
Frank Skillman Onderdont,	Manhasset
John Cortelyou Onderdont	Manhasset
Eugene Frederick Pearce	Brooklyn.
Vincent Pisek	New York.
Charles Zeblon Pond	New York
Edward Raque	Jersey City Heights.
Thomas Ridgway	Brooklyn.
Frank Alexander Searing	Mineola.
Alfred T. Sorgenfrey	New York
Charles W. Staniford	Brooklyn.
Emil Tag	Weehawken, N. Y.
Horace Grant Underwood	**New Durham, N. J.**
Adrian Vanderveer, Jr.	Flatbush

Horatio Moses Vansant	W. New Brighton.
Charles irving Webster	Boseawen, N. H.
David Weeson	Brooklyn
Frederick Seymour Wheeler	Brooklyn.

Walter Duncan Buchanan,

President of Class Association.

Page 15

Course of Instruction..

Sophomore Class.

First Term.

Chemistry, Draper.

Geometry and Trigonometry, Loomis.

Political Economy, Fawcett.

Exercises in English Composition and Translation.

Second Term.

Trigonometry and Surveying, Loomis.

German.

Demosthenes and Aeschines.

Euripides.

Lectures on Greek Literature.

Chemistry, Draper.

Exercises in English Composition.

Third Term.

Analytical Geometry and Calculus, Loomis.

Cicero.

History of English Literature, Spalding.

Page 13

Scheme of Study in the Department of Arts.

Sophomore Class.

	First Term	Second Term	Third Term
First Hour	Chemistry.	Chemistry.	Analytical Geometry, Calculus.
Second Hour	Trigonometry.	Trigonometry.	Latin.
Third Hour	Political Economy.	Greek.	English Literature.

Page 24

Attendance, Examinations, etc.

The next Academic year begins on the 18th of September, 1878, and have three terms. The first begins on that day, extends to the Christmas holidays, and is followed by a recess of one week.

The second term begins immediately after the new year, and extends to the April vacation, which begins on the first Monday of April, and lasts one week.

The third term begins on the second Monday of April, and extends to Commencement. The next annual Commencement will take place on Thursday, the 20th of June, 1878.

18790100

동정. *The University Quarterly*, 뉴욕대학교, 2(2), 1879년 1월, 77쪽.

다음 삼분기에 활동할 필로머시언 소사이어티의 임원진은 다음과 같다: 회장, 헨리 P. 모리슨; 제1부회장, 띠 O. 볼; 제2부회장, 벤저민 A. 캡웰; 감사, 조지 H. 헤이즌; 교신 총무, 세파스 브레이너드 주니어; 기록 총무, 에이치 H. 도슨; 사서, 존 W. 질레트; 편집인, 제이 H. 브레이너드 및 에이치 G. 언더우드.

Facta Actaque. *The University Quarterly,* New York University, 2(2), Jan. 1879, p. 77.

자료 2-11 필로머시언 소사이어티의 방.

The officers of the Philomathean Society for next term are as follows: President, Henry P. Morrison; First vice-President, T. O. Ball; Second vice, Benjamin A. Capwell; Supervisor, George H. Hazen; Corresponding Secretary, Cephas Brainerd, Jr.; Recording Secretary, H. H. Dawson; Librarian, John W. Gillette; Editors, J. H. Brainerd and H. G. Underwood.

필로머시언 소사이어티(Philomathean Society)

뉴욕대학교의 필로머시언 소사이어티(Philomathean Society) 대학 창립과 함께 1832년 설립된 학생 문학토론 단체였다. 학교는 이 단체에 본관의 방을 배정해 주었고, 회원들은 자신들의 도서를 수집하고 명사를 초청해 강연을 듣는 등 수시로 모임을 가졌다. 이런 학생 단체는 당시 대세였던 암기식 교과 과정에서 탈피하여 토론을 통해 정규 과정을 보완하는 기능이 있었다. 뉴욕대학교에는 필로머시언 소사이어티의 라이벌 단체로 유클리언 소사이어티(Eucleian Society)가 있었다. 필로머시언 소사이어티는 1888년 해체되었다.

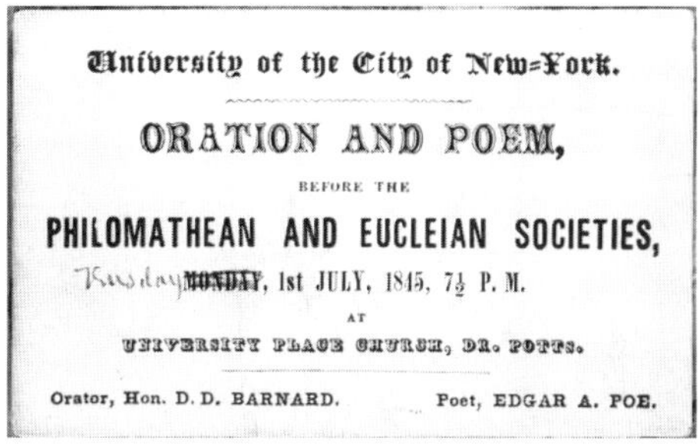

자료 2-12 필로머시언 소사이어티의 모임을 알리는 광고.

1878~9년도, 2학년, 학적부, 1853~1893년, 제2권.

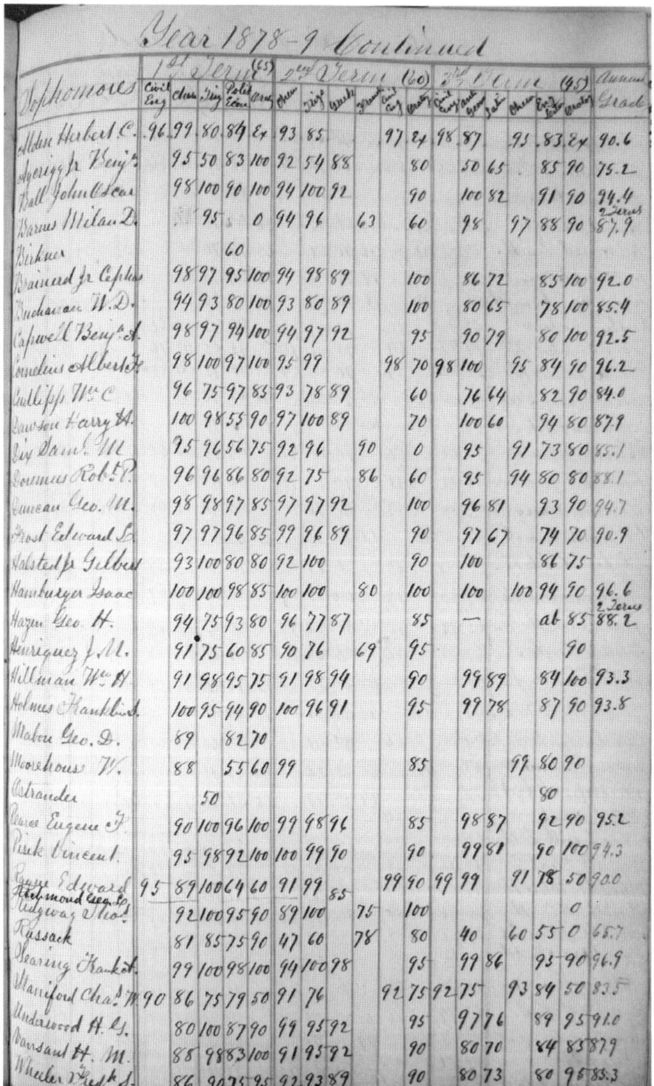

Year 1878-9 Continued

Sophomores	1st Term (65) Civil Eng	Chem	Trig	Polit Econ	Orat	2nd Term (60) Chem	Trig	Greek	French	Civil Eng	Orat	3rd Term (45) Civil Eng	Anal Geom	Lat	Chem	Eng Lit	Orat	Annual Grade
Alden Herbert C.	96	99	80	84	Ex	93	85			97	Ex	98	87		95	83	Ex	90.6
Aycrigg Jr Benjn.		95	50	83	100	92	54	88			80		50	65		85	90	75.2
Ball John Oscar		98	100	90	100	94	100	92			90		100	82		91	90	94.4
Barnes Milan D.			95		0	94	96		63		60		98		97	88	90	2 Terms 87.9
Birkner				60														
Brainerd Jr Cephas		98	97	95	100	94	98	89			100		86	72		85	100	92.0
Buchanan W. D.		94	93	80	100	93	80	89			100		80	65		78	100	85.4
Capwell Benjn. A.		98	97	94	100	94	97	92			95		90	79		80	100	92.5
Cornelius Albert F.		98	100	97	100	95	99			98	70	98	100		95	84	90	96.2
Cullipp Wm. C		96	75	97	85	93	78	89			60		76	64		82	90	84.0
Dawson Harry H.		100	98	55	90	97	100	89			70		100	60		94	80	87.9
Day Saml. M		95	96	56	75	92	96		90		0		95		91	73	80	85.1
Downes Robt. P.		96	96	86	80	92	75		86		60		95		94	80	80	88.1
Duncan Geo. M.		98	98	97	85	97	97	92			100		96	81		93	90	94.7
Frost Edward S.		97	97	96	85	99	96	89			90		97	67		74	70	90.9
Halsted Jr Gilbert		93	100	80	80	92	100				90		100			86	75	
Hamburger Isaac		100	100	98	85	100	100		80		100		100		100	94	90	96.6
Hazen Geo. H.		94	75	93	80	96	77	87			85		—			ab	85	2 Terms 88.2
Henriquez J. M.		91	75	60	85	90	76		69		95						90	
Hillman Wm. H.		91	98	95	75	91	98	94			90		99	89		84	100	93.3
Holmes Franklin		100	95	94	90	100	96	91			95		99	78		87	90	93.8
Mabon Geo. D.		89		82	70													
Moorehouse W.		88		55	60	99					85				97	80	90	
Ostrander			50													80		
Peirce Eugene F.		90	100	96	100	99	98	96			85		98	87		92	90	95.2
Pisek Vincent		95	98	92	100	100	99	90			90		99	81		90	100	94.3
Rowe Edward	95	89	100	64	60	91	99	85		99	90	99	99		91	78	50	90.0
Richmond Geo. S. / Ridgway Thos.		92	100	95	90	89	100		75		100						0	
Russack		81	85	75	90	47	60		78		80		40		60	55	0	65.7
Searing Frank A.		99	100	98	100	94	100	98			95		99	86		95	90	96.9
Staniford Chas. M.	90	86	75	79	50	91	76			92	75	92	75		93	84	50	83.5
Underwood H. G.		80	100	87	90	99	95	92			95		97	76		89	95	91.0
Van Sant H. M.		88	98	83	100	91	95	92			90		80	70		84	85	87.9
Wheeler Fredk. S.		86	90	75	95	92	93	89			90		80	73		80	95	83.3

자료 2-13 *Year 1878~9*, *Sophomore*, *Matriculation Book*, *1853~1893*, Vol. 2.

2학년(1878~9년)

1학기	화학 80, 삼각법 100, 정치 경제학 87, 웅변 90.
2학기	화학 99, 삼각법 95, 희랍어 92, 웅변 95.
3학기	분석기하학 97, 라틴어 76, 영문학 89, 웅변 95.

2학년 평균 성적 91.0

Year 1878~9, Sophomore, Matriculation Book, 1853~1893, Vol. 2.

Sophomore (1878~9)

First Term	Chemistry 80, Trigonometry 100, Political Economics 87, Oratory 90.
Second Term	Chemistry 99, Trigonometry 95, Greek 92, Oratory 95.
Third Term	Analytical Geometry 97, Latin 76, English Literature 89, Oratory 95.

Annual Grade 91.0

18790500

뉴욕대학교 일람, 1878~79년. 1879년 5월, 뉴욕: 리처드 핸디, 프린터, 듀언 가 62 및 64번지.

문리대에는 다음과 같은 학생이 재학 중이다.

2학년[68]

이름	거주지
호러스 그랜트 언더우드	뉴더햄, 뉴저지 주

유진 프레데릭 피어스
학급대표

교과 과정

3학년

제1삼분기.

자연 철학	포터, 지식 철학
독일어	영어 작문 및 독창적인 연설

제2삼분기.

근대사 비평론	
호러스의 풍자시집과 사목 서간.	자연 철학
영어 작문 및 독창적인 연설	

68) 당시 4개 학년에 114명의 학생이 재학 중이었으며, 32명인 2학년 학생의 전체 명단은 영어 원문을 참고하시오.

제3삼분기.

소포클레스, 혹은 아이스킬로스	이소크라테스
희랍문학 강의	톰슨, 논리학
자연 신학	루미스, 천문학
자작연설	

문과 시간표.

3학년

	제1삼분기	제2삼분기	제3삼분기
제1교시	독일어	근대사	천문학
제2교시	지식 철학	라틴어	논리학, 자연 신학
제3교시	자연 철학	자연 철학	희랍어

입학, 시험, 등

다음 학년은 1879년 9월 17일 시작되며, 3 삼분기로 구성된다. 제1삼분기는 개학일부터 성탄절 연휴까지 진행되며 1주일 동안의 휴식이 있다.

제2삼분기는 신년 바로 직후에 시작하며 4월 첫 월요일 시작되는 1주일 동안의 4월 방학까지 계속된다.

제3삼분기는 4월 두 번째 월요일에 시작하며, 졸업까지 계속된다. 다음 졸업식은 1879년 6월 19일 목요일에 거행될 예정이다.

Catalogue of the University of the City of New York, 1878~79. May, 1879, New York: Richard Handy, Printer, 62 and 64 Duane Street.

Page 9

In The Departments of Arts and of Science are the Following Students.

Sophomore Class.

Name.	Home.
Herbert C. Alden	New York.
Benjamin Aycrigg, Jr.	Passaic, N. J.
John Oscar Ball	Brooklyn.
Milan D. Barnes	Brooklyn.
Cephas Brainerd, Jr.	Haddam, Conn.
Walter Duncan Buchanan	New York.
Benjamin Avery Capwell	Brooklyn.
Albert F. Cornelius	Freeport.
William Charles Cudlipp	Jersey City, N. J.
Harry Hollister Dawson	Newark, N. J.
Samuel M. Dix	Staten 1sland.
Robert P. Doremus	Jersey City. N. J.
George Martin Duncan	Paterson, N. J.
Edward Lawrence Frost	East Hinsdale.
Gilbert Halsted, Jr.	Brooklyn.
Isaac Hamburger	East New York.
George Hannum Hazen	Haddam, Conn.
Julian Nunes Henriques	New York.
William Henry Hillman	Brooklyn.
Franklin Sawyer Holmes	Brooklyn.

George Deas Mabon	Weekawken, N. J.
Whitfield Moorehouse	N. Providence, N. J.
Eugene Frederick Pearce	Brooklyn.
Vincent Pisek	New York.
Edward Raque	Jersey City Heights.
Thomas Ridgway	Brooklyn.
Jacob Russak	New York.
Frank Alexander Searing	Mineola.
Charles W. Staniford	Brooklyn.
Horace Grant Underwood	New Durham, N. J.
Horatio Moses Vansant	W. New Brighton.
Frederick Seymour Wheeler	Brooklyn.

Eugene Frederick Pearce.
President of Class Association.

Matriculated Students 114

Page 14

Course of Instruction.

Junior Class.

First Term.

Natural Philosophy.	Intellectual Philosophy, Porter.
German.	English Composition and Original Declamations.

Second Term.

Modern History.	Principles of Criticism.
Horace's Satires and Epistles.	Natural Philosophy.

English Composition and Original Declamations.

Third Term.

Sophocles, or Aeschylus.	Socrates.
Lectures on Greek Literature.	Logic, Thompson.
Natural Theology.	Astronomy, Loomis.
Original Declamations.	

Page 16

Scheme of Study in the Department of Arts.

Junior Class.

	First Term	Second Term	Third Term
First Hour	German.	Modern History	Astronomy
Second Hour	Intellectual Philosophy	Latin	Logic, Natural Theology
Third Hour	Natural Philosophy	Natural Philosophy	Greek

Page 23

Attendance, Examinations, etc.

The next Academic year begins on the 17th of September, 1879, and has three terms. The first begins on that day, extends to the Christmas holidays, and is followed by a recess of one week.

The second term begins immediately after the new year, and extends to the April vacation, which begins on the first Monday of April, and lasts one week.

The third term begins on the second Monday of April, and extends to Commencement. The next annual Commencement will take place on Thursday, the 19th of June, 1879

18790700

동정. *The University Quarterly*, 뉴욕대학교, 2(4), 1879년 7월, 142쪽.

다음 삼분기에 활동할 필로머시언 소사이어티의 임원진은 다음과 같다:

회장	: 세파스 브레이너드 주니어, '81
제1부회장	: 윌리엄 C. 커드립, '81
제2부회장	: 호러스 G. 언더우드., '81
감사	: 에드워드 L. 프로스트, '81
기록 총무	: 프랭클린 S. 홈즈, '81
교신 총무	: 앨버트 F. 코르넬리우스, '81
사서	: 아이삭 햄버거, '81
제1편집인	: 찰스 W. 스태니포드, '81
제2편집인	: 제임스 W. 로렌스, '82

Facta Actaque. *The University Quarterly*, New York University, 2(4), July 1879, p. 142.

The officers of the Philomathean Society for next term are as follows:

President	: Cephas Brainerd, Jr., '81
First vice-President	: William C. Cudlipp, '81
Second vice:	: Horace G. Underwood, '81
Supervisor	: Edward L. Frost, '81
Recording Secretary	: Franklin S. Holmes, '81
Corresponding Secretary	: Albert F. Cornelius, '81

Librarian	: Issac Hamburger, '81
First Editors	: Charles W. Staniford, '81
Second Editors	: James W. Lawrence, '82

18800326

음악원에서 개최된 3학년 웅변대회. *New York Tribune*, (금, 1880년 3월 26일, 8쪽).

음악원에서 개최된 3학년 웅변대회.
뉴욕대학교 1881년 졸업반 공연.

뉴욕대학교 3학년의 연례 웅변대회가 어제 밤 1881년 졸업반 후원으로 음악원에서 개최되었다. 크로스비 총장은 대학교 가운과 모자를 쓰고 좌정한 가운데, 이 A. 존슨, 헨리 M. 베어드, 번저민 N. 마틴, 존 J. 스티븐슨, 헨리 P. 모트, T. 애디슨 리차즈, 조지 W. 코클리 및 찰스 캐롤 교수, 이 V. 톰스 박사, 럿거스 여자대학의 대니얼 S. 마틴 교수 등이 연단에 함께 자리를 했다. 웅변의 심사위원은 페어차일드 교수, 에드워드 호퍼 박사, 리처드 맥버니였나. 음악원은 학생 및 친구들로 만원을 이루었다. 연단 좌측에는 사이 업실론 클럽 회원들이 그리스어 기호로 장식된 큰 특별석에 앉았으며, 우측에는 2학년 학생들이 앉아 행사 중간에 거대한 양배추 모양의 깜작 시범을 보여주었다. 이것이 프롬프터 석과 부딪혀 '선한 사마리아인'으로 연기하는 학생들이 민첩하게 몸을 낮추었으며, 그래풀라 밴드의 연주자들 중에 수많은 작은 banquets이 흩어졌다.

2학년은 오랜 관습에 따라 정교한 "흉내 내기 프로그램"도 준비했다. "국가적인 문제"란 제목의 웅변은 흉내 내기 프로그램에서 "13-15-14"로 준비되었는데, 교수회와 신입생에 대한 일반적인 농담 이외에 크로스비 총장과 관계된 범죄 예방을 위한 단체, 구세군 및 아일랜드 구호기금 등도 언급되었다.

이날 실시된 웅변은 필로머시언 소사이어티의 대표인 조지 H. 헤이즌의 "국가적인 문제,"; 유진 피어스의 "러시아의 전제정치,"; 세파스 브렌이너드, 주니어의 "현금의 타락,"; 벤저민 A. 캡웰의 "인도의 로드 클라이브,"; 유클리언 소사이어티의 대표인 벤저민 애크리그, 주니어의 "평화와 전쟁의 관계,"; 존 O. 볼의 "기사도,"; 프랭클린 S. 홈즈의 "몰몬교에 대한 우리들의 의무,"; 호러스 G. 언더우드의

"성 바르톨로뮤의 대학살,"; 조지 M. 덩컨의 "영국의 공화주의,"; 윌리엄 H. 힐먼의 "The American Sabbath,"; 그리고 빈센트 피셱의 "휘스 전쟁," 등이었다.

덩컨과 볼로 구성된 웅변위원회의 귀한 강평이 있었고, 오랜 토의 끝에 6권의 「밴크로프트 역사서」를 수여하는 웹스터 상이 언더우드 씨에게 수여되었다. 일부 청중은 이러한 결정에 대한 불만을 토로했으며, 2학년 석의 여러 청중은 축복기도를 드리는 도중 휘파람과 야유로 버릇없게 굴었다.

Junior Eloquence at the Academy. *New York Tribune*, (Fri., Mar. 26th, 1880, p. 8).

Junior Eloquence at the Academy.

Exhibition of the Class of 1881 of the University of the City of New·York.

The annual Junior exhibition of the University of the City of New York took place last evening at the Academy of Music under the auspices of the class of '81. Chancellor Crosby, wearing the University gown and cap, presided, and with him upon the stage were Professors E. A. Johnson, Henry M. Baird, Benjamin N. Martin, John J. Stevenson, Henry P. Mott, T. Addison Richards, George W. Coakley and Charles Carroll, Dr. E. V. Thoms, Professor Daniel S. Martin, of Rutger's Female College, and others. The judges of the speaking were Professor Fairchild, the Rev. Dr. Edward Hopper and Richard McBurney. The Academy was filled with students and their friends. On the left of the stage the members of the Psi Upsilon college fraternity occupied a large box adorned with Greek symbols, and on the opposite side was the box of some members of the Sophomore class, from which, in the middle of the exercises, came an unlooked-for, demonstration in the shape of a huge cabbage. This struck the prompter's box, causing the student who was acting as "good Samaritan" to dodge low with amusing agility, and scattering innumerable small banquets among the musicians of Grafulla's band.

The Sophomores had also prepared. in accordance with immemorial custom, an elaborate "mock program." The oration entitled "The National Problem," appeared, on the mock programme as "13-15-14," and beside the usual jokes on the Faculty and the Freshmen, there were many allusions to Chancellor Crosby's connection with the Society for the Prevention of Crime, and the Salvation Army and the Irish Relief Fund did not escape mention.

The orations of the evening were as follows: "The National Problem," by George H. Hazen, representative of the Philomatheon Society; "Russian Despotism" by Eugene Pearce; "Modern Degeneracy," by Cephas Brainerd, Jr.; "Lord Clive in India," by Benjamin A. Capwell; "The Relations of Peace and War," by Benjamin Aycrigg, Jr., representative of the Eucleian Society; "Chivalry," by John O. Ball; "Our Duty to the Mormons;" by Franklin S. Holmes; "The Massacre of St. Bartholomew's," by Horace G. Underwood; "Republicanism in England," by George M. Duncan; "The American Sabbath," by William H. Hillman; and "The Hussite War," by Vincent Pisek.

Honorable mention was made by the committee of the orations of Messrs. Duncan and Ball, and after a long discussion, the Webster prize, consisting of Bancroft's History, in six volumes, was awarded to Mr. Underwood. Dissatisfaction with the decision was freely expressed by a part of the audience, and several persons in the Sophomore box displayed their ill-breeding by hissing and hooting during the benediction.

18800600

1879~80년도, 3학년, 학적부, 1853~1893년, 제2권.

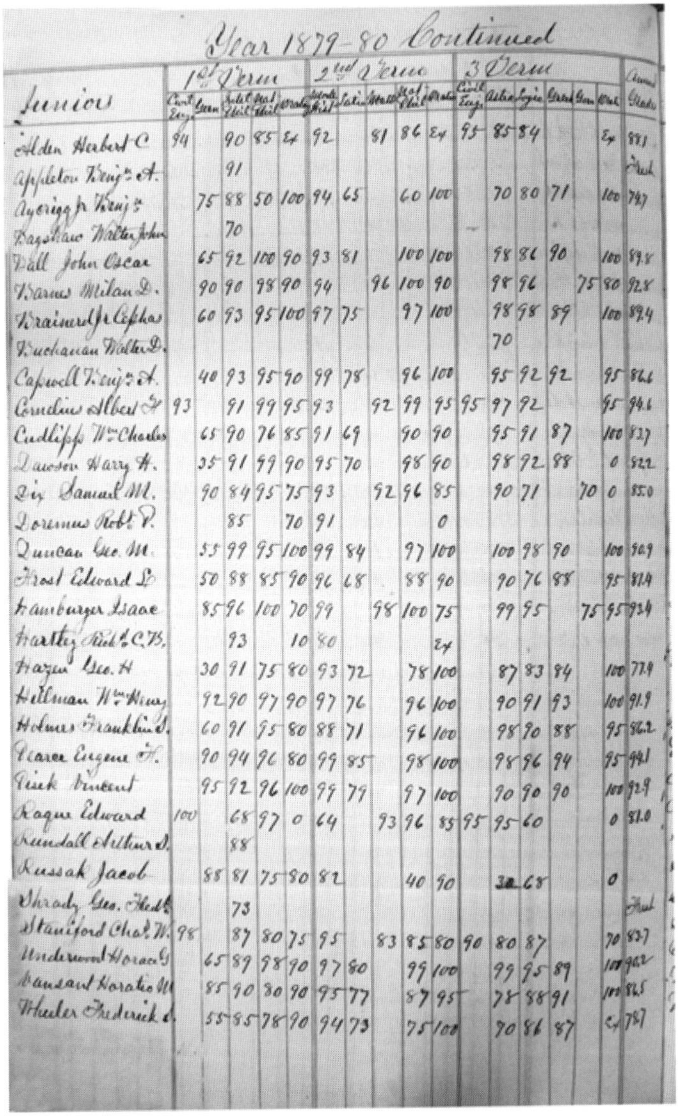

Year 1879-80 Continued

Junior	1st Term Civil Eng.	Geom.	Intel. Phil.	Nat. Phil.	Oratory	2nd Term Moral Phil.	Latin	Math.	Nat. Phil.	Oratory	3 Term Civil Eng.	Astron.	Logic	Greek	Germ.	Oral	Annual Grade
Alden Herbert C	94		90	85	Ex	92		81	86	Ex	95	85	84			Ex	88.1
Appleton Benj. A.			91														Fresh
Ayerigg Jr Benj.		75	88	50	100	94	65		60	100		70	80	71		100	79.7
Bagshaw Walter John			70														
Ball John Oscar		65	92	100	90	93	81		100	100		98	86	90		100	89.8
Barnes Milan D.		90	90	98	90	94		96	100	90		98	96		75	80	92.8
Brainerd Jr Cephas		60	93	95	100	97	75		97	100		98	98	89		100	89.4
Buchanan Walter D.												70					
Capwell Benj. A.		40	93	95	90	99	78		96	100		95	92	92		95	86.6
Condict Albert F.	93		91	99	95	93		92	99	95	95	97	92			95	94.6
Cudlipp Wm. Charles		65	90	76	85	91	69		90	90		95	91	87		100	82.7
Dawson Harry H.		35	91	99	90	95	70		98	90		98	92	88		0	82.2
Dix Samuel M.		90	84	95	75	93		92	96	85		90	71		70	0	85.0
Doremus Robt. P.			85		70	91				0							
Duncan Geo. M.		55	99	95	100	99	84		97	100		100	98	90		100	90.9
Frost Edward L.		50	88	85	90	96	68		88	90		90	76	88		95	81.4
Hamburger Isaac		85	96	100	70	99		98	100	75		99	95		75	95	93.4
Hartley Richd. C. B.			93		10	80				Ex							
Hazen Geo. H		30	91	75	80	93	72		78	100		87	83	84		100	77.9
Hellman Wm. Henry		92	90	97	90	97	76		96	100		90	91	93		100	91.9
Holmes Franklin S.		60	91	95	80	88	71		96	100		98	90	88		95	86.2
Pearce Eugene H.		90	94	96	80	99	85		98	100		98	96	94		95	94.1
Pick Vincent		95	92	96	100	99	79		97	100		90	90	90		100	92.9
Rague Edward	100		68	97	0	64		93	96	85	95	95	60			0	81.0
Rundall Arthur S.			88														
Russak Jacob		88	81	75	80	82			40	90		30	68			0	
Shrady Geo. Fredk.			73														Fresh
Staniford Chas. W.	98		87	80	75	95		83	85	80	90	80	87			70	83.7
Underwood Horace G.		65	89	98	90	97	80		99	100		99	95	89		100	90.2
Vansant Horatio M.		85	90	80	90	95	77		87	95		78	88	91		100	86.5
Wheeler Frederick S.		55	85	78	90	94	73		75	100		70	86	87		Ex	78.7

자료 2-14 *Year 1879~80*, *Junior*, *Matriculation Book*, *1853~1893*, Vol. 2.

3학년(1879~1880)

1학기	독일어 65, 지성철학 89, 자연 철학 98, 웅변 90.
2학기	근대사 97, 라틴어 80, 자연 철학 99, 웅변 100.
3학기	천문학 99, 논리학 95, 희랍어 89, 웅변 100.

3학년 평균 성적 90.2

Year 1879~80, Junior, Matriculation Book, 1853~1893, Vol. 2.

Junior (1879~80)

First Term	German 65, Intellectual Philosophy 89, Natural Philosophy 98, Oratory 90.
Second Term	Modern History 97, Latin 80, Natural Philosophy 99, Oratory 100.
Third Term	Astronomy 99, Logic 95, Greek 89, Oratory 100.

Annual Grade 90.2

18800500

뉴욕대학교 일람, 1879~80년. 1880년 5월, 뉴욕: 리처드 핸디, 프린터, 듀언 가 62 및 64번지.

문리대에는 다음과 같은 학생이 재학 중이다.

3학년[69)]

이름	거주지
호러스 그랜트 언더우드	뉴더햄, 뉴저지 주

조지 마틴 덩컨
학급대표

교과 과정

4학년

제1삼분기.

홉킨스, 도덕적 체계	계시 종교의 근거
타키투스	유베날리스
페르시우스	플라톤

희랍 신약성서 사도서신의 비평적 연구
수필, 비평, 변론적 토론 및 자작연설

제2삼분기.

포머로이, 자연법과 헌법	지질학

69) 당시 4개 학년에 110명의 학생이 재학 중이었으며, 28명인 3학년 학생의 전체 명단은 영어 원문을 참고하시오.

식물학 키케로

플라우투스	테렌스
카툴루스	루크레티우스

변론적 토론 및 자작연설

제3삼분기.

울시, 국제법	교회사와 세속사의 관계
식물학	생리학

문과 시간표.

3학년

	제1삼분기	제2삼분기	제3삼분기
제1교시	윤리학 계시 종교의 근거	라틴어	식물학
제2교시	라틴어	헌법	국제법
제3교시	희랍어	라틴어	생리학

입학, 시험, 등

다음 학년은 1880년 9월 15일 시작되며, 3 삼분기로 구성된다. 제1삼분기는 개학일부터 성탄절 연휴까지 진행되며 1주일 동안의 휴식이 있다.

제2삼분기는 신년 바로 직후에 시작하며 4월 첫 월요일 시작되는 1주일 동안의 4월 방학까지 계속된다.

제3삼분기는 4월 두 번째 월요일에 시작하며, 졸업까지 계속된다. 다음 졸업식은 1880년 6월 17일 목요일에 거행될 예정이다.

Catalogue of the University of the City of New York, 1879~80. May, 1880, New York: Richard Handy, Printer, 62 and 64 Duane Street.

Page 8

In The Departments of Arts and of Science are the Following Students.

Junior Class.

Name.	Home.
Herbert Clarendon Alden	New York.
Benjamin Aycrigg, Jr.	Passaic, N. J.
John Oscar Ball	Brooklyn.
Milan D. Barnes	Brooklyn.
Cephas Brainerd, Jr.	Haddam, Conn.
Walter Duncan Buchanan	New York.
Benjamin Avery Capwell	Brooklyn.
Albert Field Cornelius	Freeport.
William Charles Cudlipp	Jersey City, N. J.
Harry Hollister Dawson	Newark, N. J.
Samuel M. Dix	Staten Island.
Robert P. Doremus	Jersey City. N. J.
George Martin Duncan	Paterson, N. J.
Edward Lawrence Frost	East Hinsdale.
Isaac Hamburger	East New York.
George Hannum Hazen	Haddam, Conn.
Julian Nunes Henriques	New York.
William Henry Hillman	Brooklyn.
Franklin Sawyer Holmes	Brooklyn.
Whitfield Moorehouse	N. Providence, N. J.

Eugene Frederick Pearce	Brooklyn.
Vincent Pisek	New York.
Edward Raque	Jersey City Heights.
Jacob Russak	New York.
Charles W. Staniford	Brooklyn.
Horace Grant Underwood	New Durham, N. J.
Horatio Moses Vansant	W. New Brighton.
Frederick Seymour Wheeler	Brooklyn.

George Martin Duncan.
President of Class Association.

Page 15

Course of Instruction.

Senior Class.

First Term.

Moral System, Hopkins.	Evidences of Revealed Religion.
Tacitus.	Juvenal.
Persius.	Plato.

Critical Study of the Epistles of the Greek Testament.

Essays, Reviews, Forensic Discussions and Original Declamations.

Second Term.

Natural and Constitutional Law, Pomeroy.	Geology.
Botany.	Cicero.
Plautus.	Terence.
Catullus.	Lucretius.

Forensic Discussions and Original Declamations.

Third Term.

International Law, Woolsey.	Connections of Sacred and Profane History.
Botany.	Physiology.

Page 16

Scheme of Study in the Department of Arts.

Senior Class.

	First Term	Second Term	Third Term
First Hour	Moral Science, Evidence of Revealed Religion	Latin	Botany
Second Hour	Latin	Constitutional Law	International Law.
Third Hour	Greek	Latin	Physiology

Page 23

Attendance, Examinations, etc.

In the Department of Arts and in the Department of Science, examinations for admission will take place on Tuesday, the 15th of June, and on Tuesday the 14th of September, 1880; and for ensuing years, on the Tuesday preceding Commencement, and the Tuesday preceding the opening of the first term in September, in each year.

In each of these Department the full course occupies four years.

The next academic year begins on the 15th of September, 1880, and has three terms. The first begins on that day, extends to the Christmas holidays, and is followed by a recess of one week.

The second term begins immediately after the new year, and extends to the April vacation, which begins on the first Monday of April, and lasts one week.

The third term begins on the second Monday of April, and extends to Commencement. The next annual Commencement will take place on Thursday, the 17th of June, 1880.

18800700

편집인. *The University Quarterly*, 뉴욕대학교, 3(4), 1880년 7월.

편집인.

알든 A. 프리먼, '82.

벤저민 A. 캡웰, '81.
윌리엄 C. 커드립, '81.
세파스 브레이너드 주니어, Jr., '81.
호러스 G. 언더우드, '81.[70)]
존 L. 티크너, '82.
찰스 L. 브리스톨, '83.

Editors. *The University Quarterly*, New York University, 3(4), July 1880.

Editors.

Alden. A Freeman, '82.

Benjamin A. Capwell, '81.
William C. Cudlipp, '81.
Cephas Brainerd, Jr., '81.
Horace G. Underwood, '81.
John L. Ticknor, '82.
Charles L. Bristol, '83.

70) 언더우드가 언제부터 편집인의 일원이었는지는 확실하지 않지만, 이후 졸업할 때까지 편집인으로 되어 있다. *The University Quarterly* 4(1), November 1880, New York University; *The University Quarterly* 4(2), February 1881, New York University; *The University Quarterly* 4(3), May 1881, New York University.

THE

UNIVERSITY QUARTERLY.

EDITORS.

ALDEN A. FREEMAN, '82.

BENJAMIN A. CAPWELL, '81. HORACE G. UNDERWOOD, '81.
WILLIAM C. CUDLIPP, '81. JOHN L. TICKNOR, '82.
CEPHAS BRAINERD, JR., '81. CHARLES L. BRISTOL, '83.

Vol. III. NEW YORK UNIVERSITY, JULY, 1880. No. 4.

CHANCELLOR CROSBY.

LIBRARIES are filled with biographies which are never read, and many which are read, being but gross exaggerations of some sainted hero, ought never to have been printed. Leaving the dead with their mythical greatness, it is sometimes refreshing, not to say profitable, to consider the living—those who "have no life worth writing."

William B. Crosby, the father of the subject of this sketch, was a wealthy New York merchant, greatly interested in all efforts for a higher system of education, and giving largely of his wealth to charitable institutions. His father, Ebenezer Crosby, was for many years professor of Greek at Columbia College. Back another generation, and General Wm. Floyd, the Chancellor's great grandfather, signed the Declaration of Independence, fought in the Revolution, and was a member of the first Congress. Engaged in the same struggle for freedom was Colonel Henry Rutgers, an uncle of Wm. B. Crosby, who rebuilt the college in New Jersey which bears his name. And so I might fill my allotted space with interesting facts of genealogy, for it was recently my privilege to examine a book which carries the Chancellor's long line of ancestors back six centuries and a half till it starts from one of England's kings.

Returning to our text, the nineteenth descendant from Edward I, the one most valued by this generation, brings us to the year 1826, when HOWARD CROSBY was born in New York city. He has

자료 2-15 *The University Quarterly*. 편집인 명단에 언더우드의 이름이 보인다.

18810500

뉴욕대학교 일람, 1880~81년. 1881년 5월, 뉴욕: 버 프린팅 하우스.

문리대에는 다음과 같은 학생이 재학 중이다.

4학년[71]

이름	거주지
호러스 그랜트 언더우드	뉴더햄, 뉴저지 주

허러이시오 모제스 반 산트
학급대표

입학, 시험, 등

제3삼분기는 4월 두 번째 월요일에 시작하며, 졸업까지 계속된다. 다음 졸업식은 1881년 6월 23일 목요일에 거행될 예정이다.

71) 당시 4개 학년에 110명의 학생이 재학 중이었으며, 25명인 4학년 학생의 전체 명단은 영어 원문을 참고하시오.

Catalogue of the University of the City of New York, 1880~81. May, 1881, New York: The Burr Printing House, 1881.

Page 8

In The Departments of Arts and of Science are the Following Students.

Senior Class.

Name.	Home.
Herbert Clarendon Alden,	New York.
Benjamin Aycrigg, Jr.,	Passaic, N. J.
John Oscar Ball,	Brooklyn.
Milan D. Barnes,	Brooklyn.
Cephas Brainerd, Jr.,	Haddam, Conn.
Walter Duncan Buchanan,	New York.
Benjamin Avery Capwell,	Brooklyn.
Albert Field Cornelius,	Freeport.
William Charles Cudlipp,	Jersey City, N. J.
Henry Hollister Dawson,	Newark, N. J.
Samuel M. Dix,	Staten Island.
George Martin Duncan,	Paterson, N. J.
Edward Lawrence Frost,	East Hinsdale.
Isaac Hamburger,	East New York.
George Hannum Hazen, .	Haddam, Conn.
William Henry Hillman,	Brooklyn.
Franklin Sawyer Holmes,	Brooklyn.
Eugene Frederick Pearce,	Brooklyn.
Vincent Pisek,	New York.
Edward Raque,	Jersey City Heights.

Jaeob Russak,	New York.
Charles Wilkinson Staniford,	Brooklyn.
Horace Grant Underwood,	**New Durham.**
Horatio Moses Van Sant,	W. New Brighton.
Frederick Seymour Wheeler	Brooklyn.

Horatio Moses Van Sant,
President of Class Association.

Page 24

Attendance, Examinations, etc.

The third term begins on the second Monday of April and extends to Commencement. The next annual Commencement will_take place on Thursday, the 23d of June, 1881.

1880~1년도, 4학년, 학적부, 1853~1893년, 제2권.

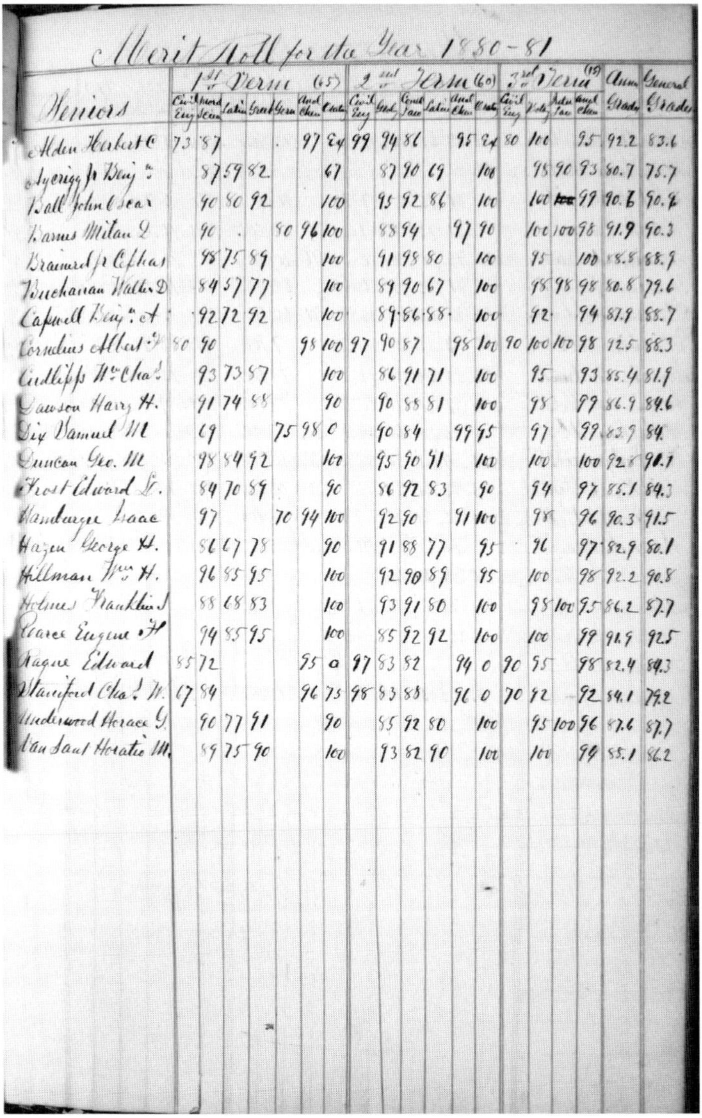

Merit Roll for the Year 1880-81

Seniors	1st Term (65)							2nd Term (60)						3rd Term (19)				Annual Grade	General Grade
	Civil Eng	Mental Science	Latin	Greek	German	Anal. Chem.	Conduct	Civil Eng	Geol.	Const. Law	Latin	Anal. Chem.	Conduct	Civil Eng	Polit.	Inter. Law	Anal. Chem.		
Alden Herbert C.	73	87				97	Ex	99	94	86		95	Ex	80	100		95	92.2	83.6
Ayerigg Jr. Benj.		87	59	82			67		87	90	69		100		98	90	93	80.7	75.7
Ball John Oscar		90	80	92			100		95	92	86		100		100	[struck out]	99	90.6	90.8
Barnes Milan L.		90			80	96	100		88	94		97	90		100	100	98	91.9	90.3
Brainerd Jr. Cephas		98	75	89			100		91	98	80		100		95		100	88.8	88.9
Buchanan Walter D.		84	57	77			100		89	90	67		100		98	98	98	80.8	79.6
Capwell Benj. A.		92	72	92			100		89	86	88		100		92		94	87.9	88.7
Cornelius Albert J.	80	90				98	100	97	90	87		98	100	90	100	100	98	92.5	88.3
Cutliffe Wm. Chas.		93	73	87			100		86	91	71		100		95		93	85.4	81.9
Dawson Harry H.		91	74	88			90		90	88	81		100		98		99	86.9	84.6
Dix Samuel M.		69			75	98	0		90	84		99	95		97		99	83.9	84
Duncan Geo. M.		98	84	92			100		95	90	91		100		100		100	92.8	90.1
Frost Edward L.		84	70	89			90		86	92	83		90		94		97	85.1	84.3
Hamburger Isaac		97			70	94	100		92	90		91	100		98		96	90.3	91.5
Hazen George H.		86	67	78			90		91	88	77		95		96		97	82.9	80.1
Hillman Wm. H.		96	85	95			100		92	90	89		95		100		98	92.2	90.8
Holmes Franklin J.		88	68	83			100		93	91	80		100		98	100	95	86.2	87.7
Pearce Eugene H.		94	85	95			100		85	92	92		100		100		99	91.9	92.5
Hague Edward	85	72				95	0	97	83	82		94	0	90	95		98	82.4	84.3
Staniford Chas. W.	67	84				96	75	98	83	88		96	0	70	92		92	84.1	79.2
Underwood Horace G.		90	77	91			90		85	92	80		100		95	100	96	87.6	87.7
Van Sant Horatio M.		89	75	90			100		93	82	90		100		100		99	85.1	86.2

자료 2-16 *Year 1880~1, Senior, Matriculation Book, 1853~1893,* Vol. 2.

4학년(1890~1881)

1학기	윤리학 90, 라틴어 77, 희랍어 91, 웅변 90.
2학기	지질학 85, 헌법 92, 라틴어 80, 웅변 100.
3학기	식물학 95, 국제법 100, 분석화학 96.

4학년 평균 성적 87.6

전학년 평균 성적 87.7

Year 1880~1, Senior, Matriculation Book, 1853~1893, Vol. 2.

Senior (1880~1)

First Term	Moral Science 90, Latin 77, Greek 91, Oratory 90.
Second Term	Geology 85, Constitutional Law 92, Latin 80, Oratory 100.
Third Term	Botany 95, International Law 100, Analytical Chemistry 96

Annual Grade 87.6

General Grade 87.7

18810600

1881년 졸업주간, 뉴욕대학교 (*Commencement Week, 1881. University of the City of New-York*).

Commencement Week, 1881.

University of the City of New-York.

SUNDAY JUNE 19th, at 7.30 P.M.

Baccalaureate Sermon by the Chancellor, Rev Howard Crosby, D. D.

TUESDAY, JUNE 21st, at 10 A.M.

Examinations for Admission, in the Council Room.

THURSDAY, JUNE 23d, at 10.30 A M.

COMMENCEMENT EXERCISES,

At the Academy of Music.

At 6 P.M.

Annual Meeting of the Alumni Association,

IN THE COUNCIL ROOM OF THE UNIVERSITY.

HORATIO MOSES VANSANT, *President of the Class,*

GEORGE HANNUM HAZEN, *Secretary of the Class.*

WILLIAM CHARLES CUDLIPP, *Grand Marshal,*

Chef d'Orchestre, - - - - - - A. BERNSTEIN.

GEO. R. LOCKWOOD & SON, 812 BROADWAY, N.Y.

자료 2-17 뉴욕대학교 1881년도 졸업식순. 모두 4쪽이다.

ORDER OF EXERCISES.

Music: Overture, "Festival," - - - - - - - *Neumann.*

Selection, "Fra Diavolo," - - - - - - - *Auber.*

March, "Athalia," - - - - - - - - *Mendelssohn.*

PRAYER.

I.—ENGLISH SALUTATORY ADDRESSES AND ORATION—"What of the Future?"

GEORGE MARTIN DUNCAN, *Paterson, N. J.*

II.—*SCIENTIFIC ORATION—"Mathematics as a Mental Discipline."

ISAAC HAMBURGER, *East New York, L. I.*

MUSIC,—"Our Lady Guests" - - - - - - BERNSTEIN.

III.—PHILOSOPHICAL ORATION—"Social Inequality and its Results."

JOHN OSCAR BALL, *Brooklyn, L. I.*

IV.—ORATION—"Individuality the Foundation of the Republic."

BENJAMIN AVERY CAPWELL, *Brooklyn, L. I.*

MUSIC,—Selection, "Olivette." - - - - - - - AUDRAN.

V.—ORATION—"The Germ of a Nation's Destruction."

FRANKLIN SAWYER HOLMES, *Brooklyn, L. I.*

VI.—ORATION—"The Valley of Glencoe—As it is and as it was."

† HORACE GRANT UNDERWOOD, *New Durham, N. J.*

VII.—ORATION—"Culture."

HORATIO MOSES VANSANT, *West New-Brighton, Staten Island.*

MUSIC,—Galop, "Tout à la Joie." - - - - - - - FAHRBACH.

VIII.—PHILOSOPHICAL ORATION—"Benevolence, the Spirit of the Age."

MILAN DAY BARNES, *Brooklyn, E. D., L. I.*

MUSIC,—Selection, "Tannhauser." - - - - - - WAGNER.

* The Scientific Oration and the Valedictory are this year equal honors; the two speakers being so equal in merit that the precedence has been determined by lot.

† Excused on account of a death in the family.

IX.—ORATION—" National Monuments."

ALBERT FIELD CORNELIUS, *Freeport, L. I.*

X.—PHILOSOPHICAL ORATION—" Doubt, its Influence and its Sphere."

WILLIAM HENRY HILLMAN, *Brooklyn, L. I.*

MUSIC,—March and Chorus, " Carmen " - - - - - - BIZET.

XI.—ORATION—" Unrestricted Suffrage."

CEPHAS BRAINERD, JR., *New York City.*

XII.—VALEDICTORY ORATION—

EUGENE FREDERICK PEARCE, *Brooklyn, L. I.*

Regular Degrees Conferred.

The Degree of Bachelor of Arts will be conferred upon

EUGENE FREDERICK PEARCE,
GEORGE MARTIN DUNCAN,
JOHN OSCAR BALL,
WILLIAM HENRY HILLMAN,
CEPHAS BRAINERD, JR.,
BENJAMIN AVERY CAPWELL,
FRANKLIN SAWYER HOLMES,
HORACE GRANT UNDERWOOD,
HORATIO MOSES VANSANT,
HARRY HOLLISTER DAWSON,
EDWARD LAWRENCE FROST,
WILLIAM CHARLES CUDLIPP,
GEORGE HANNUM HAZEN,
WALTER DUNCAN BUCHANAN,
BENJAMIN AYCRIGG, JR.

The Degree of Bachelor of Science will be conferred upon

ISAAC HAMBURGER,
MILAN DAY BARNES,
ALBERT FIELD CORNELIUS,
EDWARD RAQUE,
SAMUEL MORRIS DIX,
HERBERT CLARENDON ALDEN,
CHARLES WILKINSON STANIFORD.

The Diploma of Civil Engineer will be conferred upon

ALBERT FIELD CORNELIUS,
EDWARD RAQUE,
HERBERT CLARENDON ALDEN,
CHARLES WILKINSON STANIFORD.

The Degree of Master of Arts will be conferred upon

ROBERT ANTHONY DAVISON,
SAMUEL ALEXANDER STEVENSON,
LYMAN SEWELL LINSON,
ANDREW PURDY,
LOUIS C. WHITON,
WILLIAM L. CLARK,
CHARLES GIFFORD BUCKLEY,
CLARENCE HOPKINS,
WILSON DURACK.

The Degree of Master of Science will be conferred upon

WILLIAM A. HOWELL,
M. W. DIVINE,
CHARLES F. COOPER,
FREDERICK W. TRUE,
JOSEPH WILLIAM STICKLER, M.D.

Honorary Degrees Conferred.

AWARD OF FELLOWSHIPS.

The three Fellowships, rewards of eminent merit in the studies of the University Course, have been awarded as follows :

First Fellowship to EUGENE FREDERICK PEARCE, of Brooklyn, L. I.

Second Fellowship to GEORGE MARTIN DUNCAN, of Paterson, N. J.

Third Fellowship to JOHN OSCAR BALL, of Brooklyn, L. I.

AWARD OF SOCIETY PRIZES.

BUTLER EUCLEIAN PRIZES,

For the Best Essays in English Composition, by Members of the Eucleian Society.

First Prize to GEORGE MARTIN DUNCAN.

Second Prize to CHARLES LAWRENCE BRISTOL.

PHILOMATHEAN PRIZES.

For the Best Essays in English Composition, by Members of the Philomathean Society.

First Prize to WILLIAM CHARLES CUDLIPP.

Second Prize to HARRY WARD SKERRY.

Honorable mention of JOHN FRANCIS WILLIAMS.

BENEDICTION.

MUSIC,—"Pot Pourri," - - - - - - - COLLEGE AIRS.

Psi Upsilon Box, D, Proscenium ; Delta Upsilon Box, K, Proscenium.

The University will open for the usual Course of Study on the third Wednesday of September next.

Candidates for admission may present themselves for examination in the Council Room, at the University, on the preceding Tuesday, September 20th.

The Tuition Fees have been abolished in the Departments of Arts and Sciences. All students, therefore, of approved character, and of adequate preparation, will be received without charge for tuition, in those Departments.

18810624

흥미로운 대학 졸업식. *Truth*, (금, 1881년 6월 24일, 4쪽).

흥미로운 대학 졸업식.
뉴욕대학교 졸업식.

뉴욕대학교의 졸업식이 어제 아침 음악원에서 거행되었다. 조지 M. 덩컨 (패터슨, 뉴저지); 아이삭 햄버거, (이스트 뉴욕); 존 O. 볼, 벤저민 A. 캡웰, 프랭클린 S. 홈즈, 밀란 D. 반즈, 윌리엄 H. 힐먼 및 유진 F. 피어스 (브루클린, 롱아일랜드); 호러스 G. 언더우드 (뉴더햄, 뉴저지), 허러이시오 M. 반 산트 (웨스트 뉴브라이턴, 스태튼아일랜드); 앨버트 코르넬리우스 (프리포트, 롱아일랜드) 및 세파스 브레이너드, 주니어 (뉴욕시) 등의 웅변과 연설이 있었다..

15명의 후보자가 문학사, 7명이 이학사, 4명이 토목학사, 9명이 문학석사, 5명이 이학석사의 학위를 받았다.

수여된 명예학위는 다음과 같다:

법학박사 – 아론 J. 반데어포엘, 뉴욕 시

신학박사 – 존 B. 폴크너 목사 (저먼타운, 펜실베이니아); 윌리엄 H. S. 오브레이 목사 (런던, 영국); 찰스 D. 쇼 목사(패터슨, 뉴저지); 뉴먼 스미스 목사 (퀴니, 일리노이); 호러스 범스테드 목사(애틀란타, 조지아); 조지 B. 윌콕스 목사(시카고, 일리노이)

음악박사 – 존 M. 로레츠, 주니어(브루클린, 롱아일랜드)

철학박사 – 알렉시스 (뉴욕 시)

특별연구원은 유진 F. 피어스 및 존 O. 볼(브루클린), 그리고 조지 M. 덩컨(패터슨)에게 수여되었다.

수필 상은 윌리엄 커드립, 조지 M. 덩컨, 해리 W. 스케리 및 찰스 L. 브리스톨에게 수여되었다.

Interesting College Exercises. *Truth*, (Fri. June 24, 1881, p. 4).

Interesting College Exercises.

Annual Commencement of the University of the City of New York.

The annual commencement exercises of the University of the City of New York were held yesterday morning at the Academy of Music. Orations and addresses were delivered by George M. Duncan, Paterson, N. J.; Issac Hamburger, East New York; John O. Ball, Benjamin A. Capwell, Franklin S. Holmes, Milan D. Barnes, William H. Hillman and Eugene F. Pearce of Brooklyn, L. I.; Horace G. Underwood, New Durham, N. Y. Horatio M. Vansant, West New Brighton, S. I.; Albert Cornelius, Freeport, L. I., and Cephas Brainerd, Jr., New York City.

Fifteen candidates received thc degree of Bachelor of Arts, seven that of Bachelor of Science, four were made Civil Engineers, nine Masters of Arts, and five Masters of Science.

Honorary degrees were conferred as follows:

LL. D. - Aaron J. Vanderpoel, New York City.

D. D. - Rev. John B. Falkner, Germantown, Pa.; Rev. William H. S. Aubray, London, Eng.; Rev. Charles D. Shaw, Paterson, N. J.; Rev. Newman Smyth, Quiney, Ill.; Rev. Horace Bumstead, Atlanta, Ga.; Rev. George B. Willcox, Chicago, Ill.

Mus. Doc. - John M. Loretz, Jr., Brooklyn, L. I.

Ph. D. - Alexis A. Julien, New York city.

Fellowships were awarded to Eugene F. Pearce and John O. Ball of Brooklyn, and George M. Duncan of Paterson.

Essay prizes were taken by William C. Cudlipp, George M. Duncan, Harry W. Skerry and Charles L. Bristol.

18810624

뉴욕대학교. *New York Herald*, (금, 1881년 6월 24일, 5쪽).

뉴욕대학교

어제 아침 2,000명 이상의 사람들이 뉴욕대학교의 졸업식에 참석하기 위해 음악원에 모였다. 청중의 상당수는 숙녀 – 어머니와 누이들이었으며, 자신들의 아들과 형제들이 영광을 함께 하는 멋있는 광경의 목격하는 즐거움에 모두들 미소를 머금고 있었다. 이곳에는 대단히 많은 꽃들이 넘쳐났으며, 각 졸업생이, 만일 운 좋게 꽃들이 시들지 않는다면, 그의 남은 여생동안 사용할 수 있을 정도였다. 식장에는 A. 번스타인 씨가 지휘하는 웅장한 오케스트라가 유쾌한 선율로 대기 시간을 채워 주었다. 사이 업실론 및 델타 업실론 소사이어티를 위한 특별석이 마련되었다. 연단에는 30, 40명의 교수진과 내빈이 있었으며, 총장인 하워드 크로스비 목사, 신학박사가 좌정했다. 곳곳에서 학사모와 가운이 보였으며, 학생 봉사단이 안내를 담당했다. 학급대표는 모제스 반 산트이었고, 총무는 조지 핸넘 헤이즌이었으며, 대회장은 윌리엄 찰스 커드립이었다. 오케스트라가 여러 곡을 연주한 후 11시 직전, 총장을 선두로 행렬이 무대로 행진했다. 행렬에는 이 A. 존슨, 비 M. 마틴, 알 H. 불, 에이치 M. 베어드, 헨디 드레이퍼, 에이 스필먼, 씨 B. 브러쉬 교수; S. 이로니우스 프라임 목사, 럿거스 여자대학 학장 버차드 목사, 에스 M. 해밀턴, 에이 R. 톰슨, 샘프슨, 브렛 및 프레이너 목사, 보스턴대학교의 버든 P. 보은 교수; 레녹스 도서관의 에프 F. 버넘, 조지 H. 무어, 에이. 반데어포엘, 존 테일러 휴스턴, 스미스 E. 레인, 윌리엄 A. 휠록, 윌리엄 마틴, 제이 W. C. 리버리지 및 디 B. 세인트 존 등이 포함되어 있었다.

식순.

내빈들이 착석하자 박수가 이어졌고, 몇 곡이 연주되고 기도를 드린 후 졸업식순이 시작되어 약 3시간 동안 진행되었다.

조지 마친 덩컨, 패터슨, 뉴저지	영어 개회사 및 연설
"미래란?"	
아이삭 햄버거, 이스트 뉴욕, 롱아일랜드	과학적 연설
"정신수양으로서의 수학."	
음악 – "Our Lady Guests"	번스타인
존 오스카 볼, 브루클린, 롱아일랜드	철학적 연설
"사회적 불평등과 그 결과."	
벨저민 에이버리 캡웰, 브루클린, 롱아일랜드	연설
"개인주의 – 공화국의 토대."	
음악 – 발췌, "올리베트"	오드라
프랭클린 소여 홈즈, 롱아일랜드	연설
"국가 멸망의 근원."	
호러스 그랜트 언더우드, 뉴더햄, 뉴저지	연설
"글렌코 계곡 – 현재와 과거."	
호레이쇼 모제스 반 산트, 웨스트 뉴 브라이턴, 스태튼아일랜드	연설
"문화."	
음악 – 갤럽, "Tout a la Joie."	화르바흐
밀란 데이 반스, 브루클린, 롱아일랜드	철학적 연설
"자선, 시대정신."	
음악, – 발췌, "탄호이저."	바그너
앨버트 필드 코르넬리우스, 프리포트, 롱아일랜드	연설
"국가 기념물."	
윌리엄 헨리 힐먼, 브루클린, 롱아일랜드	철학적 연설
"회의, 그 영향과 영역."	
음악, – 행진과 합창, "카르멘"	비제
세파스 브레이너드, 주니어, 뉴욕시	연설
"제한되지 않은 참정권."	
유진 프레데릭 피어스, 브루클린, 롱아일랜드	고별사

이번 해에는 과학적 연설과 고별사가 동등하게 대우 받을 것이며, 고별사는 제비를 뽑아 결정했다고 공지되었다. 각 연자는 동일한 관심을 받아 박수를 받았으며, 연설이 끝나고 내려오면서 수 많은 꽃들이 던져졌다. 뉴저지 주 뉴더햄의 호러스 그랜트 언더우드 씨가 6번째로 하기로 했던 "글렌코 계곡 – 현재와 과거."는 집안의 부음 때문에 연설을 하지 않는 것으로 양해되었다.

〈 이하 졸업생, 학위 수여자 명단은 생략함 〉

University of New York. *New York Herald*, (Fri., June 24th, 1881, p. 5).

University of New York.

More than two thousand person were in the Academy of Music yesterday morning to listen to the commencement exercises of the University of the City of New York. A large proportion of the audience were ladies - mothers and sisters, smiling with pleasure on the handsome scene where in their sons and brothers were to share the honors. There was a profusion of flowers, each graduate getting enough, if happily they never faded, to supply him with boulonnieres for the rest of his natural lifetime. There was a large orchestra, led by Mr. A. Bernstein, who filled up the waits with agreeable melodies. Boxes were reserved for the Psi Upsilon and Delta Upsilon societies. On the platform were thirty or forty officers and friends of the University, and the Chancellor, Rev. Howard Crosby, D. D., presided. Academic caps and gowns were frequent in the place, a volunteer corps of students acting as ushers. The president of the class was Horatio Moses Van Sant, the secretary was George Nanuum Hazen and the grand marshal was William Charles Cudlipp. At a little before eleven o'clock, after the orchestra had played several selections the procession, headed by the Chancellor, marched upon the stage. Among those in the procession were Professors E. A. Johnson, B. M. Martin, R. H. Bull, H. M. Baird, Henry Draper, A. Spielman and C. B. Brush; the Rev. Dr. S. Ironeus Prime, the Rev. Dr. Burchard, president of Rutger's Female College; the Rev Drs. S. M. Hamilton, A. R. Thompson, Sampson, Brett and Phraner; Professor Berden P. Bowne, of Boston University; __ Rev. F. F. Burnham, George H. Moore, of the Lenox Library, A. J. Vanderpoel, John Taylor Houston, Smith E. Lane, William A. Wheelock, William __ Martin, J. W. C. Leveridge and Dr. D. B. St. John _____.

The Programme.

These persons were applaused as they took their seats and after more music and a prayer the regular exercises began and continued for about three hours.

George Martin Duncan, Paterson, N. J.	English Salutatory Addresses and Oration
"What of the Future?"	
Issac Hamburger, East New York, L. I.	Scientific Oration
"Mathematics as a Mental Discipline."	
Music - "Our Lady Guests"	Bernstein
John Oscar Ball, Brooklyn, L. I.	Philosophical Oration
"Social Inequality and Its Results."	
Benjamin Avery Capwell, Brooklyn, L. I.	Oration
"Individuality the Foundation of the Republic."	
Music - Selection, "Olivette"	Audran
Franklin Sawyer Holmes, Brooklyn, L. I.	Oration
"The Germ of a Nation's Destruction."	
Horace Grant Underwood, New Durham, N. J.	Oration
"The Valley of Glencoe - As it is and as it was."	

Horatio Moses Vansant, West New Brighton, S. I.	Oration
"Culture."	
Music - Galop, "Tout a la Joie."	Fahrbach.
Milan Day Barnes, Brooklyn, M. D., L. I.	Philosophical Oration
"Benevolence, the Spirit of the Age."	
Music, - Selection, "Tanhauser."	Wagner.
Albert Field Cornelius, Freeport, L. I.	Oration
"National Monuments."	
William Henry Hillman, Brooklyn, L. I.	Philosophical Oration
"Doubt, its Influence and its Sphere."	
Music, - March and Chorus, "Carmen"	Bizet.
Cephas Brainerd, Jr., New York City.	Oration
"Unrestricted Suffrage."	
Eugene Frederick Pearce, Brooklyn, L. I.	Valedictory Oration

It was announced that the scientific oration and the valedictory were equal honors this year, the two speakers being so equal in merit that the choice of valedictorian had to be determined by lot. Each speaker had seemingly paid equal attention to the substance and the delivery of his oration, and each was applauded and loaded down with flowers upon his retirement. Mr. Horace Grant Underwood, of New Durham, N. J. was down for the sixth oration on "The Valley of Glencoe: as it is and was," but had to be excused on account of a death in his family.

……

18820000

뉴욕대학교 문리대 일람, 뉴욕: 디 O. 크러포드 앤드 컴패니, 풀턴 가 62번지, 1882년.

문리대 졸업생 명단.

1881년 (22명).[72]

호러스 그랜트 언더우드	뉴더햄, 뉴저지

졸업생 요약.

문리대 졸업생,	879명
법조계, .	144명
성직자,	141명
의 사,	83명
명예학위 수여자,	340명
신학박사,	145명
문학석사,	69명
법학박사,	53명
의학박사,	37명
철학박사,	28명
음악박사	5명
공공사업박사	1명
이학석사	1명
문학사.	1명

72) 졸업생 명단은 영어 원문을 참고하시오.

A General Catalogue of the University of the City of New York, Departments of Arts and Science. New York: D. O Crawford & Co., No. 62 Fulton Street, 1882.

Graduates in the Department of Arts and Sciences.

1881.

Herbert Clarendon Alden,	New York City.
Benjamin Aycrigg, Jr.,	Passaic, N. J.
John Oscar Ball,	Brooklyn, N. Y.
Milan D. Barnes,	Brooklyn, N. Y.
Cephas Brainerd, Jr.,	New York City.
Walter Duncan Buchanan,	New York City.
Benjamin Avery Capwell,	Atlanta, Ga.
Albert Field Cornelius,	Freeport, N. Y.
William Charles Cudlipp,	Jersey City, N. J.
Henry Hollister Dawson,	Newark, N. J.
Samuel M. Dix,	Stapleton, N. Y.
George Martin Duncan,	Paterson, N. J.
Edward Lawrence Frost,	East Hinsdale, N. Y.
Isaac Hamburger,	East New York., N. Y.
George Hannum Hazen, .	Haddam, Conn.
William Henry Hillman,	Brooklyn., N. Y.
Franklin Sawyer Holmes,	Brooklyn, N. Y.
Eugene Frederick Pearce,	Brooklyn, N. Y.
Edward Raque,	Jersey City, N. J.
Charles Wilkinson Staniford,	Brooklyn, N. Y.
Horace Grant Underwood,	New Durham, N. J.
Horatio Moses Van Sant,	W. New Brighton, N. Y.

Page 55

Summary.

Graduates of Dep't of Arts and Sciences,	879
Lawyers, .	144
Clergymen,	141
Physicians,	83
Honorary Degrees conferred,	340
D. D.,	145
A. M.,	69
LL. D.,	53
M. D.,	37
Ph. D.	28
Mus. D.	5
P. S. D.	1
M. S.	1
A. B.	1

4. 뉴브런즈윅신학교 (New Brunswick Theological Seminary)

뉴욕대학교를 졸업하고 언더우드가 입학한 뉴브런즈윅의 화란개혁신학교는 3년제였으며, 교파와 관계없이 입학이 가능했다. 언더우드가 입학할 당시 신학교에는 우드브리지, 데 위트, 데마레스트 및 메이본 등의 교수진이 있었다. 특히 메이본은 언더우드가 다녔던 그로브 교회의 목사로서, 그가 뉴욕대학교가 입학할 수 있도록 가르친 분이었다.

입학 당시 학생은 1학년이 16명, 2학년이 10명, 3학년이 19명으로 전체 학생 수는 45명이었고, 언더우드는 헤르초크홀(Hertzog Hall)에서 기숙하였다.

자료 2-18 헤르초크 홀. 헤르초크 홀은 최근 해체되었다.

18810000

미국 개혁(화란)교회 신학교 교직원 및 학생 일람, 뉴브런즈윅, 뉴저지 주, 1881~82학년도. 뉴브런즈윅, 뉴저지, 제이 터휸 프레스, 올버니 가 31번지, 1881년.[73]

교수진

새뮤얼 M. 우드브리지 목사, 신학박사
교회사 및 직제학 교수

존 데 위트 목사, 신학박사
토머스 데 위트 교수 - 성서학

데이비드 D. 데마레스트 목사, 신학박사
목회신학과 수사학 교수

윌리엄 V. V. 메이본 목사, 신학박사
제임스 수이담 교수 - 설교학 및 변증신학

1학년

이름.	거주지.	방.
매리언 T. 콘크린, R. C.	킹스턴, 뉴욕	헤르초크 홀 22호
조사이어 E. 크레인, R. C.	페어 옥스, 뉴욕	헤르초크 홀 23호
조셉 P. 데이비스, U. C.	코블스킬, 뉴욕	헤르초크 홀 20호
알프레드 H. 데마레스트, R. C.	뉴브런즈윅	데마레스트 교수집
찰스 S. 더튼, H. C.,	홀랜드, 미시건	헤르초크 홀 12호
구스타부스 괴벨, B. A. D.	뉴욕시	헤르초크 홀 45호
T. 존 코머스, H. C.	뉴브런즈윅, 뉴저지	헤르초크 홀 35호
조엘 라욱스, R. C.	팔라틴 브리지, 뉴욕	헤르초크 홀 21호

73) 언더우드를 이해하는데 필요하다고 생각되는 부분만 번역했다. 하지만 영어 원문에는 모든 내용을 수록하였다.

프레데릭 W. 럴1	올버니, 뉴욕	모리스 가 30번지
윌리엄 쉬미츠, 주니어, R. C.	브루클린, 뉴욕	헤르초크 홀 28호
바스티아 N. 스미츠, R. C.	홀랜드, 미시건	헤르초크 홀 16호
조지 H. 스티븐스, R. C.	노스 브랜치, 뉴저지	베이야드 가 78번지
리빙스턴 L. 테일러, R. C.	뉴어크, 뉴저지	헤르초크 홀 14호
호러스 G. 언더우드, N. Y. U.,	뉴더햄, 뉴저지	헤르초크 홀 32호
J. 러셀 버브릭, R. C.,	뉴브런즈윅, 뉴저지	처치 가 20번지
개릿 와이코프, 주니어, R. C.,	폼프턴 프레인즈, 뉴저지	헤르초크 홀 19호

요 약

3학년	19명
2학년	10명
1학년	16명
합계	45명.

비고

U. C. – 유니온대학
R. C. – 럿거스대학
U. I. – 아이오와대학교
C. N. Y. – 뉴욕시립대학
S. G. – 슈투트가르트 체육학교
C. U. – 코넬대학교
H. C. – 호프대학
N. Y. U. – 뉴욕대학교
B. A. D. – 블룸필드 학원

입학

신학교는 모든 기독교 교파의 학생에게 입학의 문호를 개방하고 있다.

학생의 입학을 위해 전형위원회를 9월 20일 오전 11시에 개최한다.

모든 지원자는 교적 증명서와 대학 졸업장을 제출해야 한다. 정규 대학 과정을 이수하지 않은 자는 성과의 증거를 제시해야하며, 이를 위원회가 판단할 것이다.

개혁교회에서 목사가 되기 위해 준비하는 학생들과 관련된 교회법은 다음과 같다:

"성직에 종사할 것을 고려하고 있는 모든 자는, 신학 과정을 시작하기 전에, 자신이 개혁교회를 잘 다니는 교인이며, 자신의 신앙심, 역량 및 문학적 조예가 있다는 충분한 증거를 제시해야 하며, 그 후에 신학교 중 한 곳에 입학하게 될 것이다; 그리고 학업을 수행하는 동안 관련된 규례를 지켜야 하며, 규정된 신학 과정과 기간을 끝냈을 때 총회에 의해 설립된 신학교의 규칙에 따라 시험을 보게 될 것이다; 그리고 자격이 있다고 인정되면 자신이 속한 노회에서 자격시험을 치러 전문 자격을 받게 된다." – 교회법 제2조 제2항.

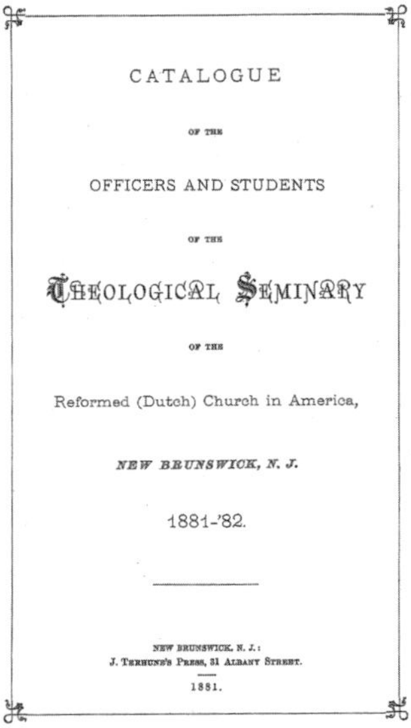
CATALOGUE

OF THE

OFFICERS AND STUDENTS

OF THE

THEOLOGICAL SEMINARY

OF THE

Reformed (Dutch) Church in America,

NEW BRUNSWICK, N. J.

1881-'82.

NEW BRUNSWICK, N. J.:
J. TERHUNE'S PRESS, 31 ALBANY STREET.

1881.

자료 2-19 뉴브런즈윅신학교의 일람.

학년.

학년은 9월 20일부터 5월 세 번째 화요일까지 8개월 학기로 이루어지며, "8~10일 동안의 성탄절 연휴"가 있다. 이러한 제도는 여름 동안에 다양한 일을 하고자 하는 사람들에게 기회를 주기 위해 만들어졌다.

학년 말에는 전형위원회 앞에서 모든 과목에 대한 시험을 5월 세 번째 화요일에 치른다.

교과 과정

교과 과정은 3년이며, 다음과 같다:

1학년

히브리어 및 헬라어.

구약과 신약성서 원전에 나오는 메시아 예언에 대한 해석학적 이해

성서 지리학 성서 고고학

성서 계보학 성서 고대역사

수사학, 설교 작성법, 설교학

사용되는 교과서는 게제니우스의 히브리어 문법 및 사전, 쿠르츠의 성서 역사, 쿠르츠의 교회사, 바이너의 갈데아어 문법, 배로우의 성서 지리학 및 성서 고고학, 그리고 미국 개혁교회의 교회법 등이다.

모든 학년의 학생들은 설교를 준비하고 연습해야 하며, 설교의 내용, 배열, 형식 및 실연 등은 학생 및 교수들의 비평을 받는다.

설교를 준비하는 전체 과정에 상당한 중점을 두는데, 학생 및 '수사학' 담당 교수가 비평을 한다. 또한 성경 및 찬송가 강독에도 중점을 둔다.

강해설교에 대한 강의와 함께 실제 연습이 진행되며, 교회법에 의해 우리 목회자들에게 필요한 하이델베르크 교리문답에 대한 대중 강연에 대한 강의도 있다.

4학년 학생들은 신학과 관련된 주제에 대한 논문을 설교학 교수에게 제출하여 비평을 받아야 한다.

시 험.

각 학년의 학년말 시험은 장학관 회의에서 5월 셋째 화요일에 시작한다.

장학관 회의는 입학 지원자들에 대한 전형을 위해 9월 20일 모인다. 모든 지원자들은 추천서를 지참해야 한다.

피터 헤르초크 신학교 홀

이 건물은 1856년 필라델피아의 제3개혁교회의 안나 헤르토크 부인이 기부한 3만 7백 달러의 기금으로 건축되었다.

이 건물은 뉴저지 주의 healthfulness로 소문난 도시인 뉴브런즈윅의 변두리에 아름답게 위치해 있다. 이와 관련된 건물 및 자산은 "뉴저지 뉴브런즈윅에 소재한 신학교의 대지 및 자산을 관리하는 신학교의 상설위원회"가 관리하에 있다. 현재 이 위원회는 가드너 A. 세이지, 존 W. 페르돈, 윌리엄 보가더스, 윌리엄 H. 커그, 에스 H. 휠러, 그리고 존 데 위트 교수로 구성되어 있다.

홀에는 예배당, 독서실, 학습실, 기숙사, 식당, 세탁실 및 화장실이 구비되어 있다. 건물은 개스로 조명을 하며, 스팀으로 난방을 한다. 수도국에서 공급되는 물이 빌딩 전체에 공급된다. 이런 설비를 완비하는데 비용을 아끼지 않았다.

홀은 랠프 윌리스 목사가 관리하고 있는데, 청결하고 조용하며 안락한 숙소를 찾는 사람들에게 기숙을 제공한다.

목사가 되려는 럿거스대학 및 공립 영재학교 학생들은 기숙하여 홀의 모든 편의를 누릴 수 있으며, 신학교 학생들에게 항상 우선권이 있다.

방에는 침대, 침구, 카펫, 의자, 옷장, 책사 등이 구비되어 있다. 각 학생은 시트, 베게닢 과 수건을 준비해야 한다.

방은 신학교가 개강하는 9월 20일, 학년 순서로 신학교 3학년부터 배정된다.

각 방의 난방 및 부차적인 경비는 매년 24달러이다. 조명비는 매년 10달러이다. 도서실, 독서실, 혹은 체육관의 이용료는 없다. 홀에 기숙하는 경비는 매주 3.25달러이다.

홀에 기숙하는 자들은 예배당에서 열리는 저녁 기도회에 참석해야 한다.

홀에 거주하지 않는 학생은 부차적인 경비로 매년 5달러를 납부해야 한다.

학생에 의한 전도

이 문제에 관한 총회의 결의는 다음과 같다:

결의, 우리 신학교의 신학생들은 4학년 학생들의 경우 신학교수 중 한 명의 지도 하에 설교의 허락을 받는 경우, 그리고 자신이 다니는 교회에서 담임 목사의 지도 하에 동일한 특권을 허락 받는 경우를 제외하고는 어떠한 교회 및 신도들을 대상으로 설교 혹은 강연을 허락하지 않는다.– 회의록, 제9권, 345쪽.

결의, 신학교의 2학년 학생들은 신학교 교수의 지도 하에 방학 중에 전도를 허용한다. – 회의록, 제8권, 535쪽.

장학 보조.

강의는 일체 무료로 진행된다.' 개혁교회에 다니면서 목사가 되려하는데 보조가 필요한 자는 교육위원회로부터 매년 150달러를 지급 받으며, 헤르초크 홀의 난방 및 전기료도 위원회가 지불한다.

교육위원회는 신학교 입학을 준비하는 과정의 젊은이를 돕는다.

Catalogue of the Officers and Students of the Theological Seminary of the Reformed (Dutch) Church in America, New Brunswick, N. J. 1881~'82. New Brunswick, N. J., J. Terhune's Press, 31 Albany Street, 1881.

Page 3

Board of Superintendents.

Rev. Rufus W. Clark, D. D. of the Classis of Albany.
Term expires, 1883.

Rev. John Scudder, M. D.	of the Classis of Arcot. Term expires, 1883.
Rev. John H. Suydam,	of the Classis of Bergen. Term expires, 1883.
Rev. William R. Duryee, D. D.	of the South Classis of Bergen. Term expires, 1884.
Rev. Evert Van Slyke,	of the Classis of Cayuga. Term expires, 1882.
Rev. Philip Furbeck	of the Classis of Geneva. Term expires, 1884.
Rev. Adrian Kriekard	of the Classis of Grand River. Term expires, 1883.
Rev. Alan D. Campbell	of the Classis of Greene. Term expires, 1883.
Rev. Nicholas M. Steffens,	of the Classis of Holland: Term expires, 1883.
Rev. Arad J. Sebring,	of the Classis of Hudson. Term expires, 1883.
Rev. Edward P. Livingston, D. D.,	of the Classis of Illinois. Term expires, 1882.
Rev. James Demarest, Jr., D. D.	of the Classis of Kingston. Term expires, 1883.
Rev. John M. Wagner,	of the North Classis of Long Island. Term expires, 1882.
Rev. Corn. L. Wells, D. D.,	of the South Classis of Long Island. Term expires, 1883.
Rev. John W. Beardslee	of the Classis of Michigan. Term expires, 1884.
Rev. Isaac P. Brokaw,	of the Cbssis of Monmouth.

Term expires, 1883.

Rev. A. J. Hageman,	of the Classis of Montgomery.
	Term expires, 1882.
Rev. William H. Gleason,	of the Classis of Newark.
	Term expires, 1883.
Rev. E. T. Corwin, D. D.,	of the Classis of New Brunswick.
	Term expires, 1884.
Rev. Talbot W. Chambers, D. D.,	of the Classis of New York.
	Term expires, 1883.
Rev. E. W. Bentley, D. D.,	of the Classis of Orange.
	Term expires, 1884.
Rev. George M. S. Blauvelt,	of the Classis of Paramus.
	Term expires, 1882.
Rev. John N. Jansen,	of the Classis of Passaic.
	Term expires, 1882.
Rev. T. X. Orr,	of the Class is of Philadelphia.
	Term expires, 1884.
Rev. C. W. Fritts,	of the Classis of Poughkeepsie.
	Term expires, 1884.
Rev. Charles T. Anderson,	of the Classis of Raritan.
	Term expires, 1882.
Rev. Edward A. Collier,	of the Classis of Rensselaer.
	Term expires, 1882.
Rev. J. Paschal Strong,	of the Classis of Saratoga.
	Term expires, 1883.
Rev. Herman Vanderwart,	of the Classis of Schenectady.
	Term expires, 1883.
Rev. Edward Miller,	of the Classis of Schoharie.
	Term expires, 1882.

Rev. Corn Van Santvoord, D. D., of the Classis of Ulster.
Term expires, 1883.

Rev. David Cole, D. D., of the Olassis of ·Westchester.
Term expires, 1883.

Rev. John H. Karsten, of the Classis of Wisconsin.
Term expires, 1882

Elders at Large.

From the Particular Synod of Albany.

William H. Van Orden, Term Expires, 1884.

Peter S. Danforth, Term Expires, 1884.

From the Particular Synod of New York.

Edward L. Beadle, M. D., Term Expires, 1884.

Henry Van Arsdale, M. D., Term Expires, 1884.

From the Particular Synod of New Brunswick.

Peter A. Voorhees, Term Expires, 1882.

Johnson Letson, Term Expires, 1884.

Stated Clerk.

Rev. P. D. Van Cleef, D. D., Jersey City, N. J.

Page 5

Faculty

Rev. Samuel M. Woodbridge, D. D.,
Professor of Ecclesiastical History and Government.
Rev. John De Witt, D. D.,
Thomas De Witt Professor of Biblical Literature.
Rev. David D. Demarest, D. D.,
Professor of Pastoral Theology and Sacred Rhetoric.
Rev. William V. V. Mabon, D. D.,
James Suydam Professor of Didactic and Polemic Theology

Page 6~7

Senior Class

Middle Class

Page 8

Junior Class

Names.	Residences.	Rooms.
Marion T. Conklin, R. C.,	Kingston, N. Y.,	22 H. H.
Josiah E. Crane, R, C.,	Fair Oaks, N. Y.,	23 H. H.
Joseph P. Davis, U. C.,	Cobleskill, N. Y.,	20 H. H.
Alfred H. Demarest, R. C.,	New Brunswick, Prof. Demarest's	
Charles S. Dutton, H. C.,	Holland, Mich.,	12 H. H.
Gustavus Goebel, B. A. D.,	New York City,	45 H. H.
T. John Kommers, H. C.,	New Brunswick, N. J.,	35 H. H.
Joel Loucks, R. C.,	Palatine Bridge, N. Y.,	21 H. H.
Frederick W. Ruhl,	A.lbany, N. Y.,	30 Morris St.
William Schmitz, Jr., R. C.,	Brooklyn. N. Y.,	28 H. H.

Bastia.N Smits, R. C.,	Holland, Mich.,	16 H. H.
George H. Stephens, R. C.,	North Branch, N.J., 78 Bayard St.	
Livingston L. Taylor, R. C.,	Newark, N.J.,	14 H. H.
Horace G. Underwood, N. Y. U.,	New Durham, N. J.,	32 H. H.
J. Russell Verbrycke, R. C.,	N. Brunswick, N. J., 20 Church St.	
Garret Wyckoff, Jr., R. C.,	Pompton Plains, N. J.,	19 H. H.

Page 9

Summary

Senior Class		19
Middle Class		10
Junior Class		**16**
	Total	45.

References.

H. H. - Hertzog Hall.

R. C. - Rutgers College.

U. I. - University of Iowa.

C. N. Y. - College of the City of New York.

N. Y. U. - New York University.

S. G. - Stuttgard Gymnasium.

B. A. D. - Bloomfield Acad. Department.

U. C. - Union College.

C. U. - Cornell University.

H. C. - Hope College.

Admission.

The Seminary is open for the admission of students from every denomination of Christians.

A Committee of the Board of Superintendents on the reception of Students, meets on the 20th of September, at 11 o'clock M.

Every applicant is required to present a certificate of church membership, and a College Diploma. Those who have not pursued a regular Collegiate course, must exhibit evidences of attainments that shall be deemed by the Committee equivalent to a liberal education.

The requirement of the Constitution in regard to students preparing for the ministry in the Reformed Church, is as follows:

"Every person contemplating the work of the Ministry, before he commences his course of Theological studies, shall furnish satisfactory evidence of his being a member in full communion and in good standing of a Reformed Protestant Church; of his piety, ability and literary attainments, and thereupon shall be admitted into one of the Theological Schools; and during the prosecution of his studies there shall be subject to the rules and regulations thereof, and when he shall have completed the prescribed course and term of Theological studies, shall be admitted to an examination according to the regulations of the schools as established by General Synod; and if found qualified, shall receive a professorial certificate to that effect, which shall entitle him to an examination for licensure before the Classis to which he belongs." - Constitution, Art. 2, Sec. 2.

The Year.

The year embraces one term of eight months of study, from the 20th of September to the 3d Tuesday in May, "with an interval of eight or ten days at the Christmas holidays." This arrangement affords opportunity for those who desire it to engage in various works during the Summer months.

At the close of the year, an examination of all the classes is held before the Board of Superintendents; commencing on the third Tuesday in May.

Course of Instruction.

This Embraces Three Years, as Follows:

Junior Class.

Hebrew and Greek Languages.

Exegetical Study of Messianic Predictions in the Original Language, and of the Greek Harmony.

Biblical Geography.

Biblical Antiquities.

Sacred Chronology.

Ancient Sacred History.

Sacred Rhetoric, Composition, and Delivery of Sermons.

Among the text-books in use are Gesenius' Hebrew Grammar and Lexicon, Kurtz's Sacred History, Kurtz's Ecclesiastical History, Winer's Chaldee Grammar, Barrow's Sacred Geography and Antiquities, and the Constitution of the Reformed Church in America.

The members of all the classes are required to prepare and deliver sermons, the matter, arrangement, style and delivery of which are criticised by the Students and Professors.

Much attention is paid through the whole course to the preparation of plans of sermons, which are criticised by the Students and the Professor of Sacred Rhetoric. Also to the reading of the Scriptures and of Hymns.

Instruction is given in Expository preaching, with practical Exercises, and also in the public explanation of the Heidelberg Catechism, which is required of our ministers by the Constitution.

Theses on subjects connected with Theology are required from the members of the Senior Class by the Professor of Didactic Theology, to whose criticism they are subject.

Page 12

Examinations.

The Annual Examination of each class before the Board of Superintendents commences on the third Tuesday in May.

A Committee of the Board of Superintendents meets on the 20th of September for the examination of candidates for admission. Applicants are requested to bring their testimonials with them.

Library.

A very valuable Library is connected with the Institution, containing more than 34,000 volumes, 3,000 of which were selected and given by Mrs. Bethune from the library of Rev. Dr. Bethune; many have been given by ministerial and other friends of the Institution; many have been purchased with moneys contributed by numerous generous donors. It also contains 6,000 pamphlets.

This Library has been placed in the very complete, spacious and elegant fire-proof building erected by the liberality of Gardner A. Sage, Esq., of New York City, and which the General Synod has named "Gardner A. Sage Library."

A considerable amount of money for the purchase of books is still in the hands of the Treasurer of "General Synod. To insure its judicious expenditure, the Synod has appointed a committee, consisting of Rev. Drs. T. W. Chambers, C. D. Hartranft, E. T. Corwin, and Prof. Jacob Cooper, of Rutgers College, to be associated with the Theological Professors, and who are to have exclusive charge of selecting the books for the Theological Library." This committee meets statedly once a month, and carefully considers the merits of every book proposed. Valuable additions are thus made to the Library from time to time.

The General Synod has resolved "that the use of the Library be extended to the whole Reformed Church, and to the citizens of New Brunswick, under silch restrictions however to be adopted by the Board of Superintendents as not to interfere with its proper use by the Faculty and Students of the Theological Seminary."

The Library is open daily from 9 A. M. to 12.30 p. M., and from 2 to 4.30 P. M., under the care of Rev. Peter J. Quick, Librarian in charge.

Page 13

Reading Room.

This is well supplied with the best Foreign and American Reviews, Magazines, and Weekly religious Newspapers.

James Suydam Hall.

This building, the noble gift of James Suydam, Esq., of New York City, contains a Chapel, Museum, Lecture Room, and a spacious and thoroughly furnished Gymnasium for physical exercises.

Society of Inquiry.

This is devoted not only to the increase of the spirit of Missions among the students, but also to the consideration and discussion of all questions that bear on their prospective work, and in which they feel an interest. The exercises consist of essays, reviews, criticisms, and debates. An anniversary is held in -the month of May.

A collection of curiosities, sent by our Missionaries from heathen lands, constitutes the foundation of an interesting Museum. Contributions to it are solicited.

Page 14

Peter Hertzog Theological Hall.

This building was erected in the year 1856, with moneys, amounting to $30,700, furnished for the purpose by Mrs. Anna Hertzog, of the Third Reformed Church of Philadelphia.

It is beautifully located in the suburbs of New Brunswick, New Jersey, a city proverbial for its healthfulness. The building and property connected with it are under the care of the Standing Committee on the Seminary grounds and property at New Brunswick, N. J. This committee is composed at present of Messrs. Gardner A. Sage, John W. Ferdon, William Bogardus, William H. Kirk, S. H. Wheeler, and Professor John De Witt.

The Hall contains a Chapel, Reading Room, Study Rooms, Dormitories, Dining Rooms, Laundry and Bath Room. It is lighted throughout by gas, and warmed by steam. Water from the City works is carried to all parts of the building. No expense has been spared to make it complete in its arrangement.

The Hall is under the care of a Rector, Rev. Ralph Willis, who furnishes board to those who desire it, and whose aim it is to secure to all a cleanly, orderly and comfortable home.

Students of Rutgers College and of the Grammar School who have the ministry in view, are permitted to reside in and enjoy all the advantages of the Hall, precedence being always given to the members of the Theological Seminary.

The rooms are furnished with beds, bedding, carpets, chairs, bureaus, tables, &c. Each student is required to provide himself with sheets, pillow cases and towels.

Rooms are chosen on the day of the opening of the Seminary year (September 20th), and in the order of the Classes, commencing with the Senior Class in the Theological Seminary.

The annual charge for heating and other incidentals for each room is $24.00. The charge for light is $10 per annum. There is no charge for the use of the Library, Reading Room, or Gymnasium. Board is furnished in the Hall at $3.25 per week.

The residents in the Hall are required to attend Evening prayers in the Chapel.

Students not residing in the Hall are required to pay $5.00 per annum for incidental expenses.

Page 15

Preaching by Students.

The following are the resolutions of the General Synod on this subject:

Resolved, That no student' of Theology in our Seminary be allowed to preach or lecture in any of our churches and congregations, except that the students of the Senior Class be allowed to deliver their own discourses under the direction of one of the Professors of Theology, with the understanding that this direction is to extend to the time when, the place where, and the discourse to be delivered; and except further that students of the Senior Class be allowed the same privileges in the churches of which they are members, under the direction of their own pastors, the direction to extend as in the case before mentioned. - Minutes, vol. ix, page 345.

Resolved, That the students of the Middle Class in our Seminaries be allowed to preach. during vacations, under the direction of their Theological Professors. - Minutes, vol. xiii, page 535.

Beneficiary Aid.

Instruction is entirely gratuitous. Young men connected with the Reformed Church, intending to enter its ministry, and needing assistance, receive from the Board of Education the sum of one hundred and fifty dollars per annum, in addition to which the charges for heating::and light in Hertzog Hall are paid by the Board.

The Board assists young men while pursuing studies preparatory to their entrance into the Seminary.

Page 16

Vedder Lecture on Modern Infidelity.

This Lectureship was founded by Mr. Nicholas F. Vedder of Utica, by a gift of $10,000, on the following among other conditions, that the General Synod should every year elect some member of the Reformed Church in America to deliver to the students of the Seminary and Rutgers College at least five lectures on the present aspects of Modern Infidelity, including its cause and cure.

The Lecturer for the year 1881~2 is Rev. William Ormiston, D. D., of New York City, and for the year 1882~3 Rev. John B. Drury, D. D., of Ghent, N. Y.

Endowment.

The Theological Seminary has no Trustees nor incorporation apart from "the General Synod of the Reformed Church in America," which has always maintained the direct guardianship and control of education for the sacred ministry. Under the provisions of the act of incorporation, granted for this express purpose by the Legislature of New York in the year 1819, and followed by an act of the Legislature of New Jersey, enabling the Church to hold property in that State, all funds designed for Theological education are held and invested for the General Synod by "the Board of Direction 0/ the Corporation."

The Board at present consists of

John Van Nest, President, J Orn Lefferts, William Bogardus, Rev. Talbot W. Chambers, D. D., Gardner A. Sage, Treasurer,	Directors.

The permanent Seminary Fund needs a large addition to make its income adequate to pay the salaries of the Professors, and to meet other necessary expenses of the institution. The kind influence and co-operation of Pastors, and liberal gifts and bequests from friends of Theological education, are earnestly solicited. No expenditure of money can be more effective in strengthening and perpetuating the Church.

18820000

미국 개혁(화란)교회 신학교 교직원 및 학생 일람, 뉴브런즈윅, 뉴저지 주, 1882~83학년도. 뉴브런즈윅, 뉴저지, 제이 터휸 프레스, 올버니 가 31번지, 1882년, 11쪽.

교과 과정

교과 과정은 3년이며, 다음과 같다:

2학년

설교학 및 변증신학	교회사
직제학	성서비평
갈데아어 및 시리아어	
메시아 예언의 해석학	
바울서신 중 하나의 해석학적 연구	
예전학	요리문답
설교의 구성 및 실제	

Catalogue of the Officers and Students of the Theological Seminary of the Reformed (Dutch) Church in America, New Brunswick, N. J. 1882~'83. New Brunswick, N. J., J. Terhune's Press, 31 Albany Street, 1882, p. 11.

Didactic and Polemic Theology

Ecclesiastical History

Church Government

Biblical Criticism

Chaldee and Syriac Languages

Exegetical Study of Messianic Predictions continued.

Exegetical Study of one of the Pauline Epistles.

Liturgics

Catechetics

Composition and Delivery of Sermons

18830501

1883년 5월 1일 뉴브런즈윅에서 개최된 뉴브런즈윅 특별 노회 회의록. 서머빌, 뉴저지 주: The Unionist-Gazetter Printing House, 1883년, 31쪽.

교적 변동.

폼프턴에 있는 교회와 존 N. 얀센 사이의 목회 관계가 1883년 4월 4일 해지되었다.

***Minutes of the Particular Synod of New Brunswick, Convened at New Brunswick, May 1, 1883.* Somerville, N. J.: The Unionist-Gazetter Printing House, 1883, p. 31.**

Ecclesiastical Changes.

The pastoral relation between the church at Pompton and the Rev. John N. Jansen was dissolved April 4, 1883.

18830000

미국 개혁(화란)교회 신학교 교직원 및 학생 일람, 뉴브런즈윅, 뉴저지 주, 1883~84학년도. 뉴브런즈윅, 뉴저지, 제이 터휸 프레스, 올버니 가 31번지, 1883년, 11쪽.

교과 과정

교과 과정은 3년이며, 다음과 같다:

3학년

설교학 및 변증신학
교회사
목회신학
예언서의 해석
바울서신의 해석학
논문.
설교의 구성 및 실제
개혁교회 헌법.
학생들은 그들이 학습하는 사도서신을 완전히 석의해야 한다.

Catalogue of the Officers and Students of the Theological Seminary of the Reformed (Dutch) Church in America, New Brunswick, N. J. 1883~'84. New Brunswick, N. J., J. Terhune's Press, 31 Albany Street, 1883, p. 11.

Didactic and Polemic Theology continued.

Ecclesiastical History continued.

Pastoral Theology.

Exegetical Study of the Prophecies continued.

Exegetical Study of the Pauline Epistles continued.

Theses..

Composition and Delivery of Sermons.

Constitution of the Reformed Church.

The students are also required to write out full paraphrases of the Epistles which they study.

18840506

1884년 5월 6일 뉴욕 주의 워윅에서 개최된 뉴브런즈윅 특별 노회 회의록. 서머빌, 뉴저지 주: The Unionist-Gazetter Printing House, 1884년, 29쪽.

폼프턴의 교회 보고: "목사가 없었던 우리 교회는 정체되거나 뒷걸음질 치지 않았다. 여름 동안 신학교 학생을 구했고, 그의 열성적인 활동과 전임 목사가 뿌린 씨앗의 결과 29명의 신자가 더 늘어났다."

***Minutes of the Particular Synod of New Brunswick, Convened at Warwick, N. Y., May 6, 1884.* Somerville, H. J.: The Unionist-Gazetter Printing House, 1884, p. 29.**

The Church of Pompton reports: "Although without a pastor we have neither been standing still nor going back. During the Summer the services of a student from the Theological Seminary were obtained, and as a result of his efforts, and the good seed sown by himself and the former pastor, there have been added to the church twenty-nine."

5. 졸업 후 교육 (Postgraduate Study)

1881년 언더우드는 화란개혁신학교에 입학함과 동시에, 9월 20일 시작하는 럿거스대학(Rutgers College)의 대학원 과정에도 등록했다.[74] 그런데 이 과정은 현재와 같이 연구논문을 작성하고 심사를 통과하면 석사학위를 받는 것이 아니었다. 당시 럿거스대학은 다음의 여러 조건 중 한 조건에 해당하는 문학사 학위 소지자가 신청을 하는 경우, 졸업 3년 후에 문학석사를 수여할 수 있었다.[75] 그 조건이란 첫째, 신학교, 법과대학, 의과대학, 혹은 변호사 혹은 의사 면허증 등의 증명서를 제시하는 경우, 둘째, 교수진이 인정할 만한 기타 학문적 진전의 증거를 제시하는 경우, 셋째, 이수 받은 교육 과정에 대한 교수진의 시험을 통과하거나 교수진이 인정하는 논문을 제출하는 경우 등이었다. 언더우드의 경우 특별히 강의나 연구 논문 작성이 아니라 신학교를 졸업하는 것으로 문학석사를 청구할 수 있었던 것이다.

언더우드가 입학할 당시 학생은 15명, 1882년 9월 20일 시작하는 이듬해에는 14명이었는데, 1883학년도에 언더우드는 대학원 학생 명단에 빠져 있다. 그 이유는 럿거스대학이 대학원 규정을

---

74) 럿거스대학교는 화란개혁신학교에 인접해 위치해 있는, 뉴저지에서 가장 큰 고등 교육 기관이다. 이 대학은 네덜란드 개혁교회가 운영하는 사립대학으로 1770년 퀸즈 칼리지(Queen's College)란 이름으로 개교했으며, 당시에는 남자들만 입학할 수 있었다. 미국 독립 이전에 정식 학위를 수여할 수 있었던 9개 대학 중에 8번째로 설립되었으며, 독립 전쟁의 영웅인 헨리 럿거스(Henry Rutgers, 1745~1839) 대령을 기념하기 위해 1825년 교명을 바꾸었다. 1945년 뉴저지 주에 의해 공립(주립) 대학교로 되었다.

75) *Catalogue of the Officers and Students of Rutgers College, New Brunswick, N. J.*, 1881–'82, pp. 7, 35; *Catalogue of the Officers and Students of Rutgers College, New Brunswick, N. J.*, 1882~'83, 1882, p. 7.

변경했기 때문이었다.[76] 즉, 본인의 신청이 아닌 실제 성과에 의해서만 석사 학위를 수여하기로 강화하면서 첫째, 럿거스대학에서 최소한 1년 동안 과정을 이수하고 시험은 물론 관련된 주제의 논문을 제출하거나, 둘째, 럿거스대학 출신으로서 신학교, 법과대학, 의과대학, 혹은 변호사 혹은 의사 면허증 등의 증명서를 제시하거나, 셋째, 특정 분야의 교육이나 저술이 뛰어나다는 충분한 근거를 제시하는 경우로 국한시켰던 것이다.

이렇게 1년을 남겨두고 석사학위 신청의 길이 막혀버린 언더우드는 아직도 자신이 럿거스대학에 입학할 당시처럼, 신청에 의해 석사학위를 수여하고 있던 뉴욕대학교로 적을 옮겼다.[77] 그리하여 언더우드는 1884년 6월 19일 뉴욕대학교의 졸업식에서 문학석사의 학위를 받았다.[78]

---

76) *Catalogue of the Officers and Students of Rutgers College, New Brunswick, N. J.*, 1884~'5, 1884, p. 46.

77) 뉴욕대학교에 연구를 위한 대학원 과정이 개설된 것은 1886년 10월이었다. Theodore Francis Jones, *New York University, 1832:1932*, The New York University Press, 1933, pp. 139~40.

78) *University of the City of New York. Catalogue and Announcements 1884~1885*, May 1885, p. 46.

18810000

럿거스대학 교직원 및 학생 일람, 뉴브런즈윅, 뉴저지 주, 1881~82학년도, 7, 35쪽.

1881년 9월 20일 시작하는 학년의 학생 목록[79)]

대학원 학생

이름	거주지	방
호러스 G. 언더우드,	뉴더햄,	헤르초크 홀 32호

학위 및 대학원 교육

문학사 및 이학사는 다음의 조건 중 하나에 충족될 경우, 졸업 후 3년이 경과한 후 신청에 의해 문학석사 및 이학석사의 학위를 수여 받는다.

1. 신학교, 법과대학 혹은 의과대학의 졸업 증명서 혹은 법률 혹은 의료업을 허락하는 증명서를 제시하는 경우.

2. 교수회가 인정할 만한 다른 지적 진전의 증거를 제시하는 경우.

3. 앞에 기술된 교육 과정에 대해 교수 위원회의 시험을 보고, 교수회가 심사할 논문을 제시하는 경우.

4. 하지만 1882년까지는 제시한 논문과 관련된 것을 제외하고, 시험을 보지 않을 것이다.

철학박사 및 이학박사는 교수의 지도아래 전술한 과정을 2년 동안 전담으로 수행한 졸업생에게 수여될 것이다.

조건은 지원 시 알려줄 예정이다.

---

79) 전체 명단은 영어 원문을 참고하시오.

Catalogue of the Officers and Students of Rutgers College, New Brunswick, N. J., 1881-'82, pp. 7, 35.

Page 7

Catalogue of Students for the Year Beginning Sept. 20, 1881.

Post-Graduate Students.

Name	Residence	Rooms
Willy Muss Arnoldt,	New York City.	Hertzog Rail.
Theo. Burges Booraem, Jr.,	New Brunswick,	54 Bayard Street.
Myron T. Conklin,	Kingston, N. Y.,	22 Hertzog Hall.
Josiah E. Crane,	Fair Oaks, N. Y.,	23 Hertzog Hall.
Alfred H. Demarest,	New Brunswick,	Seminary Place.
Charles H. Dutton,	Holland, Mich.,	12 Hertzog Hall,
Abel H. Huinzinga,	Zealand, Mich.,	40 Hertzog Hall.
T. John Kommers,	New Brunswick,	35 Hertzog Hall.
Chas. T. Pomeroy,	Newark,	Newark.
John Scarlet,	South Branch,	50 Hertzog Hall.
Edwin F. See.	Tarrytown, N. Y.,	44 Hertzog Hall.
John L. Stillwell,	Somerville,	49 Hertzog Hall.
Livingston L. Taylor,	Newark,	14 Hertzog Hall,
Horace G. Underwood,	New Durham,	32 Hertzog Hall.
Irving S. Upson,	Marion, Conn.,	College avenue.
J. Russel Verbrycke,	New Brunswick,	20 Church Street.

Page 35

Degrees and Post-Graduate Studies.

Bachelors of Art and Bachelors of Science shall be entitled on application to receive three years after graduation the degrees of A. M. and M. S. respectively, on one of the following conditions:

1. On presenting a certificate of graduation from a Theological Seminary, Law School or Medical College, or a certificate of admission to the practice of Law or Medicine.

2. On presenting evidence of other intellectual progress satis factory to the Faculty.

3. On passing an examination before a committee of the Faculty on a prescribed course of study, and presenting a thesis to be approved by the Faculty.

4. Until 1882, however, no examination will be required except on the subject of the thesis presented.

The degrees of Ph. D. and D. Sc. will be conferred upon resident graduates of the College who shall pursue for two years prescribed courses of study under the direction of the Faculty.

The conditions will be made known on application.

18820000

럿거스대학 교직원 및 학생 일람, 뉴브런즈윅, 뉴저지 주, 1882~83학년도, 7쪽.

1882년 9월 20일 시작하는 학년의 학생 목록[80)]

대학원 학생

이름	거주지	방
호러스 G. 언더우드,	뉴더햄,	헤르초크 홀 32호

Catalogue of the Officers and Students of Rutgers College, New Brunswick, N. J., 1882~'83, 1882, p. 7.

Catalogue of Students for the Year Beginning Sept. 20, 1882.

Post-Graduate Students.

Name	Residence	Rooms
W. Muss Arnoldt, B. S.,	New York City.	51 Hertzog Rail.
Theo. Burgess Booraem, Jr.,	New Brunswick,	54 Bayard Street.
J. Chester Chamberlain	Madanapalle, India,	George & Albany Sta.
William I. Chamberlain	Madanapalle, India,	31 Hertzog Rail.
Charles L. Edgar,	New Brunswick,	New Brunswick.
John G. Fagg,	Madison, Wis.,	48 Hertzog Hall.
Abel H. Huinzinga,	Zealand, Mich.,	46 Hertzog Hall.

80) 전체 명단은 영어 원문을 참고하시오.

Jorl Loucks,	Palatine Bridge, N. Y.,	21 Hertzog Hall.
Chas. T. Pomeroy,	Newark,	Newark.
John Morrison,	Fishkill-on-Hud'n, N. Y.,	36 Hertzog Hall.
Henry DuBois Mulford,	Hudson, N. Y.,	45 Albany St.
Edwin F. See.	Tarrytown, N. Y.,	44 Hertzog Hall.
Livingston Ludlow Taylor,	Newark,	14 Hertzog Hall,
Horace Grant Underwood,	New Durham,	32 Hertzog Hall.

18840000

럿거스대학 교직원 및 학생 일람, 뉴브런즈윅, 뉴저지 주, 1884~5학년도, 1884년, 46쪽.

학위 및 대학원 교육.

문학석사 및 이학석사의 학위는 더 이상 "때가 되면" 수여되지 않고, 수행한 실적만으로 수여되고 있다.

교수회는 학사 학위를 받고 적절하게 검증을 받은 자를 문학석사 혹은 이학석사의 후보자로 추천한다.

1. [후보자는] 럿거스대학에서 교수로부터 인증 받은 인문 및 비직업적 과정을 최소한 1년 동안 수료해야 하고, 학기 시험 이외에 그 과목의 시험을 통과해야 하며 그 과목과 연관된 어떤 주제에 대한 논문을 제출하거나; 혹은

2. 럿거스대학을 졸업한 지 3년이 되지 않은 자가 석사학위를 신청하는 경우 신학교, 법과대학 혹은 의과대학의 졸업증명서를 제출하던가 법호사 혹의 의사 개업 허가를 제출하거나; 혹은

3. 특정 분야의 교육 혹은 저술에서 성공적인 성과를 거두었다는 충분한 증거를 엄선하여 제출하거나; 혹은

4. 이학사의 경우, 실제 수행한 성공적인 전문 분야의 성과 및 수행했던 진 선도적인 전문 연구를 제출해야 한다.

철학박사 및 이학박사는 교수의 지도하에 2년 동안 규정된 과정을 수행한 럿거스대학의 전일제 졸업생에게 수여할 수 있다.

조건은 지원 시에 공지할 예정이다.

Catalogue of the Officers and Students of Rutgers College, New Brunswick, N. J., 1884~'5, 1884, p. 46.

Degrees and Post-Graduate Studies.

The degrees of A. M. and M. S. are no longer given "in course," but only for work done.

The Faculty will recommend for the degree of Master of Arts or Master of Science candidates otherwise properly qualified, who, after taking the appropriate Bachelor's degree,

1. Shall pursue for at least one year at Rutgers College a course of liberal and non-professional study, approved by the Faculty, and shall, besides the term examinations, pass a thorough examination on that course and present a thesis on some topic connected with it; or,

2. Who, not less than three years after taking the Bachelor's degree at Rutgers College, shall make application for the Master's degree, presenting at the same time a certificate of graduation from a Theological Seminary, a Law School, or a Medical School, or of admission to the practice of Law or Medicine; or,

3. Satisfactory evidence of successful labor in that field of education or literature which may have been chosen; or,

4. In case of Bachelors of Science, satisfactory evidence of successful professional work actually done and advanced professional studies prosecuted.

The degrees of Ph. D. and D. Sc, may be conferred upon resident graduates of the College who shall pursue for two years prescribed courses of study under the direction of the Faculty.

The conditions will be made known on application.

19330000

시어도어 프랜시스 존스, 뉴욕대학교, 1832~1932, 뉴욕대학교 출판부, 1933, 139-40쪽.

아는 바와 같이 크로스비 박사는 대학원 교육의 필요성이 증대될 것이고 이를 조직할 필요성이 있음을 깨달았다. 구체적인 방안이 정해지지 않은 상황에서, 1885년 당시 대학교는 아직도 오랜 동안 해왔던 것처럼, 통상적으로 졸업 후 3년이 경과하고, 지원 시 일정 수준의 학문적 관심의 증거를 제시하면, 지원한 졸업생에 대해 무시험으로 문학석사 학위를 수여하고 있었다. 분석화학을 위한 드레이퍼 교수의 분석화학학교가 없어진 이래 드물기는 하지만 명예 학위로서 철학박사 학위가 수여되었다. 이러한 제도는 미국 대학에서 오래 동안 관행적으로 실시되어 온 것이었지만, 시대가 변해 1885년 당시 자존심 있는 미국 대학교의 대부분은 전일제로 최신 연구에 몰두한 보상으로 석사와 박사 학위를 수여하고 있었다. 당시 맥크라켄 박사는 필요한 기부금이 아직도 부족한 상황이었지만 원래 계획을 실현하자고 제안하여 대학교의 체면을 살렸고, 당시 상황에서 최선을 다해 대학원 과정을 구축함으로써 대학의 교수진을 북돋았다.

따라서 1886년 6월, 1870년 조직된 문과와 이과가 다시 합쳐져 문리학부가 설립되었으며, 대학평의회는 문학석사, 이학석사 및 철학박사를 심사에 의해서만 수여하며, 학부는 그러한 심사를 위해 준비하는 교육 과정을 결정하고 구성하도록 허용해야 한다는 지침을 내렸다.

대학교 또한 졸업 성적이 최상위인 4학년 학생 2명에게 각 300달러를 지급하는 특별 연구원 제도를 마련했으며, 1명은 고전 분야에 1명은 철학 분야에 배정했다. 캐롤 교수를 제외한 학부의 모든 교수들은 1886년 10월에 시작되는 대학원 교육을 위한 "서클"로 발표되었다. 강사는 12명의 전일제 학생들이 납부하는 강사료를 받는다. 그리고 학년 말에 2명으로 구성된 위원회는 시험을 치러 1명에게 석사 학위를. 2명에게 철학박사 학위를 수여한다. 학위를 받기 위한 "필요 자격"이 무엇이었는지 정확하게 알기는 어렵다. 박사학위를 받은 사람 중의 하나였던 엠 G. 벌체프 씨는 분명히 4번의 시험, 즉 휴튼 교수의 영국 역사, 맥크라켄 박사의 현대 윤리, 고대 철학 및 현대 철학을 통과했다.

Theodore Francis Jones, *New York University, 1832: 1932*, The New York University Press, 1933, pp. 139~40.

Dr. Crosby had, we know, realized the growth of the demand for, and the necessity of organizing postgraduate instruction. The means had not been provided and in 1885 the University was still conferring the A. M. degree, as it had long done, without examination upon such of its alumni as applied for it, ordinarily three years after graduation, and who, perhaps by that very application, showed a certain amount of academic interest. Since the disappearance of Professor Draper's School of Analytical Chemistry, the degree of Ph. D. was, although but rarely, conferred as an honorary degree. Such had long been the practice of other American universities; but times had changed, and by 1885 most self-respecting American universities were using the master's and the doctor's degrees only as a reward for advanced study in residence. Dr. MacCracken now proposed, although the all but necessary endowment was still lacking, to fulfill the original plan, save the face of the University, and invigorate the faculty of the College, by organizing graduate work as best he could under the circumstances.

In June, 1886, therefore, at the same time that the two departments of Arts and Science, organized in 1870, were again reunited to form one faculty of Arts and Science, the Council ordered that the degrees of M. A., M. S., and Ph. D. should henceforth be given upon examination only, and that the faculty of the College should be authorized to determine and organize the course of study preparatory for such examinations. The University also agreed to confer two graduate fellowships, each of $300, upon the two seniors highest in rank at graduation, one for study in the classics, and one in philosophy. The first organization was necessarily informal. All the members of the faculty, except Professor Carroll, announced "circles" for postgraduate work, which began in October, 1886; the instructors received the fees paid by the students, of whom twelve resident graduates appeared; and, after examination conducted at the end of the year by a committee of two professors, one degree of M. A. and two degrees of Ph. D. were conferred. It is difficult to discover precisely what the "requirements" for the degrees were. Mr. M. G. Vulcheff, who received one of the doctorates, apparently passed four examinations: one in English History, under Professor Houghton, and three under Dr. MacCracken, in Contemporary Ethics, in Ancient, and in Modern Philosophy.

18840600

제51회 졸업식, 1884. 뉴욕대학교, 1884년 6월 19일. (*Fifty-first Commencement, 1884. University of the City of New York, June 19th, 1884*).

Fifty-first Commencement,

1884.

University of the City of New York.

Thursday Morning, June 19th, 1884,

AT HALF PAST TEN O'CLOCK,

At the Academy of Music,

AT SIX O'CLOCK P. M.

Annual Meeting of the Alumni Association,

IN THE COUNCIL ROOM OF THE UNIVERSITY.

GRAND MARSHAL, - - - - - - FRANK LEGRAND TOWNSEND.

Chef d' Orchestre, - - - - - A. BERNSTEIN.

GEO. R. LOCKWOOD & SON, NEW YORK.

Order of Exercises.

Music : Overture, "La Belle Galathe," *Suppe.*

Selection, "The Beggar Student," *Millocker*

March, "Prophete," *Meyerbeer*

Prayer.

MUSIC, "La Gioconda," (Dance of the Hours,) PONCHIELLI.

I.—LATIN SALUTATORY ORATION,
CARL HENRY LELLMANN, New York City.

II.—ENGLISH SALUTATORY ORATION,—"Poverty and Progress,"
JOHN DAYTON BLAKE, Jersey City Heights.

III.—PHILOSOPHICAL ORATION,—"Originality,"
LEWIS BAYLES PATON, Newark, N. J.

MUSIC, Selections, "Prince Methusalem," STRAUSS.

IV.—DISSERTATION,—"Monopolies,"
HOMER LEWIS BARTLETT, Brooklyn.

V.—ORATION,—"Philanthropy, the Aim of Life,"
CLARENCE THWING, Brooklyn.

MUSIC, Waltz, "Our Guests," BERNSTEIN.

VI.—DISSERTATION,—"The Futility of Political Theorizing,"
CHARLES FLETCHER HALSTEAD, Harrison, N. Y.

VII.—DISSERTATION,—"Oliver Cromwell,"
AMORY THOMPSON SKERRY, JR., Brooklyn.

MUSIC, Selections, "Aida," VERDI.

VIII.—ORATION,—"The Permanency of Governments,"
THOMAS WATTERS, Brooklyn.

IX.—ORATION,—"Socialism,"
WITH VALEDICTORY ADDRESSES, ALEXANDER STEELE LYMAN, New York City.

MUSIC, Galop, "Fedora," DIEDRICH.

Regular Degrees Conferred

By the Rev. WILLIAM M. TAYLOR, D. D, LL. D., in absence of Dr. JOHN HALL, Chancellor *ad interim.*

The Degree of Bachelor of Arts will be conferred upon :

JOHN DAYTON BLAKE, ALEXANDER STEELE LYMAN,
CHARLES FLETCHER HALSTEAD, LEWIS BAYLES PATON,
CARL HENRY LELLMANN, THOMAS WATTERS.

The Degree of Bachelor of Science will be conferred upon :

HOMER LEWIS BARTLETT, CLARENCE THWING,
FREDERICK M. CROSSETT, FRANK LEGRAND TOWNSEND,
AMORY THOMPSON SKERRY, JR., HENRY BEACH WINDSOR.

The Diploma of Civil Engineer will be conferred upon :

HOMER LEWIS BARTLETT, AMORY THRMPSON SKERRY, JR.,
FRANK LEGRAND TOWNSEND.

The Degree of Master of Arts will be conferred upon :

BENJAMIN AYCRIGG, JR BENJAMIN AVERY CAPWELL,
CEPHAS BRAINERD, JR., GEORGE MARTIN DUNCAN,
WALTER DUNCAN BUCHANAN, GEORGE HANNUM HAZEN,
HORACE GRANT UNDERWOOD.

The Degree of Doctor of Medicine will be conferred upon :

JOHN BUNYAN ACKEN,	New York.	JOHN WILLIAM KEEFE,	New York.
JOHN FORD BARBOUR, A.B.,	Kentucky.	JACOB SWARTLEY MANCHA,	New York.
HENRY TITIAN BOYLE,	New York.	HENRY PEREIRA MENDES,	New York.
LUCIEN DARWIN CRANE,	New York.	CHAS. ERNESTUS PHILLIPS,	New York.
JOHN FRANKLIN DE COSTER,	Maine.	THOS. AQUINAS PURCELL, A.B.,	Mass.
FRANCIS WILLIAM COWAN,	New York.	HENRY HURD RUSBY,	New Jersey.
RICHARD BLACK CUMMINGS,	Canada.	SAM'L MARSTON STOCKER, Ph.B.,	Illinois.
JAMES CHAUNCEY FITCH,	New York.	HENRY PARKER DEVOURSNEY,	New York.
JOSEPH ALLISON JARRETT,	Georgia.	JOHN EVANS WALKER,	South Carolina.

BICKERTON LYLE WINSTON, Minnesota.

Honorary Degrees Conferred.

Award of Fellowships.

The First Fellowship to ALEXANDER S. LYMAN,

The Second Fellowship to CARL HENRY LELLMAN,

The Third Fellowship to JOHN DAYTON BLAKE.

Award of Society Prizes.

BUTLER EUCLEIAN PRIZES, for the best Essays in English Composition by Members of the Eucleian Society.

Benediction.

MUSIC, - - - - - COLLEGE AIRS.

The University will re-open for the usual Course of Study on the third Wednesday of September next.

Candidates for admission may present themselves for examination in the Council Room on the preceding Tuesday, September 16th, at 10 oclock, A.M.

There are no Fees for Tuition in the Departments of Arts and Sciences.

18850500

뉴욕대학교, 1884~5학년도 일람 및 알림. Printed for the University, 1885년 5월, 65쪽.

학위 수여

문리과, 1884년 6월

문학석사[81]	벤저민 애크리그, 주니어
	세파스 브레이너드, 주니어
	월터 덩컨 뷰캐넌
	벤저민 에이버리 캡웰
	조지 마틴 덩컨
	조지 핸넘 헤이즌
	호레이스 그랜드 언너우드

University of the City of New York, Catalogue and Announcements 1884~1885. Printed for the University, May, 1885, p. 65.

Degrees Conferred.

In the Departments of Arts and Science, June, 1884

Master of Arts[82]	Benjamin Aycrigg, Jr.
	Cephas Brainerd. Jr.

81) 모두 언더우드의 뉴욕대학교 졸업 동기생들이다.

82) Classmates of Mr. Underwood in New York University.

Walter Duncan Buchanan.

Benjamin Avery Capwell.

George Martin Duncan.

George Hannum Hazen.

Horace Grant Underwood.

18920600

제60회 졸업식, 1892. 뉴욕대학교, 1892년 6월 9일. (Sixtieth Commencement, 1892. University of the City of New York, June 9th, 1892.)[83]

SIXTIETH COMMENCEMENT,

1892

University of the City of New York,

THURSDAY EVENING, JUNE 9, 1892,

AT EIGHT O'CLOCK.

AT THE

METROPOLITAN OPERA HOUSE.

Grand Marshal, - - CHARLES HENDRE KELBY.

Conductor of Music, - - C. A. CAPPA.

Seventh Regiment Band.

83) 이 식순지는 8쪽이며, 이곳에는 1쪽과 7쪽만을 실었다.

THE HONORARY DEGREE OF DOCTOR OF DIVINITY

WILL BE CONFERRED UPON:

ISAIAH B. HOPWOOD, A.M., *New York University*, '59. . . . Newark, N. J.
HORACE GRANT UNDERWOOD, A.M., *New York University*, '81, . . . Corea.
WILLAM TAYLOR, A.M., ... Windemere, England.
WILLIAM B. RICHARDS, A.M., ... Plainfield, N. J.

THE HONORARY DEGREE OF MASTER OF LAWS

WILL BE CONFERRED UPON:

MYER S. ISAACS, A.M., CHRISTOPHER G. TIEDEMAN, A.M.,
E. F. SHEPARD, HENRY W. JESSUP, A.M.

ANNOUNCEMENTS.

The Special Opening Exercises of the School of Pedagogy for the next year, 1892–93, will be held Saturday, October 1st, 1892, at 11 A.M., in the Asbury Church, next the University Building, Washington Square, East.

The University will re-open in its Department of Arts and Science on the Fourth Wednesday of September next.

Candidates for admission to College or to the Schools of Engineering and Chemistry, will present themselves for examination at the Council Room on Monday, September 26th, 1892.

Candidates for enrollment in the Graduate Seminary may present themselves October 1st, 1892, or enroll by printed form obtainable by addressing the Chancellor.

ASSOCIATION OF THE ALUMNI.

The Annual Meeting of the Association will be held to-morrow (Friday) Evening, June 10, 1892, at seven o'clock, precisely, in the Council Room.

DR. HENRY D. NOYES, '51,
President.

DR. C. S. BENEDICT, '78,
Secretary.

BURR PRINTING HOUSE, NEW YORK.

18940000

뉴욕대학교 문리과 학장, 교수, 졸업생의 인명 편람. 동창회, 뉴욕, 1894년, 165, 222, 293쪽.[84)]

문리과

1881년.

언더우드, 호러스 그랜트. (비지 가 30번지, 뉴욕 시)　　서울, 한국.

존 언더우드와 엘리자베스 (메어) 언더우드의 아들; ; 출생. 런던, 영국, 1859년 7월 19일.

웹스터 3학년 웅변상. 졸업식 연설자. 「University Quarterly」의 편집인. 필로머시언 소사이어티의 편집인 및 부회장. 델타 업실론.

화란개혁교회 신학교, 뉴브런즈윅, 뉴저지, 1881~4년.; 대학원 과정, 럿거스 대학, 1882~4년.; 안수 목사, 화란개혁교회, 1884년.; 목사, 솜프턴, 뉴저지, 1884년.; 1885년 이래 한국 파송 선교사.; 한국 제중원의학교 화학 및 물리 교수, 1887-90년.; 목사, 유니언처지, 한국, 1888~9년.; 대한 성서위원회 의장, 1887~91년.; 한국어 성경 번역을 위해 임명된 2명 중의 1명.; 장로회 한국선교부 회계, 1885~89년.; 장로회 한국선교부 회장, 1888-90년.; 교신총무, 조선성교서회, 1889년.

뉴욕대학교 문학사, 1881년 및 문학석사, 1884년, 그리고 신학박사, 1892년.

결혼, 1889년 3월 13일, 의사 릴리어스 스털링, 제임스 맨더빌 호튼.; 자녀: 호러스 호튼.

(이력을 볼 것.)

84) 언더우드가 뉴욕대학교를 졸업한 13년 후 다른 동기생들의 동정은 영어 원문을 참고하시오. 언더우드를 이해하는데 조금이나마 도움이 될 것으로 생각하여 실었다.

222쪽

명예학위

1892년.

신학박사

이사야 B. 합우드, '59	뉴어크, 뉴저지
윌리엄 R. 리처즈	플레인필드, 뉴저지
*필립 샤프, 신학박사, 법학박사, 교수	뉴욕시
윌리엄 테일러	윈더미어, 영국
호러스 그랜트 언더우드, '81	서울, 한국

293쪽

이 력

언더우드, 호러스 그랜트. 1881년.

1887년	마가 및 요한복음을 한국어로 번역함. 요코하마, 일본.
–	한국어의 축약본 사전을 2부분, 한영 및 영한,으로 출판함. 4 6판, 196쪽 및 293쪽.
1889년	한영문법, 문법 및 실제. 런던 4 6판, 425쪽.
1889~91년	여러 소책자를 한국어로 번역하고 직접 저술하기도 함.

***Biographical Catalogue of the Chancellors, Professors and Graduates of the Department of Arts and Science of the University of the City of New York*. The Alumni Association, New York, 1894, pp. 161~5, 222, 293.**[85]

pp. 161~5

Department of Arts and Science

1881.

Alden, Herbert Clarendon. P. O. Box 197, Yonkers, N. Y. Δ. Φ.

Civil Engineer.

B. S., 1881, and C. E., 1881, from Univ., City of N. Y.

Aycrigg, Benjamin, Jr. 107 Washington St., Paterson, N. J.

Son of Charles Aycrigg and Julia Elizabeth (Ellsworth) Aycrigg b. Passaic, N. J., Mar. 16, 1857.

Eucleian Junior Orator. Vice-Pres. of Eucleian. Ψ. γ.

Columbia Coll. Law School, 1881~3; Admitted to Bar of State of N, J., 1884; Lawyer; Trustee for Public Schools of Passaic, N. J., 1881~6.

A. B., 1881, and A. M., 1883, from Univ., City of N. Y. LL. B., 1883, from Columbia Coll.

Married, June 23, 1887, Abbie, da. of George Brown. Children: Charles Benjamin and George Brown.

Father: Charles, 1844 (special). Cousin: Benjamin B., 1844.

Ball, John Oscar. Mott Ave. and 163d St., N. Y. City.

Son of James Harvey Ball and Mary Smith (Farrand) Ball b. Hanover, N. J.,

---

85) 언더우드를 이해하는데 조금이나마 도움이 될 것으로 생각하여 뉴욕대학교를 졸업한 13년 후 다른 동기생들의 동정도 함께 실었다.

Mar. 24, 1859.

Junior Orator. Philosophical Orator and Third Fellow ($100). Pres. of Philoxnathean. Φ. B. K.

Columbia Coll. Law School, 1881~3 Lawyer.

A. B., 1881, from Univ., City of N. Y. LL.B., 1883, from Columbia Coll.

Married, I., Nov. 20, 1889, Frances L., da. of Edwin H. Babcock. II., Sept. 22, 1891, Elizabeth B., da. of DeWitt C. Weeks. Child: Lois Frances.

Barnes, Milan Day. 318 E. 13th St., N. Y. City.

Son of Aaron B. Barnes and Lavinia (Van Deusen) Barnes b. Brooklyn, N. Y., Apr. I, 1863.

Junior Orator. Philosophical Orator. F. B. K.

Am. Institute of Phrenology, 1888; Metropolis Law School, 1891~3; Stenographer and Sec'y since 1884l with Southern Pacific R. R. since 1892.

B. S., 1881, from Univ., City of N. Y. LL. B., 1893, from Metropolis Law School.

Member of Am. Institute of Phrenology.

Married, Aug. 13, 1890, Rosanna, da. of Francis Keene. Child: Clarence S

Brother: Amos W., 1885.

Brainerd, Cephas, Jr. 49 Cedar St., N. Y. City.

Son of Cephas Brainerd and Eveline (Hutchinson) Brainerd b. Cromwell, Conn., Dec. 28, 1859.

Junior Orator. Commencement Orator. Editor of University Quarterly.

Pres. of Philomathean. Class Orator. Δ. γ.

Law Student, 1881~3 Lawyer.

A. B., 1881, and A. M., 1884, from Univ., City of N. Y.

Married, Oct. 4, 1887, Harriet Tyler, da. of Wm. P. Arnold.

Brother: Ira H., 1882.

Buchanan, Walter Duncan. 139 W. 13th St., N. Y. City.

Son of the Rev. Dr. John Mairs Buchanan and Jane McElderry (Douglass) Buchanan b. Milwaukee, Wis., Apr. 13, 1859.

Class Pres., Freshman Year. Member of Glee Club and of Quartette.

Union Theol. Sem., 1879~80 and 1881~3. Ordained Minister, Presb. Church, 1884; Pastor, Seventh Ave. Chapel of Fifth Ave. Presb. Church, 1883-9; Chalmers Presb. Church, Seventh Ave., N. Y. City, 1889-92; 13th St. Presb. Church since 1892.

A. B., 1881, and A. M., 1884, from Univ., City of N. Y.

Married, May 16, 1882, Grace, da. of John H. Mortimer. Children: Grace Douglass and Mary Dun.

Cousin: George D. Young, 1887.

Capwell, Benjamin Avery. 108 Franklin St., N. Y. City.

Son of Albert Bently Capwell and Julia Ann (Sook) Capwell b. Brooklyn, N. Y., Dec. 17, 1858.

Junior Orator. Commencement Orator. Editor of University Quarterly, Sec'y and Pres. of Eucleian. Ψ. γ. and Φ. B. K.

With Phelps Publishing Co., Springfield, Mass.; in business in N. Y. City.

A. B., 1881, and A. M., 1884, from Univ., City of N. Y.

Cornelius, Albert Field. Hempstead, N. Y.

Son of Carman Cornelius and Phebe Jane (Combs) Cornelius b. East Meadow, N. Y.

Commencement Orator. Editor of University Quarterly. Sec'y and Vice-Pres. of Philomathean. Δ. Φ.

Columbia Coll. Law School, 1881~3; Lawyer; Dist. Attorney's office of Oueens Co. N. Y.

B. S., 1881, and C. E., 1881, from Univ., City of N. Y. LL.B., 1883, from

Columbia Coll.

Cudlipp, William Charles. 641 Jersey Ave., Jersey City, N. J.

Son of William Henry Cudlipp and Harriet Lavina (Edison) Cudlipp; b. Jersey City, N. J., June 15, 1860.

Sec'y, Vice-Pres. and Pres. of Philomathean. First Philomathean Essay Prize, 1881. Class Sec'y. Editor of University Quarterly. Marshal at Commencement. Δ. Φ.

Columbia Coll. Law School; Counselor-at-Law, at 1 Montgomery St., Jersey City

A. B., 1881, from Univ., City of N. Y.

Dawson, Henry Hollister. 750 Broad St., Newark, N. J.

Son of Edwin H. Dawson and Julia M. (HoUister) Dawson b. Newark, N. J., Oct. 31, 1860.

Senior Regent, 1880~1, and appointed Alternate in Mathematics for the Univ., 1881, in Intercollegiate Literary Ass'n. Class Treas., Senior Year. Class Prophet. Pres. and Sec'y of Philomathean. Editor of University Quarterly. Δ. γ.

Columbia Coll. Law School, 1881~3; Lawyer, N. Y. City, 1883-5; Newark, N. J., since 1885.

A. B., 1881, from Univ., City of N. Y. LL.B., 1883, from Columbia Coll.

Member of N. J. Historical Soc'y.

Married, May 7, 1890, Ida A., da. of John Wharton.

Dix, Samuel Morris. P. O. Box 153, Stapleton, N. Y.

Son of John Dunning Dix and Lorinda Morris (Kingsley) Dix b. Clifton, N. Y., July 22, 1860.

Ψ. γ.

Clerk with Henderson Bros., 1881~4; Dix & Co., 1884~5; Rochester and Pittsburgh Coal and Iron Co., 1885~7; United States Rolling Stock Co., 1888.

B. S., 1881, and M. S., 1888, from Univ., City of N. Y.

Brother: Joseph K., 1880 (non-grad.). Cousins: Wm. M. Kingsley, 1883; Louis L. Tribus, 1885, and Wm. P. H. Bacon, 1886.

Duncan, George Martin. 28 York Square, New Haven, Conn.

Son of James Duncan and Jane Martin (Torbet) Duncan b. Haledon, N. Y., Nov. 26, 1857.

Junior Orator, with Hon. Mention. First Butler Eucleian Essay Prizes, 1880 and 1881. Junior Regent, 1879~80, and appointed Univ. Contestant in Mental Science in 1881, in Intercollegiate Literary Ass'n. English Salutatorian and Second Fellow ($200). Pres. of Class, Junior Year. Sec'y, Librarian, Vice-Pres. and Pres. of Eucleian. Ψ. γ. and Φ. B. K.

Yale Divinity School, 1881~4; Yale Univ., 1884; Univ. of Jena, Germany, 1885; Leipsic Univ., 1885-6; Heidelberg Univ., 1886; Berlin Univ., 1886~7; Univ. of Paris, France, 1887~8; Instructor in Philosophy, Yale Univ., 1888~91; Ass't Prof, of Philosophy, Yale Univ., since 1891.

A. B., 1881, and A. M., 1884, from Univ., City of N. Y. B. D., 1884, from Yale Univ.

Married, Aug. 29, 1889, Mary A., da. of Theodore R. Carter. (See bibliography.)

Frost, Edward Lawrence. Floral Park, N. Y.

Son of Marshall S. Frost and Cornelia (Valentine) Frost b. Glen Cove, N. Y., Oct. 4, 1859.

Sec'y and Pres. of Philomathean. Class Treas. Ψ. γ.

Columbia Coll. Law School, 1881~3; Lawyer.

A. B., 1881, from Univ., City of N. Y. LL.B., 1883, from Columbia Coll.

Married, Oct. 21, 1885, Aletta M., da. of Thomas H. Frederick. Children: Herbert E. and Roswell.

Hamburger, Isaac. 915 N St., N. W., Washington, D. C.

Son of Morris Hamburger and Anna (Levy) Hamburger b. N. Y. City, Sept. 15, 1860.

Junior Orator. Scientific Orator (First Honor with E. F. Pearce). Treas. of Class. Sec'y of Philomathean. Appointed Univ. Contestant in Mathematics in Intercollegiate Literary Ass'n, 1881. Δ. γ. and Φ. B. K.

Stenographer and Ass't Sec'y, Montana Stock Growers' Ass'n, and State Board of Stock Commissioners, Montana, 1886~8; Stenographer, U. S. Judicial District Court, Montana, 1886~9; Private Sec'y, Hon. T. H. Carter; Clerk of Committee on Mines and Mining, U. S. House of Representatives, since 1889 Private Sec'y of Senator T. C. Power, Montana; Clerk of U. S. Senate Committee on Civil Service Reform.

B. S., 1881, from Univ., City of N. Y.

Hazen, George Hannum. 33 E. 17th St., N. Y. City.

Son of Miner C. Hazen and Lemira R. (Judson) Hazen b. Middletown, Conn., Jan. 17, 1858.

Philomathean Junior Orator. Editor of University Quarterly. Pres. of Philomathean. Class Sec'y. Ψ. γ.

With the Century Co. since 1881.

A. B., 1881, and A. M., 1884, from Univ., City of N. Y.

Married, July 9, 1885, Ella, da. of William Gardner. Children: Charles Sumner and William Gardner.

Hillman, William Henry. 214 Division Ave., Brooklyn, N. Y.

Son of Alexander Campbell Hillman and Anna Cochran (McGinness) Hillman b. Brooklyn, N. Y., Apr. 21, 1862.

Junior Orator. Philosophical Orator. Δ. γ. and Φ. B. K.

Clerk with Phelps, Dodge & Co. since 1881.

A. B., 1881, from Univ., City of N. Y.

Brother: James W., 1873.

Holmes, Franklin Sawyer, 455A Macon St., Brooklyn, N. Y.

Son of Franklin Holmes and Martha Chickering (Sawyer) Holmes.

Pres. of Philomathean. Junior Orator. Commencement Orator. Newspaper Work, 3 years; Salesman of Electric Goods; Manager of Electric Light Station, St. George, S. I., N. Y., 1888~9; Electrical Engineer with C. H. Davis, since 1889.

A. B., 1881, from Univ., City of N. Y. Member of Am. Soc'y of Electrical Engineers.

Pearce, Eugene Frederick. 95 Henry St., Brooklyn, N. Y.

Son of Frederick Pearce and Margaretta E. (Keane) Pearce b. Brooklyn, N. Y., Sept. 12, 1858.

Junior Orator. Valedictorian (First Honor with I. Hamburger) and First Fellow {$300). Ψ. γ. and Φ. B. K.

Long Island Coll. Hosp., 1881~3; Interne, Long Island Coll. Hosp., 1883-4; Physician.

A. B., 1881, from Univ., City of N. Y. M. D., 1883, from Long Island Coll. Hosp.

Married, Feb. 3, 1885, Emily S., da. of Charles H. Lyons. Children: Frederick Kingsley and Edna Serviss.

Raque, Edward. P. O. Box 53, West Nyack, N. Y.

Son of Charles Godfrey Raque and Anna Francisco (Jaeckel) Raqu6 b. Jersey City, N. J., Sept. 2, 1861.

Δ. Φ.

Draughtsman, C. B. and Q. R. R., 1881; Topographer and Ass't Engineer, South Penna. R. R., 1882~5; Ass't Engineer, Harlem River Bridge Construction,

1886~9; Ass't Engineer French Co., Venezuelan Railways, 1889; Resident Engineer, Harlem River Bridge Commission, 1890~1; Ass't Engineer, Atlas Iron Construction Co. since 1892.

B. S., 1881, and C. E., 1881, from Univ., City of N. Y.

Married, Feb. 22, 1893, Lillie D., da. of George W. Nickerson.

Staniford, Charles Wilkinson. 62 Berkeley Place, Brooklyn, N. Y.

Son of Daniel Staniford and Caroline Cecilia (Fawcett) Staniford b. Rockport, Mass., Feb. 19, 1861.

Leveler, Construction of Coney Island Elevated R. R., 1880; Surveyor of Routes, and Inspector of Construction of Mutual Union Telegraph Co., 1881~3; Topographer of Survey, South Penna. R. R., 1883~5; 5 Resident Engineer in Charge of 9 miles Construction of South Penna. R. R., 1885~6; Charge of Party Surveying Extension, Lake Chautauqua R. R., 1886; Topographer of Survey of Buffalo Extension, Lehigh Valley R. R., 1886~7; Charge of Parties Surveying North Western and South Atlantic R. R. from Wilmington, N. C, to Bristol, Tenn., 1886~7; Div. Engineer, Louisville and Nashville R. R., 1887~8; Charge of Construction of 32 miles of Cumberland Valley Branch and Terminal, Florence, Ala., 1888; Ass't Survevor, Dept. of Docks, N. Y. City.

B. S., 1881, and C. E., 1881, from Univ., City of N. Y.

Member Am. Soc''y Civil Engineers.

Married, June 8, 1886, Julia M., da. of Capt. Wm. M. Schrock. Children: Charles Wilkinson and Foye Fawcett.

Underwood, Horace Grant. (30 Vesey St., N, Y. City.) Seoul, Korea.

Son of John Underwood and Elizabeth (More) Underwood; b. London, Eng., July 19, 1859.

Webster Junior Oratory Prize. Commencement Orator. Editor of University Quarterly. Editor and Vice-Pres. of Philomathean. Δ. γ.

Theol. Sem. of Ref. Dutch Church, New Brunswick, N. J., 1881~4.; Post-Graduate Course, Rutgers Coll., 1882~4.; Ordained Minister, Ref. Dutch Church, 1884.; Pastor, Pompton, N. J., 1884.; Missionary to Korea, since 1885.; Prof, of Chemistry and Nat. Philosophy, Royal Korean Hosp. Med. Coll., 1887-90.; Pastor, Union Church, Korea, 1888~9.; Chairman Korean Bible Committee, 1887~91.; One of the two Translators Appointed to Translate the Bible into Korean.; Treas., Korea Presb. Mission, 1885~89.; Chairman of Mission, 1888-90.; Cor. Sec'y, Korea Tract Soc'y, 1889.

A. B., 1881, and A. M., 1884, and D. D., 1892, from Univ., City of N. Y.

Married, Mar. 13, 1889, Dr. Lillias Sterling, da. of James Mandeville Horton.; Child : Horace Horton.

(See bibliography.)

Van Sant, Horatio Moses. 327 N. 7th St., Newark, N. J.

Son of Nicholas Van Sant and Amelia Paulina (Moses) Van Sant b. Haverstraw, N. Y., Nov. I, 1859.

Junior Orator. Commencement Orator. Pres. of Class, Senior Year. Ψ. γ. Clerk and Ins. Agt. Member of firm, Wood & Van Sant.

A. B., 1881, from Univ., City of N. Y.

Married, Apr. 24, 1884, Essy A., da. of Joseph S. Morriss. Children: Robert Morriss and Catharine Roxanna.

p. 222

Honorary Degrees.

1892.

D. D.

Isaiah B. Hopwood, '59 Newark, N. J

William R. Richards	Plainfield, N. J
*Philip Schaff, D. D., LL. D., Prof	New York City
William Taylor	Windermere, England
Horace Grant Underwood, '81	Seoul, Korea

p. 293

Biography

Underwood, Horace Grant, 1881.

1887. Translation of the gospels of Mark and John into Korean. Yokohama, Japan.

- Concise dictionary of the Korean language in two parts, Korean-English and English-Korean. 12 mo, pp. 196 and 293.

1889. An introduction to the Korean spoken language in two parts, grammar and practice. London. 12 mo, pp. 425.

1889~91. Various original and translated tracts in Korean.

19120605

뉴욕대학교, 제80회 졸업, 1912년 6월 5일. (*New York University, Eightieth Commencement, June 5th, 1912.*)

NEW YORK UNIVERSITY

EIGHTIETH
COMMENCEMENT

WEDNESDAY, JUNE 5th, 1912
AT ELEVEN, AND AT THREE O'CLOCK

IN THE
AUDITORIUM, UNIVERSITY HEIGHTS
NEW YORK CITY

MUSIC BY
Shannon's Twenty-Third Regiment Band, Thomas F. Shannon, Director;
and Orchestra, D. R. Philippi, Organist and Director

ROLL OF CANDIDATES, 1912

Honorary Degrees

THE FOLLOWING CANDIDATES WILL BE PRESENTED BY
REV. GEORGE ALEXANDER, D.D.,
President of the University Council.

For the Degree of Doctor of Divinity

Shepherd Knapp .... Worcester, Mass.
Pastor of the Central Congregational Church, Worcester, Mass.
John R. Mackay .... New York City
Pastor of the North Presbyterian Church, New York City.

For the Degree of Doctor of Laws

Edward Everett McCall .... New York City
N. Y. U., LL.B., 1884. Justice of the Supreme Court of the State of New York.
Horace Grant Underwood .... Seoul, Korea
N. Y. U., A.B., 1881; A.M., 1884; D.D., 1892; Missionary; Chairman of the Korean Educational Federation; Professor of Theology in the Korean Theological Seminary; Principal of John D. Wells Training School of Seoul, Korea.

Degrees Upon Examination

THE FOLLOWING CANDIDATES WILL BE PRESENTED BY
DEAN FRANCIS HOVEY STODDARD, PH.D.

For the Degree of Bachelor of Arts

Ralph Romaine Bruster, *cum laude* .... New York City
Frederick Amerman Dale .... New York City
John Wesley Dutcher .... Paterson, N. J.
Bhupendra Nath Dutt .... Calcutta, India
Emanuel Ralph Engel .... Brooklyn, N. Y.
James Vincent FitzGerald .... Saratoga Springs, N. Y.
Ion Carl Holm .... Brooklyn, N. Y.
Raymond Wright Masters .... Chester, N. Y.
Albert John Murphy .... New York City
Hamilton Sherborne Peltz .... Elmhurst, L. I.
John Preston Phillips .... Yonkers, N. Y.
Elmo Eugene Spoerl .... Hempstead, L. I.
Samuel David Stein, *summa cum laude* .... New York City
Presley Downs Stout, *summa cum laude* .... East Orange, N. J.
John Patrick Tiernan .... Tompkinsville, S. I.
Charles Shepperd Trimmer .... New York City
Horace Horton Underwood .... Seoul, Korea
17

For the Degree of Bachelor of Science in Pure Science

Yngve Pierre Brundin .... Corona, L. I.
Thomas Joseph Crawford .... New York City
Orlando Hayford Daniels .... New York City
Richard Edward Elliffe .... New York City
Benjamin Fischler .... Brooklyn, N. Y.
Morris Bernard Fleischer .... New York City
Herman Henneberger .... New York City
Raymond Hamilton Mathews .... Jersey City, N. J.
George Harvey Nicholls .... New Rochelle, N. Y.
Ira Streusand .... New York City
10

19180000

Lillias H. Underwood, *Underwood of Korea*. Fleming H. Revell Company, New York, 1918, pp. 19~21, 23~29.[86)]

Chapter I
Ancestry And Training

At the age of ten, Horace, with a brother Fred, had been sent to a boys' boarding school in Boulogne Sur Mer, France.

It was a Roman Catholic school carried on by a Professor Die, whom the boys found to be good, wise and kind and who won their lasting affection and respect. No attempt at proselyting was made; the boys attended their own English church and kept their Protestant faith unshaken, but learned too a certain tolerance and good feeling toward Christians of that other church.

Many were the reminiscences related by Horace of these days at the seaside school, but one incident, a bed-time experience in the big dormitory full of French and English boys, is worth recounting, as it shows the caliber of these two boys as well as the sort of training they had had. Our little Underwoods, entering this cage of wild animals, entire strangers, calmly proceeded, after undressing, to kneel down as usual and say their prayers; upon the first glimpse of which unheard-of performance, loud yells of derision, cat calls and other persuasive signs of disapproval were in evidence. These, having no effect, were followed by tornados of pillows, boots, hair brushes, etc., but all to no purpose. The boys finished their prayers and calmly climbed into bed. For a few nights this scene was repeated but it finally dawned on the consciousness of the other English boys that, religion entirely aside, they ought to stand by their own nationals. At any rate, all of them began to say their prayers,

---

86) 호러스 언더우드의 학생시절에 대해 부인 릴리어스의 저서인 *Underwood of Korea*에서 해당 부분의 원문을 이곳에 실었다.

probably more as patriotic Englishmen than as good Christians. Henceforth shoes and other projectiles were a little less freely bestowed where so many gallant lads might be counted on to defend their faith with their fists next morning. So, little by little, it became quiet at prayer time, and one by one the French boys, too, began to pray, so that after a while all the boys in their dormitory said prayers at bed time, all through the persistence of two unafraid, determined little fellows.

While in New Durham, the boys helped in the garden, in the house and in the ink factory with willing hands, but somehow the father seemed to think that Horace must not go into business. It may have been because even as a child he had expressed a wish to become a minister and a missionary. However that may be, he was sent to Hasbrooke Seminary for boys in Jersey City and later on, placed under the care of the Rev. Dr. Mabon, then of Grove Church, to be tutored in preparation for college. He took to his books with the avidity of a real scholar and in six months had learned all the Greek necessary to admit him to college. During these early years in America, the boys were engaged in much evangelistic work. Besides three or four regular services of church and Sunday school, they attended a mission school and engaged in tract distribution in some of the worst localities of Union Hill. They met active opposition in one of the saloons and were roughly ordered to keep away. They bowed politely and calmly went again the following week quite undisturbed by bluster and profanity. They were threatened with the police but boys who could pray against a rabid dormitory, at ten years of age, were not deterred at sixteen and seventeen by one or two mere saloon keepers. So, like the French schoolboys, the saloon men eventually capitulated with what grace they might and even grew to be friendly with the indomitable and polite young evangelists.

Horace began his course of study at New York University in 1877, walking back and forth from New Durham to the college in New York, about seven miles, each day, taking the lightest of so-called luncheons, studying until twelve at night, and rising at five o'clock, with the same energy that characterized his whole life. He seemed absolutely incapable of sparing himself in any way, under any conditions. While at the University, he joined the Delta Upsilon, a non-secret society, and became an ardent and enthusiastic member. It was in the early days of the fraternity in that college, and the branch in New York University was very weak and in rather a critical condition, but with foresight, energy, diplomacy and skill, they managed, against a determined fight of other societies, to claim and initiate, apparently at the risk of life and limb, enough first-rate men of an incoming class to insure the future life of their fraternity.

Often have I heard him tell with infinite zest of that early contest. He had a great love for and pride in both his university and fraternity and later on, when a missionary and a Doctor of Divinity, one dark night, in walking down Broadway with another D. U. man they found themselves suddenly in a crowd from another college giving their fraternity yell with all the abandon of college boys out for a lark. Waiting an instant until they had paused for breath, our missionary divine and his brother raised stentorian voices and gave their own yells until the welkin rang, and before the astonished crowd could capture and punish, made good their escape in the dark, bubbling with glee. Horace entered college in 1877 and two years later his father began to fail. A malignant growth in the throat necessitated repeated, terribly painful treatments which he bore with the quiet courage of a Christian hero, but the cruel disease continued to progress until, on June 7th, 1881, this rare and good man passed away. He was a Christian of wonderful faith and spirituality. We hear of his engagement in much evangelistic work. A book of hymns constantly used by him during those last years is marked in a way which clearly, shows how bright was his hope, and how deep and far reaching his Christian experience. One of his closest and most intimate friends was Dr. Muller, the founder of the great orphanage in Bristol, carried on only by faith and prayer. John Underwood lived a rich, full life. In his business he had made a number of useful inventions, one of which was a safety check paper on which writing could not possibly be altered; another, an ink which would make seventy-five copies. Also, he invented the first copiable printing ink. He improved on the typewriter ribbons so that no others since made have been able to compare with them. He carried his experiments in making diamonds far enough to produce tiny specimens, the manufacture of which, however, was far too costly for profit, and so, not filling the family bread basket half so well as ink, nor proving half so nourishing, they were dropped as they deserved to be. Not his least service was in leaving sons bred and trained to carry on the work of the Kingdom of God with all their father's zeal, faith and devotion; a zeal often expressed in his and their favorite motto: "Laughs at impossibilities and says it shall be done"

Although his stay in America had been only nine years, John Underwood had made his mark, made easier the world's work, and left that undying influence for good which follows a righteous man after his body has gone to dust.

Horace graduated with high standing from New York University in 1881, taking the degree of A. B., and in the fall of that year entered the Dutch Reformed Theological Seminary at New Brunswick. Dr. Mabon, his much beloved pastor, at the same time assumed the chair of Systematic Theology in the institution. One who observed Horace as he entered the seminary, writes: "I shall never forget the first time I saw him. He was walking up the path toward the seminary in New Brunswick, at the beginning of his student days and I asked somebody who he was. The earnestness and concentration of purpose in his face impressed me very strongly even at that thnc." Another writes: "He made the impression of consecration and the possession of spirituality and intellectual power even then." Perhaps it may not be amiss to attempt a sketch of the young fellow as he appeared at that time. He was about five feet, eight or nine inches in height; broad shouldered, with a rather uncommonly large double-crowned head thatched with thick dark chestnut curly hair, growing low on the forehead. His features were all finely chiseled ; delicate, refined and yet strong. The nose was slightly aquiline and somewhat large but not noticeably so; the mouth sweet in expression without being effeminate; the chin firm and strong. The eyes were clear and dark brown and the whole expression told of sincerity, earnestness of purpose, enthusiasm and kindliness. But there was more: an indescribable something about the pure, calm brow and those dear eyes; a gentleness and other-worldliness, probably conferred by that saintly mother who had so long ago gone to rest.

The three years spent in New Brunswick were crowded to overflowing, pressed down, shaken together and running over with every form of evangelistic work which an active and intense young student could manage to crowd in between seminary duties. An old classmate writes: "I used to say you could see Horace with his coat-tails flying around some New Brunswick street on some religious work almost any day in the week, during his three years' stay in the seminary." This was much to the distaste of the faculty, who believed it could not but be to the disadvantage of his studies, but they tried in vain to interfere. They had come in contact with a personality not easily controlled. "Woe is me if I preach not the gospel," was his feeling, and as all he did seemed not to prevent his high standing in his classes, or interfere with a wonderful constitution which stood like iron the strain of only five hours' sleep, and nineteen of study and work, they really found little to say and nothing to do. A Doctor Easton, the pastor of the largest Dutch Reformed Church of New Brunswick at that time, was a man after our student's own heart. On fire with a passion for souls, he soon had the staid and at one time rather cold, old church at white heat crowded to overflowing with continual revivals, wonderful conversions, early and late prayer meetings, after-meetings and an awakened interest in all the neighboring churches. In all this, Horace took the part which might have been expected of an assistant pastor. One who knew him well reports that he would attend seven or eight different services on Sunday during that period.

The Salvation Army also set up a station in New Brunswick for the first time while he was in the seminary. In those days they were looked upon with more or less disapproval if not positive distrust by most conservative church people, among whom the Dutch Reformed are the first. So the feelings of the faculty and family may be better imagined than described when he threw himself heart and soul into this work, marched and spoke in their street and barrack meetings, and so identified himself with them that his sisters became greatly alarmed lest he should join the army out and out. He always loved them, and often in later years, when passing a little group of them at a street comer, he and I would stop and join in their singing and prayers with zest and give them the right hand of fellowship. On the foreign field he was one of the warmest supporters and friends of the Salvationists there. The truth was that whenever he saw people working for Christ he saw brothers who had a claim upon his great sympathy and service. He never had any strong sectarian, class, or race bias. More than any one else I have ever seen he seemed to feel a real brotherhood with people of all races, nationalities, classes, ages, and sects. The whole current of his being set toward unity. He involuntarily tended to draw into close, helpful, loving fellowship with all living souls. No one was too low or too high, too broad or too narrow; too white or too black for his sympathy, interest and love.

He belonged to that fraternity of which Paul writes: "There is neither Jew nor Greek; there is neither bond nor free; there is neither male nor female, for ye are all one in Christ Jesus." This marked trait of character was often illustrated in his life in the East, in a foreign community made up of European? and Americans of all classes of society, all shades of religious beliefs, from the titled diplomat to the flotsam and jetsam of wandering ne'er do wells ; from the high Anglican church missionary to the atheist ; and all in the midst of the great non-Christian Oriental races of China, Japan and Korea. He was the friend and brother of everybody, from the king to the coolie, and sooner or later found an opportunity to succor, sympathize with, or show his good-will to one and all, realizing the often over-looked truth that everybody in this sad world needs a friend. But especially did he make light of or set aside altogether all sectarian barriers in his relations with other Christian workers, longing to bring them all into the closest unity. This was one of the great desires of his life, "that they all should be one."

I have made quite a digression from my story, but this which had been characteristic of the lad, was so strengthened and developed with years, it deserves to be well understood at the beginning of a study of his life.

제3부

선교사 임명과 내한

Part 3.
Appointment as a Missionary and Coming to Korea

1.
선교사 지원 (Application as a Missionary to Korea)

언더우드가 한국 선교에 나서기로 결심하는 데에는 이수정의 호소가 가장 큰 영향을 미쳤다. 이수정의 글은 *The Missionary Review* 1884년 3월호에 실렸으므로 그가 한국행을 고려한 것도 이즈음이었던 것으로 추정된다. 그는 자신이 속해 있던 개혁교회에 한국 파송을 요청했다. 하지만 개혁교회는 예산이 부족하고 한 명의 선교사로 새로운 선교지부를 설립하는 것은 적절하지 않다며 이 요청을 거절하였다. 한국행을 두고 계속 고민하던 언더우드는 마침 미국 북장로회에서 한국으로 파송할 목회선교사를 필요로 한다는 소식을 듣고 지원하였다.

언더우드는 7월 10일자로 나이, 건강, 가족, 어학 능력, 기혼이나 미혼 중 어느 상태로 파송되기를 원하는지, 선호 사항, 희망하는 사역지, 신앙 경력, 선교에 지원하게 된 특별한 이유 등의 내용이 담긴 지원 편지를 보냈다. 이와 함께 각종 추천서 및 증명서가 미국 북장로회 해외선교본부로 보내졌다. 학력과 관련하여 뉴욕대학교(크로스비 전 총장, 코클리 수학 교수, 베어드 그리스어 및 문학 교수)와 신학교 교수들(우드브리지, 데마레스트, 메이본)의 편지가 선교본부로 보내졌다. 그리고 교회와 관련하여 개혁교회의 추천서(이스턴, 뉴브런즈윅 제1개혁교회 목사)를 받았고, 또한 건강 상태에 관한 주치의사의 소견서도 보내졌다. 언더우드의 한국행 지원과 관련하여 특히 미국 개혁교회의 해외선교본부 교신총무인 콥도 미국 북장로회 해외선교본부로 편지를 보내 언더우드를 적극 추천하였다.

언더우드의 선교사 지원과 관련된 편지들은 1884년 7월 14일에 열린 미국 북장로회 해외선교본부 실행위원회에 제시되었고, 7월 28일 개최된 실행 위원회에서 논의되어 미국 북장로회의 해외선교사로 임명됨과 동시에 한국이 임지로 정해졌다. 이로서 언더우드는 미국 북장로회 최초의 한국 파송 목회선교사로 임명되었는데, 언더우드의 선교사 지원과 임명은 예외적으로 상당히 신속하게 이루어진 것이었다.

선교사로 임명 받은 언더우드에게 아직 해결해야 할 문제가 남아 있었다. 아직 목사 안수를 받지 못했던 것이다. 결국 언더우드는 11월 3일 버겐노회로부터 강도사 자격을 받았고, 11월 14일 뉴브런즈윅노회로부터 목사안수를 받았으며, 같은 날 저지 시(市)의 장로회 노회로 적이 변경되었다.

이로서 언더우드는 화란개혁교회 소속이 아닌 미국 북장로회 소속의 목사가 되었다.

언더우드는 1884년 12월 샌프란시스코로 가기 위해 뉴욕에서 시카고를 향해 떠났는데, 이때 형 존 T. 언더우드가 동행하였다. 결국 언더우드는 12월 말경 미국을 떠나 다소 험난한 항해 끝에 1885년 1월 25일 일본 요코하마에 도착하였다. 헵번 선교사의 집에 머물던 언더우드는 3월 26일 요코하마를 출발했고, 4월 2일 부산을 거쳐, 5일 제물포에 도착하였다.

1-1 선교사 지원 편지

Application Letter of Horace G. Underwood

18840710

뉴더햄의 호러스 G. 언더우드가 프랭크 F. 엘린우드에게 보낸 편지, (1884년 7월 10일).

접수? 7월 11일

뉴더햄, 뉴저지
1884년 7월 10일

장로교회 해외선교본부 귀중,

안녕하십니까 -

저는 뉴브런즈윅신학교에서 신학 과정을 방금 마쳤으며, 미국 개혁교회의 뉴저지 주 버겐 노회에서 강도사 자격을 받았습니다.

신학교에 갓 입학했을 때 저는 이교도 지역에서 사역할 필요성이 막대함에도 아직도 그런 일꾼들이 턱없이 부족함에 주목했고, 기도를 통해 심사숙고한 끝에 제 일생을 해외 선교 사역에 헌신하기로 결심하였습니다. 처음에 이러한 결심은 단순히 이교도들에게 전도하겠다는 소망에 불과했지만, 이 소망은 점점 확대되어 지금 저는 "만일 내가 이교도들에게 복음을 전하지 않는다면 사랑은 없다"고 생각하고 있습니다.

저는 해외 선교 사역에 나서려 하고 있지만 몇 개월 전에 한국인들 중에 선교사를 파견해 달라는 이수정의 진지한 호소를 읽기 전까지 어느 선교지로 가야하는

지 결정하지 못했습니다.[87] 저의 심장은 이 호소에 의해 꿈틀거렸으며, 어떤 결과가 이루어질지 조마조마하며 주시해 왔습니다. 하지만 한동안 아무 것도 이루어지지 않았으며, 제가 속해 있는 (개혁교회의) 선교본부에 파송해달라고 억지로 요청해야 함을 느꼈습니다. (하지만) 그들은 기금의 부족으로 제 요청을 받아들일 수 없었습니다.[88] 그렇다면 다른 교회의 선교본부에 요청해야 하는가? 혹은 다른 선교지로 파송되어야 만 하는가? 혹시 하나님의 손길이 내가 한국으로 들어가지 말도록 말씀하시는 것은 아닌가? 이러한 질문들이 제 마음 속에 가득 찼습니다. 저는 어느 길로 가야 할지 몰랐습니다.

이에 대한 기도와 고민 끝에 저는 하루하루, 그리고 매주일 마다 주님께서 주신 일을 하다 보면, 제 차례가 올 것이라는 결론을 내렸습니다. 그렇게 지내오다 몇 주 전에 저는 장로회 선교본부에서 한국에 선교부를 개설할 예정이며, 이미 의료 선교사는 임명했고, 그와 함께 파송할 안수 받은 목사를 구한다는 소식을 들었습니다.[89]

저는 이 사안에 대해 며칠 동안 기도와 심사숙고한 끝에 귀 선교본부에 한국에서의 선교 사역을 위해 저를 임명해 줄 것을 요청하기로 결심하였고, 이에 지원하는 바입니다.

---

87) 이수정(李樹廷, Rijutei, 1842?~1886?)은 임오군란이 일어났을 때 민비를 충주로 피신시킨 공로로 1882년 9월 수신사 박영효의 수행원으로 일본으로 건너갔다. 그는 1883년 4월 29일 일본에서 한국인 최초의 세례를 받았고, 이후 루미스를 도와 성경을 한글로 번역하였다. 그가 세례를 받은 사실은 미국 북장로회의 녹스에 의해 미국으로 전해져 여러 선교본부의 관심을 받았다. 당시 일본의 기독교인과 일부 선교사들은 한국에 대한 선교를 일본인이 시작해야 한다는 주장을 하고 있었으나, 이수정은 이를 강력하게 반대했고 1883년 12월 13일자로 미국의 기독교인들에게 편지를 보내 한국에 선교사들을 파송해 줄 것을 요청했다. 이 요청은 기존에 알려진 것처럼 한국에 대한 선교 개시를 주시하고 있던 미국 북장로회의 맥윌리엄스를 움직여 한국 선교부 개설을 위해 5천 달러를 기증하게 했을 뿐 아니라, 이 편지에서 나타나듯 신학교 졸업을 앞둔 언더우드에게도 영향을 미쳤고 결국 언더우드는 미국 북장로회가 임명한 한국 최초의 목회 선교사가 되었다. Rijutei, "Rijutei to the Christian of America. Greeting." *Missionary Review of the Word* 7(1884), 145~6.

88) 1884년 2월의 일이었다.

89) 미국 북장로회는 한국에 파송할 첫 선교사로 1884년 4월 28일 의사 헤론을 임명한 바 있다.

저는 지금 거의 25세가 되며, 건강하고 거의 철(鐵) 같은 체질을 갖고 있습니다.

저는 뉴브런즈윅(신학교)의 메이본 교수의 지도로 대학 입학 준비를 했으며, 1881년 뉴욕대학교를 졸업했고, 지난 5월 뉴브런즈윅에 있는 신학교를 졸업했습니다. 저는 강도사 자격을 받았으며, 해외 선교 사역을 위해 안수해 주도록 요청한 상태입니다.

저는 언어 배우는 것을 대단히 좋아하며, 어떤 언어이든 어렵지 않게 배울 수 있을 것으로 생각합니다. 미혼 상태로 파송될 것으로 예상되지만, 결혼을 하고 파송될지 혹은 독신으로 파송될 지는 현재로서는 분명하지 않습니다. 제가 해외 선교지로 가려는 이유는 그곳에서 일꾼들이 많이 필요하지만 그 사역에 나서는 사람의 수가 적기 때문입니다. 또한 (제가) 언어에 대한 소양, 철 같은 체질, 그리고 더위와 추위, 고된 일 및 수면 부족 등을 견디어내는 힘 등 사역을 위한 분명한 적합성을 갖고 있기 때문입니다.

저는 이 사안에 대해 올바르게 인도되었다고 믿으며, 답장을 기다리고 있겠습니다. 안녕히 계십시오,,

호러스 G. 언더우드

Horace G. Underwood (New Durham, N. J.), Letter to Frank F. Ellinwood, (July 10th, 1884). PHS RG 31 37-10, #490~1.

Rec? July 11

New Durham, N. J.

July 10th, 1884

To the Board of Foreign Missions of the Presbyterian Church,

---

90) PHS means Presbyterian Historical Society.

Gentlemen: -

I have just finished my theological course at the New Brunswick Theological Seminary & have been licensed to preach by the Classis of Bergen (N. J.) of the Ref. Ch. of America.

During the early part of my first year in the Seminary my attention was called (I believe by the spirit of God) to the great & enormous need & yet the scarcity of workers among the heathen & after prayerful consideration I determined to devote my life to Foreign Missionary labors. At first it was not much more than a desire to preach to the heathen but this desire has so steadily grown upon me that now there seems a "love is nil if I preach not the Gospel to the heathen" hanging over me.

While my attention had been called to Foreign labor I had not decided which field I ought to enter until some months ago I read the earnest appeal of Rijutei for missionaries among the Coreans. My heart was stirred by the appeal & I anxiously watched to see what would be done. For some time nothing was done & I felt forced to ask my own Board to send me to Corea. This they felt they could not do on account of lack of funds. Should I apply to another Board? Ought I to go to some other field? Was not this the hand of God telling me that it was not for me to go to Corea? Such questions as these filled my mind. I did not know which way to turn.

After praying & worrying over it a good deal I concluded that I ought to go on with what the Lord gave me to do from day to day & week to week & in my own time be would open by the way. Thus it rested until a few weeks ago I heard that the Presbyterian Board were about to open a mission in Corea, that they had appointed a physician & wished to send with him an ordained minister.

After give to the matter several days of prayerful consideration I concluded to & do now apply to you for an appointment to Mission work in Corea.

I am now almost turned 25 & have a strong & almost iron constitution.

I prepared for college under Prof Mabon of New Bruswick graduated from the New York University in 1881, & from the Theological Seminary at New Brunswick in

May last. I have been licensed to preach & have applied to the Classis of Bergen for Ordination to Foreign Mission work.

I have a decided fondness for languages & think that I can acquire them with ordinary facility. Relative to my going out married or single I am at present undecided though I expect to go out unmarried. My reasons for desiring to enter to Foreign Mission field were the great need of workers there, the smallness of the number entering the work & an apparent fitness for the work, consisting in a fondness for languages an iron constitution & the power of enduring heat & cold, hard labor, & loss of sleep.

Trusting that I have been guided aright in this matter & awaiting a reply. I remain,

Yours most respectfully
Horace G. Underwood

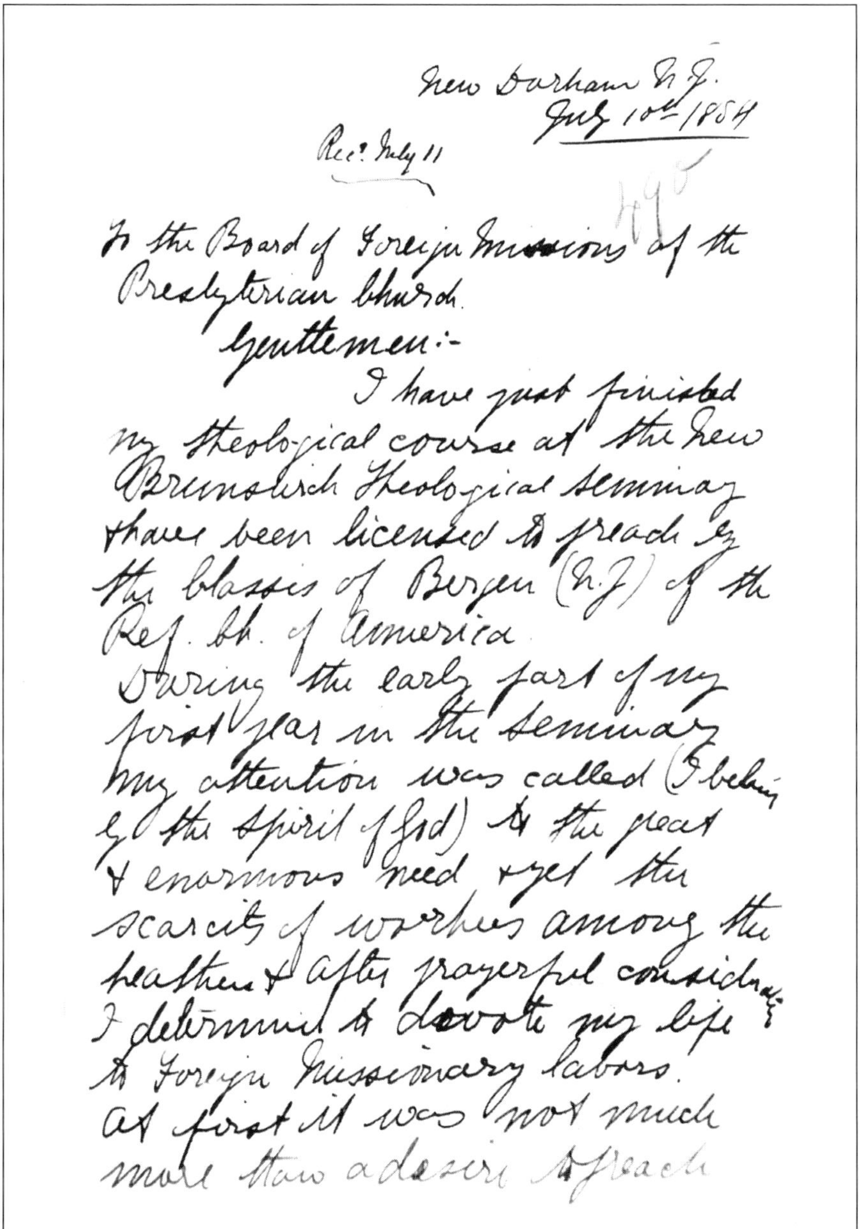
New Durham N.J.
July 10th 1884

Rec'd July 11

490

To the Board of Foreign Missions of the Presbyterian Church.

Gentlemen:-

I have just finished my theological course at the New Brunswick Theological Seminary & have been licensed to preach by the Classis of Bergen (N.J.) of the Ref. Ch. of America.

During the early part of my first year in the Seminary my attention was called (I believe by the Spirit of God) to the great & enormous need & yet the scarcity of workers among the heathen & after prayerful consideration I determined to devote my life to Foreign Missionary labors.

At first it was not much more than a desire to preach

자료 3-1 언더우드의 선교사 지원 편지. 모두 5쪽이다.

to the heathen but this desire has so steadily grown upon me that now there seems a "Woe is me if I preach not the Gospel to the heathen" hanging over me.
While my attention had been called to Foreign labor I had not decided which field I ought to enter until some months ago I read the earnest appeal of Ripintic for Missionaries among the Coreans. My heart was stirred by the appeal & I anxiously watched to see what would be done. For some time nothing was done & I felt forced to ask my own Board to send me to Corea. This they felt they could not do on account of lack of funds. Should I apply to another Board? Ought I to go to some other

field? Was not this the hand of God telling me that it was not for me to go to Korea? Such questions as these filled my mind. I did not know which way to turn.

After praying & worrying over it a good deal I concluded that I was going to go on with what the Lord gave me to do from day to day & week to week & in his own time he would open up the way. Thus it rested until a few weeks ago I heard that the Presbyterian Board were about to open a Mission in Korea, that they had appointed a Physician & wished to send with him an ordained minister. After giving to the matter several days of prayer put consideration I concluded to & do now apply to you for an appointment to Mission work in Korea.

I am now almost turned 25 & have a strong & almost iron constitution.

I prepared for college under Prof Mabon of New Brunswick graduated from the New York University in 1881 & from the Theological Seminary at New Brunswick in May last. I have been licensed to Preach & have applied to the Classis of Bergen for Ordination to Foreign Mission Work. I have a decided fondness for languages & think that I can acquire them with ordinary facility. Relative to my going out married or single I am

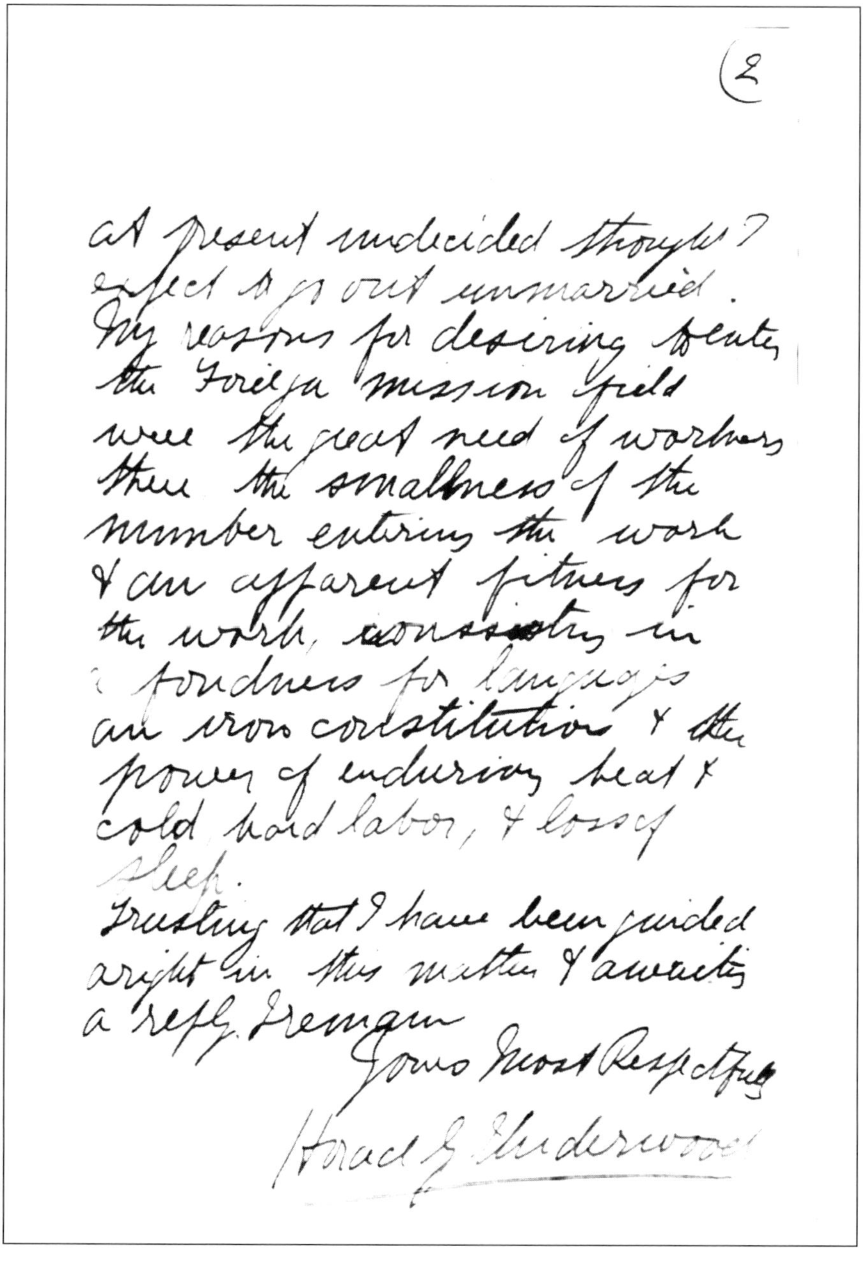

(2

at present undecided though I
expect to go out unmarried.
My reasons for desiring to enter
the Foreign mission field
were the great need of workers
there the smallness of the
number entering the work
& an apparent fitness for
the work, consisting in
a fondness for languages
an iron constitution & the
power of enduring heat &
cold, hard labor, & loss of
sleep.
Trusting that I have been guided
aright in this matter & awaiting
a reply I remain

Yours Most Respectfully

Horace G. Underwood

1-2 언더우드의 선교사 임명과 관련된 각종 추천서

Various Testimonials for Horace G. Underwood

18840703

뉴욕대학교 헨리 M. 베어드의 추천서, (1884년 7월 3일).

뉴욕대학교

1884년 7월 3일

저는 호러스 G. 언더우드 씨가 한국으로 파송되겠다고 [귀 교회의] 해외선교본부에 지원한 것을 알게 되었으며, 대단히 기쁘게 그의 기독교적인 품성과 능력에 대한 저의 판단에 대해 몇 자 적습니다.

언더우드 씨는 뉴욕대학교에서 4년 동안 저의 학생이었으며, 1881년 졸업반입니다. 그는 대학생으로서 모든 일들을 수행함에 있어 성실하고 양심적이었으며, 자신의 동급생들, 더 나아가 동료 학생들과의 관계에 관한 한 매우 건전한 영향력을 발휘했습니다. 그의 성적은 나무랄 데 없었으며, 그의 학식은 만족스러울 뿐 아니라 장차 학문의 진보 및 지적 발달에 대한 큰 기대를 주었습니다. 그가 한국인들 중에서 선교 사역을 위해 일생을 바치도록 부름을 받은 것은 하느님의 뜻임에 틀림없으며, 저는 그가 유능하고 헌신적이며, 따라서 자신이 진정으로 성공적인 – 그의 사역이 그 자신이나 그를 파송할 교회에 어떠한 부끄럼도 주지 않을 – 일꾼임을 증명할 것으로 기대하고 있으며, (저 또한) 그렇게 되도록 열렬하게 기도드릴 것입니다.

헨리 M. 베어드,

희랍어문학 교수

Henry M. Baird (University of the City of New York), Testimonial, (July 3rd, 1884). PHS RG 31 37-10, #471.

University of the City of New York,

July 3, 1884

Learning that Mr. Horace G. Underwood contemplates offering himself to the Board of Foreign Missions, to go to Corea, it is with great pleasure that I write these lines to express my appreciation of his Christian character and abilities.

Mr. Underwood was a pupil of mine in the institution for four years, graduating with the class of 1881. Faithful and conscientious in the performance of all his college duties, he exerted, so far as his relations with his classmates and fellow students extended, a very healthful influence. His record was beyond reproach, and his scholarship was not only satisfactory, but gave great promise of study improvement and intellectual growth in years to come. Should it be the will of God that he be called to devote his life to missionary work among the Coreans, it is my expectation, as it will be my fervent prayer, that he will prove an able and a consecrated, and therefore a truly successful worker - one of whose labours neither he nor the Church that sent him will have any reason to be ashamed.

Henry M. Baird,

Professor of the Greek Language and Literature

베어드(Henry Martyn Baird, 1832~1906)는 1832년 1월 17일 펜실베이니아 주 필라델피아에서 태어난 미국의 역사학자 및 교육자로서, 특히 위그노 교도(Huguenots)에 대한 연구로 유명하다. 그의 부친 로버트(Robert Baird, 1798~1863)는 미국과 유럽에서 장로교회의 전도사 및 저술가로 활동했다. 베어드는 유소년기에 8년 동안 파리와 제네바에서 살았으며, 1850년 뉴욕대학교를 졸업한 후, 2년 동안 이태리와 그리스에서 살았다. 이후 1853년부터 2년 동안 뉴욕의 유니언신학원에서 수학했으며, 1856년 프린스턴신학원을 졸업했다. 그는 4년 동안 뉴저지대학(지금의 프린스턴대학교)에서 강사로 활동했으며, 1859년부터 1906년 타계할 때까지 뉴욕대학교의 그리스어 및 문학 교수로 재임했다.

자료 3-2 베어드 교수(Henry M. Baird)

18840703

뉴욕의 헨리 N. 콥이 미국 북장로회 해외선교본부로 보낸 편지, (1884년 7월 3일).

미국 개혁교회 해외선교본부

비지 가(街) 34번지

뉴욕, 7월 3일, 1884년

북장로교회

해외선교본부 귀중.

친애하는 형제들께:

얼마 전 호러스 G. 언더우드 씨는 우리에게 선교사로서 한국으로 파송해 달라고 지원하었습니다. 낭시 우리 선교본부는 새로운 선교부를 설립할 수 없었으며, 아직까지도 설립할 수 없기에, 어쩔 수 없이 그 요청을 거절할 수밖에 없었습니다. 하지만 (우리 선교본부는) 그를 중국의 아모이(厦門) 선교부로 파송할 수 있을 것으로 기대하였습니다. 만일 신의 섭리에 의해 어떤 방도가 생긴다면, 그는 한국으로 파송되려는 자신의 원래 의지를 추구하는 것이 자신의 특권이며 의무라고 생각하고 있습니다. 저는 귀 본부가 설립하려는 한국 선교부에 그가 적합한 인물로 판단한다면, 비록 제한된 범위일지라도 새로 열리는 왕국에 복음을 전하려는 시도에 있어 그는 자신과 관계되는 선교본부와 교회를 만족시킬 것이며, 우리는 그와 [그가 설립할] 선교부가 하느님의 손에 의해 성공하기를 소원하며 기도할 것입니다.

널리 확장되고 번성하는 귀 선교본부의 사역에 하나님의 은총이 내리기를 기원하면서,

그럼 안녕히 계십시오,

헨리 N. 콥

교신 총무

Henry N. Cobb (New York), Letter to the Board of Foreign Missions of the Presbyterian Church, (July 3rd, 1884). PHS RG 31 37-10, #462.

Board of Foreign Missions
of the
Reformed Church of America,
34 Vesey Street,

New York, July 3rd, 188 4

To the Board of Foreign Missions
of the Presbyterian Church.

Dear Brethren:

Mr. Horace G. Underwood applied to us some time ago to be sent as a missionary of the Board to Corea. As the Board were unable under pressive of exciting engagements, to esta[blish] a new mission at that time, and are still unable, as one reluctantly obliged to decline the offer, hoping, however, that we might [be] able to secure his services for our Amoy Mission in China. As he feels it his privilege and duty, if the way be Providentially open, to pursue his original intention a__ go to Corea. I have only to say that if you should judge him a suitable person for that mission, which we understand you are about [to] establish, I have no doubt it will give plea[sure] to the Board and the Church to be associated, even to so limited an extent, in the attempt to evangelize that newly opened Kingdom, and that he and the mission will be followed by our best wishes and prayers for the wishes to success from the hand of the Lord.

Praying the blessing of God upon all your widely extended and growing work, I am

Yours sincerely,
Henry N. Cobb
Cor. Sec.

자료 3-3 콥(Henry Nitchie Cobb)

콥(Cobb, Henry Nitchie, 1834~1910)은 1834년 11월 15일 뉴욕에서 출생했으며, 1910년 4월 17일 75세의 나이로 뉴저지 주 이스트 오렌지에서 사망했다.

그는 1855년 예일대학, 1857년 유니온신학교를 졸업했으며 1860년 뉴욕 제3장로교회에서 안수를 받고 American Board of Foreign Missions에 의해 페르시아와 쿠르디스탄의 선교사로 파송되었다. 건강 악화로 2년 만에 귀국한 콥은 1866년부터 뉴욕 밀브룩의 개혁교회의 목사로 시무했다. 1877년 그는 해외선교본부의 위원으로 선임되었으며, 1882년 교신총무로 임명되어 1910년까지 활동했다.

따라서 화란개혁교회에 선교사로 파송해 줄 것을 요청한 언더우드의 편지는 바로 교신총무 콥이 받았던 것이다.

18840703

뉴저지 주 뉴브런즈윅의 윌리엄 V. V. 메이본이 미국 북장로회 해외선교본부로 보낸 편지, (1884년 7월 3일).

미국 북장로회 해외선교본부 귀중,

뉴 브런즈윅, 뉴저지 주

1884년 7월 3일

근계(謹啓):

호러스 지 언더우드 씨는 오늘 아침 제게 보낸 편지에서 자신을 한국으로 파송해 달라며 [귀 선교본부로] 지원한 것과 관련하여, 그 사역을 할 수 있다는 자신의 자질과 자격에 대한 분명한 평가를 귀 선교본부로 보내 달라고 요청하였습니다.

언더우드 씨는 약 10년 전 하나님의 뜻에 의해 런던에서 뉴욕으로 이주해 온 화학자인 집사 존 언더우드의 막내아들입니다. 그는 훌륭한 사람으로 ________. 호러스는 런던 혹은 에든버러에서 장로교회 목사였던 고(故) 워 박사의 손자입니다.

저는 이 젊은이와 그의 형에게 세례를 주었으며, 미국에서 그동안 죽 그의 선생이었고 유일한 목사였기에, 그의 자질을 사진과 같이 [정확하게] 설명할 수 있습니다. 간단히 말해 그는 기독교 사역의 열정, 능력 및 인간적 태도에 있어 모든 개혁교회에서 가장 전도가 유망한 청년입니다. 만일 그가 어떠한 결점이라도 갖고 있다면, 그것은 자신의 개인적인 편리를 넘어 자신의 양심이 인정한 그 무엇을 강하게 추진하도록 이끄는 풍부한 삶에 기인하거나 혹은 그가 열정적인 사람이기 때문일 것입니다.

그의 지적 능력과 관련하여, 그가 희랍어 알파벳을 처음 배운 것이 1877년 1월 1일이었는데, 그 해 6월 15일 아무런 조건 없이 뉴욕대학교에 입학한 사실만으로 충분할 것입니다.

그의 도덕적 측면과 관련하여, 그는 부친에게 행운이 따르기 전 오래 동안 부족함과 빈곤을 알았습니다.

그가 자신의 눈을, (한국) 정부의 보호를 받지 않고, '은자의 나라'로 돌리는 것을 목격하고 저에게 드리웠던 구름의 그림자가 걷혔습니다. 그가 교회, 해외 선교, 그리고 장로회 선교본부에 영광을 돌린 것에 하나님께 감사드립니다.

윌리엄 V. V. 메이본
제임스 루이텀 교수 설교학 및 변증신학

주의
언더우드 씨는 이 편지를 보지 않았습니다.

더불유 V. V. 에이본

Wm. V. V. Mabon (New Brunswick, NJ), Letter to the Sec'y of the Board of Foreign Missions, (July 3rd, 1884). PHS RG 31 37-10, #470.

To the Board of the Presbyterian Board of Foreign Missions

New Brunswick, N. J.
July 3rd, 1884

Dear Sir:

In a letter from Mr. Horace G. Underwood to me this morning he asks me to send to your Board accompanying his application to be sent to Corea, a discriminating account of his qualities and qualifications for the work in prospect.

Mr. Underwood is the youngest son of John Underwood deacon, a practical and theoretical Chemist who came in the Providence of God from London to New

York about ten years since. He was a magnificent person and had been ___d to the higher walks of life. Horace is the grandson of the late Rev. Dr. Waugh, Presbyterian Minister either in London or Edinburg.

As I baptized the young man and his brother, and have been his teacher throughout and his only Pastor in America, I might be relieved from a photographic description of his qualities, by the simple statement, that he is the most promising young man in the whole Reformed Church in the matter of zeal, efficiency in Christian work and personal manner. If he has any fault it is possibly in an abundance of life leading him to push whatever has the approval of his conscience beyond the convenience or it may be the taste of his ardent persons.

In regard to his brain power, it may be enough to say that he was introduced to the greek alphabet on the 1st of January 1877 and entered the N. Y. University without conditions on the 15th June the same year.

As to his moral hardihood, he knows what it is to have borne scantiness and penury during a number of years before his fathers fortunes turned for the better.

A shadow of a cloud passes over me as I see him bend his eyes toward a hermit nation without the security of a constitutional government, but thank God for the honor of presenting to the church, to the cause of Foreign Missions and to the Presbyterian Board the best possession in our hand.

Wm. A. Mabon
James Luydam Prof. of Dch. and Pol. Theology

N. B.
Mr. Underwood is not to see this note.

W. V. V. Mabon

메이본(William Van Vranken Mabon, 1822~1892)은 1822년 1월 24일 뉴저지 주 버겐 군 뉴브런즈윅에서 출생하였으며, 1854년 뉴브런즈윅신학교를 졸업한 후 그로브개혁교회에서 시무하였다. 그는 언더우드가 신학교에 입학하던 1881년 신학교 교수로 취임한 후 1892년 3월 11일 사망하였다.

자료 3-4 메이본 (William V. Mabon)

18840710

하워드 크로스비 (얼스터 카운티, 파인 힐), 추천서, (1884년 7월 10일).

호러스 G. 언더우드 씨는 뉴욕대학교의 1881년도 졸업반이었습니다. 그는 항상 성실한 학생이었으며, 교수들로부터 높은 평가를 받았습니다.

하워드 크로스비
뉴욕대학교 전 총장

파인 힐, 얼스터 카운티
1884년 7월 10일

Howard Crosby (Pine Hill, Ulster Co.), Testimonial, (July 10th, 1884). PHS RG 31 37-10, #489.

Mr. Horace G. Underwood was a member of the class of '81 in the University of the City of New York. He was always a faithful student and highly esteemed by the Faculty.

Howard Crosby
Ex Chancellor, N. Y. U.

Pine Hill, Ulster Co.
July 10, 1884

하워드 크로스비(Howard Crosby, 1826~91)는 미국 장로교회의 전도사, 학자 및 교수로서, 뉴욕에서 태어나 1844년 뉴욕대학교를 졸업했다. 그는 1851년 뉴욕대학교의 희랍어 교수로 임명되었으며, 1859년 럿거스대학의 그리스어 교수로 임명되었다. 1861년 그는 뉴브런즈윅 제1장로교회에서 목사 안수를 받았고, 1863년부터 사망할 때까지 뉴욕의 제4애버뉴 장로교회의 목사로 시무했다. 그는 영어본 신약성사의 역자 중의 한 명이었다.

그는 1870년부터 1881년까지 뉴욕대학교의 총장으로 활동했으며, 정치적으로도 뚜렷한 역할을 수행하였다. 그는 미국 철학협회의 회장으로도 활동했다.

자료 3-5 하워드 크로스비(Howard Crosby).

18840710

제임스 A. 블레이크 (브룩클린, 뉴욕), 증명서, (1884년 7월 10일).

브룩클린, 1884년 7월 10일

나는 호러스 언더우드 씨와 약 10년 동안 아는 사이였으며, 그의 건강 상태가 양호하고 보통보다 더 원기 왕성함을 증명합니다.

제임스 A. 블레이크, 의학박사.
퍼트넘 가(街) 194번지

Jas. A Blake (Brooklyn, New York), Testimonial, (July 10th, 1884). PHS RG 31 37-10, #465.

Brooklyn, July 10, 1884

I hereby certify that I have been acquainted with Mr. Horace Underwood about 10 years and I know that he is in good health and possessed of a physique more than ordinarily vigorous.

Jas. A. Blake, M. D.
194 Putnam Ave.

18840705

새뮤얼 M. 우드브리지 학장이 장로교회 해외선교본부로 보낸 편지, (1884년 7월 5일).

장로교회 해외선교본부 귀중.

나는 개혁교회 신학교를 최근 졸업한 호러스 G. 언더우드 씨가 해외 선교지에서 유능한 선교사가 될 것으로 판단하여 기꺼이 추천하는 바입니다. 3년 과정 중에 그는 자신이 갖고 있는 지적 재능을 보여주었고, 많은 것을 습득했으며, 기독교 사역에 열의와 헌신을 보여주었을 뿐 아니라 그가 받아들이기로 한 선교 사역에의 관심을 믿을 수 있을 실제적인 재능을 보여 주었습니다.

나는 개혁교회의 선교본부가 그를 파송할 수 없다는 점이 유감스러울 뿐입니다.

에스 M. 우드브리지
학장
1884년 7월 5일

S. M. Woodbridge (Dean of the Faculty), Letter to the Board of Foreign Missions Presbyterian Church, (July 5th, 1884). PHS RG 31 37-10, #473

To the Board of Foreign Missions of the Presbyterian Church.

I take pleasure in commending Mr. Horace G. Underwood, a recent graduate of the Theological Seminary of the Reformed Church as one fitted, in my judgement to be an efficient missionary in the foreign field. During his three years course, he has shown himself possessed of the intellectual gifts, and has made the acquirements, has manifested a zeal and devotion in christian work and withal a practical talent which indicated his fitness to be entrusted with the interests of a mission such as he proposes to accept.

I only regret that he could not have been sent out by the Board of the Reformed Church.

S. M. Woodbridge
Dean of the Faculty.
Inogue July 5th, 1884

새뮤얼 M. 우드브리지(Samuel Merrill Woodbridge, D.D., LL.D., April 5, 1819~June 23, 1905)는 미국의 목회자, 신학자, 저술가 겸 대학교수였다. 그는 매사추세츠 주의 그린필드에서 태어나 목사인 부친의 6남매 중 셋째로 태어나 1838년 뉴욕대학교를, 1841년 뉴브런즈윅신학교를 졸업했다. 그는 뉴욕과 뉴저지의 개혁교회 목사로 16년 동안 활동하다가 1857년 12월 뉴브런즈윅에 정착한 후 신학교에서 1901년까지 44년 동안 교회사와 직제학의 교수로 근무했다. 또한 럿거스대학에서도 7년 동안 교수로 강의를 담당했으며, 1883년부터 1901년까지 신학교 학장으로 재임했다.

자료 3-6 새뮤얼 M. 우드브리지(Samuel Merrill Woodbridge)

18840705

뉴저지 뉴브런즈윅의 토머스 C. 이스턴이 장로교회 해외선교본부로 보낸 편지, (1884년 7월 5일).

뉴브런즈윅, 뉴저지
1884년 7월 5일

해외선교본부
장로교회

사랑하는 형제께:

목사 호러스 그랜트 언더우드 씨는 우리 신학교의 졸업생이며, 주 예수 그리스도의 가장 열성적인 종으로 알고 있습니다.

그는 선교사로 한국으로 파송되기를 갈망하고 있습니다. 우리 교회는 현재로서는 한국으로 파송할 수 없으며, 그는 임명될 수 있다는 간절한 희망으로 귀 선교본부에 지원하였습니다.

지난 4년 동안 목사로서 그를 면밀하게 관찰한 결과 그의 자격 요건에 대해 감히 말씀드리고자 합니다.

첫째, 그의 학식. 그는 빨리 배우며 언어를 습득합니다. 그는 모든 과목에서 높은 점수를 받았으며, 새로운 언어를 즉시 습득할 것입니다.

둘째, 그의 신앙심. 그는 영혼을 개종시키는데 열렬한 열정을 소유하고 있습니다. 수 백 명이 그리스도께 인도되는 것을 목도했던 위대한 부흥회에서 그는 나의 가장 유능한 조력사요 동역자였습니다. 그는 전도 사역을 사랑하며, 선교사로서 크게 성공할 것입니다.

셋째, 그의 일반적인 자격 요건. 그는 인성에 대한 예리한 통찰력을 갖고 있습니다. 그는 사람을 빠르게 이해하며, 얻은 친구들을 유지합니다. 그는 인정이 있고 자비롭습니다. 그는 실제적인 상식이 풍부하여 곤경에 빠지지 않고 전진할 수 있으며,

어느 면에서나 선교본부를 복잡하게 만들지 않을 것입니다.

넷째, **그의 결점 및 약점.** 그는 과로하는 경향이 있으며, 자신의 건강을 충분히 고려하지 않습니다.[91] 그는 자신의 체력이나 지식 습득보다 더 복음 전도의 가치에 시간을 더 할애하는 경향이 있으며, 선교지로 들어가는 마당에 이 점을 분명해야 할 것입니다. 그는 지나치게 관대합니다. 그는 가난한 자를 돕기 위해 마지막 한 푼까지도 나누며, 자주 그가 주어야 하는 것보다 훨씬 더 많은 것을 도와줍니다.

여러 면에서 나는 언더우드 목사를 우리 주님의 고결한 종으로 여기며, 우리 교단이 우리의 힘으로 그를 붙잡기를 원합니다.

그러나 20년 이상동안 장로회 목사로 시무해 온 나는 그가 귀 선교본부로 지원했고, 귀 선교본부가 그를 한국으로 파송할 방도를 분명하게 모색하리라는 것에 기뻐하고 있습니다.

형제의 우의로,
토머스 C. 이스턴
목사
제1(화란)개혁교회
뉴브런즈윅
뉴저지

---

91) 과로하는 경향은 일에 몰두하면 다른 일을 잊어버리는 경향과 일맥상통한다고 볼 수 있다. 호튼은 언더우드의 이러한 특성을 나타내는 일화로 '5달러 지폐를 찢었던 일'을 소개하였다.

Thomas C. Easton (New Brunswick, NJ), Letter to the Board of Foreign Missions Presbyterian Church, (July 5th, 1884). PHS RG 31 37-10, #478.

New Brunswick, New Jersey
July 5th, 1884

Board of Foreign Missions
Presbyterian Church

Beloved Brother

Mr. Rev. Horace Grant Underwood, A. M. Graduate of our Theological Seminary is well known to me as a most zealous servant of the Lord Jesus Christ.

He is anxious to go to Corea as a missionary. Our Church cannot send men there at the present time and he applies to your body in earnest hopes that he may be appointed.

In regard to his qualifications after a close watch __ him as Paster for three years let me state.

1st His scholarship. He is quick to learn and master a language. He has ever ranked high in all his studies and will readily grasp a new language.

2nd His Piety. He has a burning zeal for the conversion of souls. In revivals of great power where we have seen hundreds led to Christ, he has been my most efficient helper and co-laborer in the work. He loves evangelistic work and as a missionary would prove a great success.

3rd His General Qualifications. Has a keen perception of human nature. Reads men quickly and wins and holds his friends. Is sympathetic and charitable. Has a rich view of practical common sense that steers him clear of difficulties and would not complicate the Board in any manner by rush injudicious modes.

자료 3-7 First Reformed Church, New Brunswick, N. J.

4th His Faults and Defects. Tendency to overwork and not study his health sufficiently. Tendency to give more time to the worth of evangelization than either his strength or studies might allow and here he must sound himself in entering mission field. Overgenerous. He parts with the last dime to help the poor and too often assists where it costs him more than he should give.

In many ways I regard Rev. Underwood as a novel servant of our Lord and wish it were in our power to hold him in our own denomination.

But as a Presbyterian Minister for over 20 years I rejoice that he comes to you and hope you will see find way clear to engage him for Corea.

Most Fraternally
Thomas C. Easton
Pastor
1st Reformed (Dutch) Church
New Brunswick
N. J.

토머스 C. 이스턴

이스턴 (Thomas Chalmers Easton, 1836~1923)은 스코틀랜드 록스버러셔의 제드버러에서 출생하여 1860년 미국으로 이주하였다. 블루클린에서 활동하던 그는 1881년 5월 11일 지난 6개월 동안 시무하던 목사가 없던 뉴브런즈윅 제1교회에 부임했다. 그는 1923년 사망하여 뉴저지 주 미들섹스 카운티의 스포츠우드 개혁교회 묘지에 묻혔다.

18840707

조지 W. 코클리 (켐프스테드, 롱아일랜드), 증명서, (1884년 7월 7일).

켐프스테드, 롱아일랜드
1884년 7월 7일

호러스 지 언더우드 씨는 뉴욕대학교의 정규 학생으로서 여러 과목을 수강했고 학년말에 시험을 무난히 통과했으며, 품행, 근면 및 학문적으로 훌륭한 성격을 가졌음을 보증합니다. 그는 3년 전에 졸업했으며, 지난 6월 19일 졸업식에서 문학석사의 학위를 받았습니다.

대학교를 졸업한 후 그는 뉴브런즈윅에서 신학을 공부했으며, 그것에 관해서는 신학교 당국자들이 증명할 것입니다.

조지 W. 코클리, 수학 교수

George W. Coakley (Kempstead, Long Island), Certification, (July 7th, 1884). PHS RG 31 37-10, #481.

Kempstead, Long Island
July 7th, 1884

This is to certify that Mr. Horace G. Underwood was a regular member of the University of the City of New York, passing through its several classes, with satisfactory examinations at the end of each year, and that he bore a good character for conduct, industry and scholarship. He graduated three years ago, and received the degree of A. M. at the Commencement on the 19th of June last.

Subsequent to his graduation at the University he studied theology at New Bruswick, his mean in which studies will be attested by the authorities of the Seminary.

George W. Coakley, Prof. Math, etc.

코클리(George W. Coakley, Feb. 22, 1814 ~Aug. 2, 1893)는 West Indies에서 출생했으며, 1836년 럿거스대학을 졸업했으며 저명한 수학자 및 천문학자였다. 그는 1846년부터 1860년까지 메일랜드의 성 제임스대학에서 수학 교수로 활동했으며, 1850년부터 1893년 브룩클린에서 사망할 때까지 뉴욕대학교의 수학 및 천문학 교수로 활동했다.

자료 3-8 코클리(George W. Coakley).

1-3 언더우드의 선교사 임명

Appointment of Horace G. Underwood as a Missionary to Korea

18840714

미국 북장로회 해외선교본부 실행이사회 회의록 제4~5권, 에이치 G. 언더우드 - 지원, (1884년 7월 14일).

에이치 G. 언더우드 - 지원. 선교사 임명을 지원하는 에이치 G. 언더우드 목사의 편지가 제출되었으며, 공람되었다.

PHS Minutes V4~5, #322, H. G. Underwood - Application, (July 14th, 1884).

H. G. Underwood - Application. A letter was presented from Rev. H. G. Underwood applying for appointment as a missionary and it was laid over.

18840728

미국 북장로회 해외선교본부 실행이사회 회의록 제4~5권, 에이치 G. 언더우드 – 임명이 확정되고 한국으로 배정됨, (1884년 7월 28일).

에이치 G. 언더우드 – 임명이 확정되고 한국으로 배정됨. 지난 번 회의에서 제출되었던, 선교본부로부터 선교사로 임명 받기 위한 호러스 G. 언더우드 씨의 지원을 심사하였다.

언더우드 씨를 선교본부에 기꺼이 추천하는 다음 사람들로부터의 편지들이 제출되었다. 1884년 7월 3일자 윌리엄 V. 메이본 목사, 신학박사, 7월 3일자 뉴욕대학교의 에이치 M. 베어드 목사, 신학박사, 7월 3일자 에이치 N. 콥 목사, 7월 5일자 뉴저지 뉴브런즈윅의 제이 C. 이스턴 목사, 7월 10일자 하워드 크로스비 목사, 신학박사, 그리고 7월 10일자 제이 A. 블레이크 의사.

언더우드 씨는 선교본부에 의해 선교사로 임명되었으며, 한국선교부로 배정되었다.

PHS Minutes V.4~5, #324, H. G. Underwood - Appointment Confirmed & Assigned to Corea, (July 28th, 1884).

H. G. Underwood - Appointment Confirmed & Assigned to Corea. The application of Mr. Horace G. Underwood for appointment as a missionary of the Board, which had been presented at the last meeting, was taken into consideration.

Letters commendatory of Mr. Underwood and recommending him warmly to the Board, were presented from the following persons. Rev. Wm. V. Mabon, D. D. of July 3rd/ 84, Rev. H. M. Baird, D. D., of New York University, of July 34d, Rev. H. N. Cobb, of July 3rd, Rev. J. C. Eastern of New Brunswick, N. J., of July 5th, Rev.

Howard Crosby, D. D. of July 10th and J. A. Blake, M. D. of July 10th.

Mr. Underwood was appointed by the Board as a missionary and assigned to the Corean Mission.

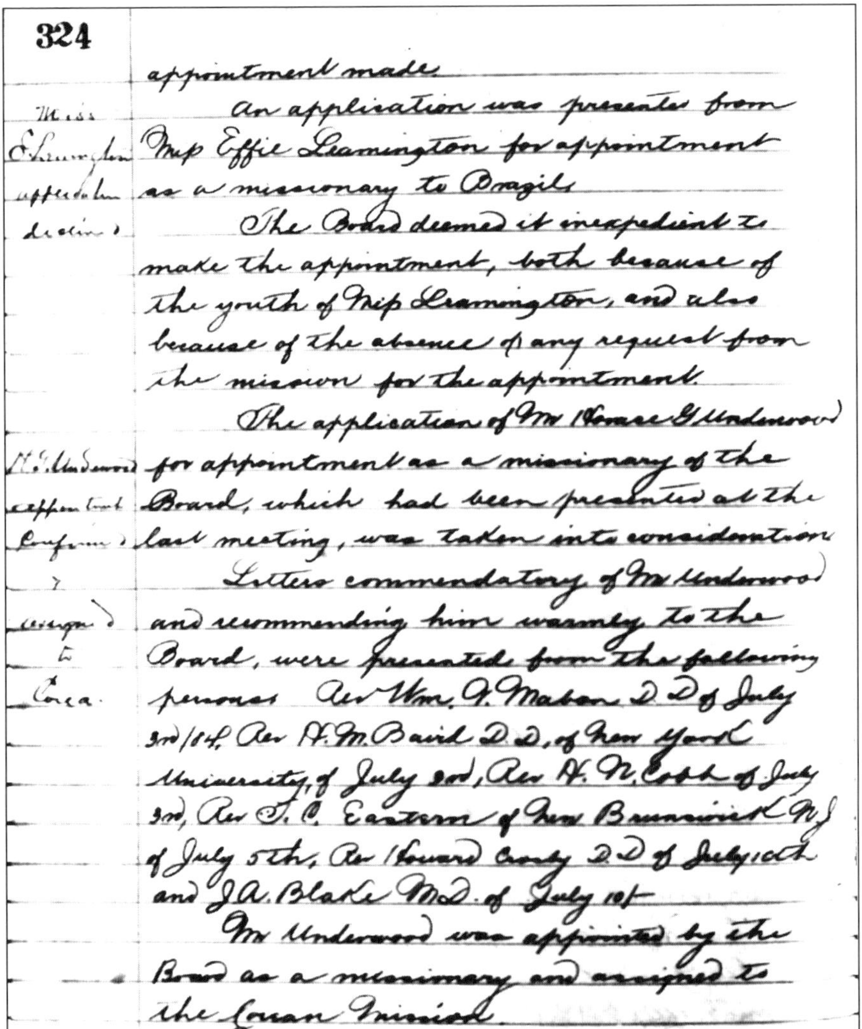

324

Miss E. Leamington application declined

appointment made.

An application was presented from Miss Effie Leamington for appointment as a missionary to Brazil.

The Board deemed it inexpedient to make the appointment, both because of the youth of Miss Leamington, and also because of the absence of any request from the mission for the appointment.

H. G. Underwood appointment confirmed & assigned to Corea.

The application of Mr Horace G. Underwood for appointment as a missionary of the Board, which had been presented at the last meeting, was taken into consideration.

Letters commendatory of Mr Underwood and recommending him warmly to the Board, were presented from the following persons Rev Wm. G. Mabon D.D. of July 3rd/84, Rev H. M. Baird D.D. of New York University, of July 3rd, Rev H. N. Cobb of July 3rd, Rev T. C. Easton of New Brunswick N.J. of July 5th, Rev Howard Crosby D.D. of July 10th and J.A. Blake M.D. of July 10th

Mr Underwood was appointed by the Board as a missionary and assigned to the Corean Mission.

자료 3-9 *PHS Minutes V.4~5*, #324, H. G. Underwood – Appointment Confirmed & Assigned to Corea, (July 28th, 1884). 장로회 역사관 소장.

2.
언더우드의 내한 (Coming to Korea)

신학교를 졸업한 언더우드는 뉴욕 시에 있는 협동개혁교회(Collegiate Reformed Church) 중의 한 곳에서 목회를 맡아 달라는 요청을 받았다고 한다.[92] 조건은 연봉 1,500달러에, 언더우드의 의학 공부에 지장을 주지 않도록 일요일에 설교를 한 번하고 주중 기도회를 주관하는 매우 파격적인 것이었다고 한다. 하지만 언더우드는 해외 선교에 나서기 위해 다각도로 노력하다가 결국 이를 수락하는 편지를 보내기 직전, 마지막으로 기회를 찾던 중 미국 북장로회의 선교사로 임명되면서 요청을 거절하였다고 한다.

92) Lillias H. Underwood, 앞의 책, 1918, p. 33.

2-1 언더우드의 내한 준비

Preparation for Korea

18840908

프랭크 F. 엘린우드가 상하이의 호러스 N. 알렌에게 보낸 편지, (1884년 9월 8일).

뉴욕, 1884년 9월 8일

에이치 N. 알렌 박사

상하이, 중국

친애하는 박사님:

서울의 미국 공사관에서 자리를 확보하는 데 실패했다는 소식이 담긴 귀하의 편지를 잘 받았습니다. 우리는 자리를 얻지 못한 것에 유감스러우며, __________ 합니다. 우리는 조만간 한국으로 가서 어떤 기회가 있는지 살펴보겠다는 귀하의 생각을 지지하며, 그것은 한국에 선교부를 설치하는데 긍정적인 효과를 보일 것입니다.[93] 나는 이미 루셔스 H. 푸트[94] 공사에게 우리의 계획을 알리는 편지를 썼

---

93) 1883년 10월 중국으로 파송되었던 의료 선교사 알렌은 부인의 건강 악화 등으로 정착하지 못하고 1884년 6월 9일자로 한국행을 지원했고, 9월 8일 개최된 해외선교본부 실행위원회는 알렌을 한국 선교부로 이적시켰다. 따라서 이 편지는 미국 북장로회의 한국 선교부가 탄생한 날 알렌에게 보낸 것이다.

94) 푸트(Lucius H. Foote, 福德)는 미국 캘리포니아 주 새크라멘토 시(市)의 판사, 캘리포니아 법원장을 역임한 후, 1878년부터 81년까지 칠레 주재 영사 및 대리 공사를 거쳐 1883년 2월 26일 초대 주한 미국 특명 전권공사(Envoy Extraordinary and Minster Plenipotentiary)로 임명됐다. 푸트는 일본에서 윤치호를 통역관으로 고용하여 5월 16일 서울에 도착했다. 푸트는 문호가 갓 개방된 한반도의 외교 무대에서 열강과의 정치·외교 문제에 관하여 고종에게 많은 조언을 했다. 그러나 한국에 별로 관심을 두지 않았던 미국이 1884년 7월 7일부로 외교 및 영사법령에 의해 공사 자리가 변리공사(辨理公使) 겸 총영사(Minister Resident and Consul General)로 격하되자 푸트는 1885년 1월 10

습니다. 언더우드 씨가 목회 선교사로 임명되었지만, 그는 12월 이전에 파송되지 않을 것이며 귀하가 의사로서 자리를 확보하기 전까지 한국 외부에서 언어를 배우다가 귀하에 합류할 것으로 예상하고 있습니다. 그는 정부가 허가하는 대로 ___ 것입니다. 그는 학교를 열 때까지 귀하를 도울 것입니다. 아마 그는 한 동안 복음 전도의 허락을 받지 못할 것입니다.

에프 F. 엘린우드

Frank F. Ellinwood, Letter to Horace N. Allen (Shanghai), (Sept. 8th, 1884). PHS China V68-84, #7.

New York, Sept. 8th, 1884

Dr. H. N. Allen

Shanghai, China

Dear Dr.:

Your letter in which you speak of having failed to secure the position at the American Legation at Seoul was duly read. We are sorry that you did not get it and yet it may turn out for __ ___. We ___ ____ned to favor the idea of your seeking the earliest opportunity to go to Corea and see what the chances are, and is possible effect on establishment there. I have already written to our Minister Hon. Lucius H. Foote, indicating our plans. As Mr. Underwood has been appointed as a clerical missionary but will not go out before Dec. and his plan is to study the language outside of Corea

일 사임하고 12일 제물포를 떠났다. 후임으로는 민영익 보빙사의 통역으로 활동하다 1884년 5월 31일 내한했던 포크(C. C Foulk, 福久)가 6월 5일 임시 대리공사로 임명되었으며, 1886년 6월 9일 파커(W. H. Parker)가 내한할 때까지 활동했다.

for a time until you shall get established as a physician, after which he will expect to join you. In___ he will be as soon as permitted by the Government. He might go in the ____ity of a assistant to you until he could get a school. Probably he would not be permitted to preach the Gospel for some time.

Yours truly,
F. F. Ellinwood

18841003

아서 미첼이 뉴욕의 호러스 G. 언더우드에게 보낸 편지, (1884년 10월 3일).

뉴욕, 1884년 10월 3일

에이치 G. 언더우드 목사,
비지 가 30번지, 뉴욕

친애하는 형제여:

귀하의 목사 안수와 관련하여 진전된 성과가 있다면 알려 주시겠습니까. 당연히 우리는 그것에 관해 관심이 있으며, 귀하의 상황을 알고 싶습니다.

아서 미첼

Arthur Mitchell, Letter to Horace G. Underwood (New York), (Oct. 3rd, 1884). PHS RG 31 44-13, #339.

New York, Oct. 3rd, 84

Rev. H. G. Underwood,
30 Vesey St., N. Y.

Dear Bro:

Will you please let me know what experiences you have made, if any, with regard to your ordination. Of course, we yet make interest in it, and at every way I am glad to know of your places.

Yours truly,
Arthur Mitchell

18850505

더블유 R. 고든, 버겐 노회, 1885년 5월 5일 뉴저지 주의 오렌지에서 개최된 뉴브런즈윅 특별 노회 회의록. 서머빌, 뉴저지 주: The Unionist-Gazetter Printing House, 1885년, 13쪽.

버겐 노회.

윌리엄 H. 스커더 목사는 시카고 회중연합으로; 찰스 파커 목사는 브루클린의 노회로, 알렉산더 쇼는 롱아일랜드의 노스노회로, 강도사 호러스 G. 언더우드는 저지 시티의 노회로 각각 떠났다.

W. R. Gordon, Classis of Bergen, Minutes of the Particular Synod of New Brunswick, Convened at Orange, N. J., May 5, 1885. Somerville, N. J.: The Unionist-Gazetteer Printing House, 1885, p. 13.

Classis of Bergen.

Rev. William H. Scudder has been dismissed to the Congregational Association of Chicago; Rev. Charles Parker, to the Presbytery of Brooklyn; Rev. Alexander Shaw, to the North Classis of Long Island, and the Licentiate, Horace G. Underwood, to the Presbytery of Jersey City.

18850505

교적 변동, 1885년 5월 5일 뉴저지 주의 오렌지에서 개최된 뉴브런즈윅 특별 노회 회의록. 서머빌, 뉴저지 주: The Unionist-Gazetter Printing House, 1885년, 25쪽.

교적 변동.

호러스 G. 언더우드는 1884년 11월 3일 버겐 노회로부터 받아들여졌고, 11월 11일 목사 안수를 받았으며, 장로회 선교본부에 의해 한국 선교사로 파송을 위해 같은 날 저지 시티의 노회로 이적되었다.

Ecclesiastical Changes, *Minutes of the Particular Synod of New Brunswick, Convened at Orange, N. J., May 5*, 1885, Somerville, N. J.: The Unionist-Gazetteer Printing House, 1885, p. 25.

Ecclesiastical Changes.

Horace G. Underwood was received from the Classis of Bergen on Nov. 3d, and on Nov. 11th, 1884, ordained to the ministry, as a missionary to Corea, and dismissed on the same day to the Presbytery of Jersey City, as he intended to go thither under the Presbyterian Board.

18850505

1885년 5월 5일 뉴저지 주의 오렌지에서 개최된 뉴브런즈윅 특별 노회 회의록. 서머빌, 뉴저지 주: The Unionist-Gazetter Printing House, 1885년, 31쪽.

폼프턴 [교회는] 1년 이상 목사가 없었다가 은총으로 정규 예배를 볼 수 있게 되었다. 많은 사람들이 종교집회에 참석하며, 그리스도를 위해 베푸는 일과 사역에 자원하고 있다.

***Minutes of the Particular Synod of New Brunswick, Convened at Orange, N. J., May 5, 1885.* Somerville, N. J.: The Unionist-Gazetteer Printing House, 1885, p. 31.**

Pompton rejoices that after being vacant for a little more than a year they are enjoying the regular administration of the means of grace. All religious meetings are well attended and a willing spirit is manifested to labor and give for the cause of Christ.

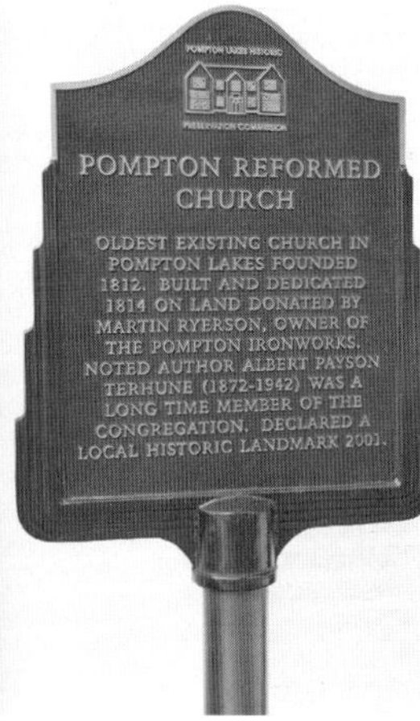

자료 3-10 언더우드가 내한하기 전에 잠시 시무했던 폼프턴 개혁교회.

18850505

교적 변동, 1885년 5월 5일 뉴저지 주의 오렌지에서 개최된 뉴브런즈윅 특별 노회 회의록. 서머빌, 뉴저지 주: The Unionist-Gazetter Printing House, 1885년, 32쪽.

교적 변동.

〈전략〉

호러스 G. 언더우드는 1884년 11월 3일 버겐 노회로부터 이적되어 11월 11일 목사 안수를 받았으며, 장로회 선교본부의 한국 선교사로 파송 받기 원하기 때문에 같은 날 저지 시티의 노회로 이적되었다.

〈후략〉

Ecclesiastical Changes, *Minutes of the Particular Synod of New Brunswick, Convened at Orange, N. J., May 5, 1885*, Somerville, H. J.: The Unionist-Gazetteer Printing House, 1885, p. 32.

Ecclesiastical Changes.

......

Horace G. Underwood was received from the Classis of Bergen on Nov. 3d, and on Nov. 11th, 1884, ordained to the ministry, as a missionary to Corea, and dismissed on the same day to the Presbytery of Jersey City, as he intended to go thither under the Presbyterian Board.

......

18841200

에드윈 A. 벌클리 (서기, 저지 시티 노회), 증명서, (1884년 12월).

저지 시티 노회의 회원인 호러스 G. 언더우드 목사는 1884년 12월 2일 노회 모임에 참석하였으며, 해외 선교지에서의 사역을 위해 해외선교본부로 추천되었습니다. 그의 자질과 동기를 면밀히 검토한 끝에 그에 대한 노회의 승인을 정식으로 증명하는 바입니다.

증명서:

에드윈 A. 벌클리,
서기

Edwin A. Bulkley (Stated Clerk, Presbytery of Jersey City), Attest, (Dec. 1884). PHS RG 31 37-10, #488.

The Rev. Horace G. Underwood, a member of the Presbytery of Jersey City, was at its meeting on Dec. 2, 1884, recommended to the Board of Foreign Missions, for labor in the foreign field, and this may duly certify the Presbytery's approval of him, after careful inquiry as to his qualifications and motives.

Attest:

Edwin A. Bulkley,
Stated Clerk.

18841222

호러스 G. 언더우드가 헬렌 M. 언더우드에게 보낸 편지, (1884년 12월 22일).

기차 속에서, 1884년 12월 22일

사랑하는 헬렌에게, –

토머스는 얼마 전 나와 헤어졌다. 나는 이 편지를 시작으로 너에게 2~3통의 편지를 보낼 예정이다. 의심할 여지없이 이미 들었던 것처럼 나와 함께 바다에 있었던 일본인 관리들이 같은 기차의 같은 칸에서 샌프란시스코로 가고 있어 즐겁다. 나는 (유타 주의) 오그덴에서 그들과 헤어져 솔트 레이크 시(市)로 갔다가 미국[서쪽] 끝에서 증기선을 탈 때 그들을 다시 만날 것이다. 그들 중 한 명은 요코야마(橫山) (네가 기억하는 대로 내가 영국에서 만난) 씨의 파트너인데, 그는 다소 몸이 불편해 하루 종일 침대에 누워 있어 아직 그를 만나지 못했다. 스위스 인 통역자는 매우 멋진 친구인데, 거의 전 세계를 여행했으며 따라서 상당히 좋은 이야기꾼이란다.

지금 체격이 건장한 국방대신은 식사 후 낮잠을 자고 있다 (호화 침대칸에서의 선잠이지만 그런 직책을 가진 사람에게는 위엄이 있다.) 다른 7명의 일행은 카드놀이에 열중?하고 있다. 그들은 카드놀이를 매우 즐기는 것 같이 보이며, 그들은 통역자를 통해 계속 지더라도 그 유혹을 떨칠 수 없다고 내게 말했다. 놀이에 진 사람은 이긴 사람만큼 분명 패배를 즐기는 것 같다. 그들은 작은 조개껍질로 계산을 하며, 계속 놀이를 하고 있다; 통역자는 소설을 심취해 시간을 보내려하고 있다. 기차간 이곳저곳을 내려다보니 머리, 책의 윗모서리, 두 발의 발가락, 모자의 장식이 보이며, 어떤 팔의 손가락과 팔꿈치는 내가 보는 것 말고도 기차 칸에 무엇인가 있다는 것을 알려주고 있다. 그것은 내게 "장미는 보는 이 없이 붉어진다"는 사실을 상기시키며, 때때로 그리 멀지 않은 곳에서 들리는 소리(나는 그것을 음악 혹은 불협화음이라 부를 것이다)는 일본인들이 분명 자신들의 "찬송가"를 갖고 있음을 알려 준다.

차창 밖을 쳐다보니 우리는 산이나 평원, 혹은 그것들의 아름다움이나 수수함, 혹은 문인들이나 시인들 때문이 아니라; (우리는 방금 호손 및 에머슨 역을 통과했다) 놀랄 만한 것이 아무 것도 없어 놀랄 만한 그런 지역을 지나고 있음을 알 수 있다.

이 대목에서 너는 왜 호러스 오빠는 멋있는 편지를 쓸 수 없지 하고 이야기 할 것 같구나. 내가 그런 것에 신경을 쓰지 않는다는 것을 오빠는 알텐데.

헬렌아, 사실 나는 그렇게 할 수 없고 결코 할 수 없었단다. 이제 너는 나의 허약함에 동정할 필요가 없다. 이제 이 편지를 끝내야 할 것 갔다. 네가 이 편지를 읽고 매우 기뻐하며, 내가 오래 동안 편지하기를 원하고 있다고 확신한다. 나의 사랑, 키스 그리고 메리 크리스마스를 모두에게 보내며.

너를 사랑하는 오빠가,
호러스 그랜트 언더우드

Horace G. Underwood, Letter to Helen M. Underwood, (Dec. 22nd, 1884).

On Train. Dec. 22nd 1884

Dearest Helen, -

Thomas left me only a little while ago, and I thought I would start a letter to you expecting of course two or three from you for this one. It has turned out very nicely, as doubtless have already heard, that the party of Japanese officers who were to have been on the ocean with me are on the same train and in the same car going to San Francisco with me. I shall leave them at Ogden while I go to Salt Lake City, but I shall meet them again when I get on the Steamer at the end of America. One of them is Mr. Yokoyama's (whom as you will remember, I met in England) partner, but I have not seen him yet as he is a little indisposed and has been in bed all day. The interpreter is a Swiss and a very nice fellow, he has travelled almost all over the world and is therefore quite a good talker.

Just at this moment the Minister of War, who is a thick set broad shouldered fellow though rather short of his breadth is taking his after dinner siesta (If a broken and disturbed sleep in a Pullman car can be dignified by such a title) & a party of seven others are hard at work? over a game of cards. They seem to enjoy them very much, and I am told by their interpreter that no matter how much they may get beaten they never lose their temper, and it does certainly seem as if those who are beaten enjoy their defeat as much as their opponents. They do their counting by means of little shells and keep on playing as if wound up to go forever; the interpreter is try to while away the hours by diving into the pages of a novel and here and there as I glance down the car I can see the head, the top of a book, the toes of two feet, the tassel of a cap, or the fingers and elbow of some arm which warn me that there are more in the car than those I see, and remind me of "Roses born to blush unseen" and now and then a not far off rumbling (shall I call it music or discord) reminds me that the Japanese have a "hymnology" distinctively their own.

As I look outside I see that we are going over a section of country that is remarkable not for its mountains, not for its plaines, for neither its beauty, nor its homeliness; for neither its literati, nor its poets; (we just passed the stations Hawthorne & Emerson) but is remarkable for its entire lack of anything that is remarkable. Now I suppose you will say why is it that Horace can't write a decent letter? He might know that I wouldn't care for such stuff as that.

Well the truth is Helen I can't and never could. Now you need not take pity upon my weakness and get to business which just now chances to be the closing & signing of this letter of which you I am sure will be very glad & wish I had done it long ago. Love, kisses, & a merry Christmas to all with a Lion's share for yourself.

Your loving brother,

Horace Grant Underwood

ON TRAIN . Dec.22'nd 1884

Dearest HELEN, -

Thomas left me only a little while agoand I thought I wuld start a letter to you expecting of course two or three from you for this one . It has turned out very nicely, as doubtless have already heard, that the party of Japanese [illegible] who were to have been on the ocean with me are on the same train and in the same car going to San Fransisco with me I shall leave them at Ogden while I go to Salt Lake City but I shall meet them again when I get on the Steamer at the end of America. One of them is Mr. YOKOYAMA'S (whom as you will remember ,I met in England)partner, but I have not seen him yet as he is alittle indisposed and has been in bed all day The interpreter is a Swiss and a very nice fellow, he has travelled almost all over the world and is therefor quite agod talker .Just at this moment the Minister of War ,who is a thick set broad shouldered fellow though rather short fo his breadth is taking his after dinner siesta(If a broken and disturbed sleep in a Pullman car can be dignified by such a title)& a party of seven others are hard at work? over a game of cards they seem toenjoy them very much and I am told by their interpreter that no matter how much they may get beaten they never lose their temper and it does certainly seem as if those who

자료 3-11 *Horace G. Underwood, Letter to Helen M. Underwood, (Dec. 22nd, 1884).*

2-2 선교지에 도착한 언더우드

Underwood at the Field

18850126

요코하마의 호러스 G. 언더우드가 프랭크 F. 엘린우드에게 보낸 편지, (1885년 1월 26일).

요코하마, 일본
1885년 1월 26일.

엘린우드 박사님께,

친애하는 박사님:

저는 다소 험한 항해 끝에 어제 아침 이곳에 도착했으며, 지금은 헵번 박사님 댁에 머무르고 있습니다.[95] 알렌은 헵번 박사께 보낸 편지에서 저에게 즉시, 아니면 최대한 빨리 한국으로 올 것을 부탁했습니다. 한국으로 가는 선편과 연결되기 위해서는 오늘 오후에 이곳을 떠나 나가사키로 가는 증기선이 있었습니다. 그러나 저는 필요할지도 모르는 약간의 물품을 구할 수 없었고 그렇게 빨리 떠날 수 없었으며, 더욱이 이곳의 선교사들이나 한국인들과 친분을 맺어 두는 것이 바람직하

95) 헵번(James C. Hepburn, 1815~1911)는 새로 조직된 미국 북 장로회가 해외선교를 위해 임명한 최초의 의료 선교사로서 싱가포르에서 2년 동안 활동하다가 1843년부터 2년 동안 중국에서 활동했다. 1845년 미국으로 돌아와 뉴욕 시에서 개업을 하던 헵번은 1853년 일본이 미국과 화친 조약을 맺은 이후, 1859년 10월 미국 북 장로회 최초의 선교사로 일본에 도착하였다. 의사였다. 일본 정부가 모든 외국인이 요코하마에 거주하도록 하자 헵번을 이곳에서 진료소를 차리고 활동했다. 그는 1867년 첫 일영사전을 편찬했고 1887년에는 성경 번역을 완료했다. 1872년 자신의 진료실에서 교회가 시작되었으며, 1883년 메이지학원 총장을 지냈다. 그는 1892년 미국으로 돌아갔으며, 1911년 9월 뉴저지 주 이스트 오렌지에서 96세의 나이로 사망했다.

자료 3-12 미국 북장로회의 재동경 선교사와 가족들. 1883~4년경. 별표(*)한 사람이 헵번이다. 장로회 역사관 소장.

다고 생각했습니다. 루미스 씨는 이번 주에 한국인들에게 저에게 소개시켜 주겠다고 했습니다. 그래서 저는 2~3주일 후에 있을 다음 증기선을 기다리기로 결정했습니다.

호레이스 G. 언더우드 올림

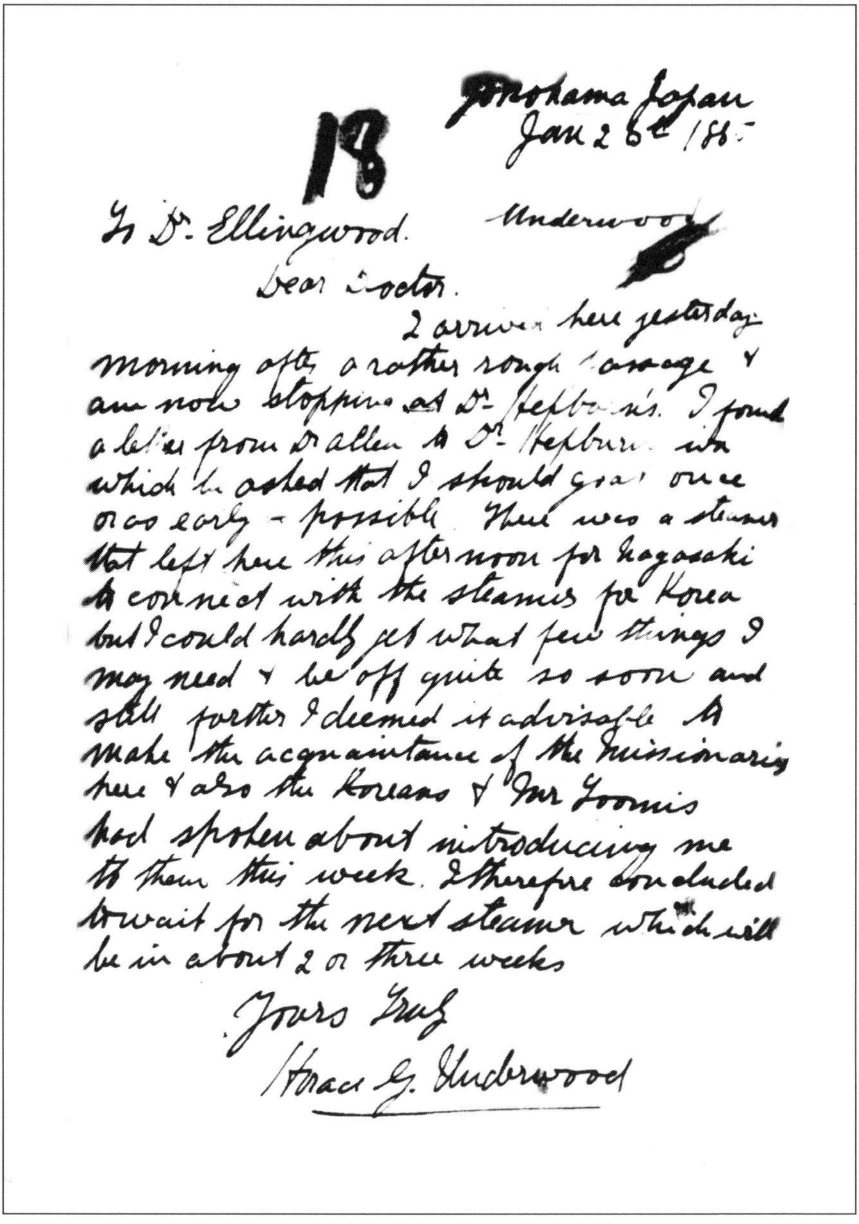

18

Yokohama Japan
Jan 26th 1885

To Dr. Ellingwood. Underwood

Dear Doctor.

I arrived here yesterday morning after a rather rough passage & am now stopping at Dr. Hepburn's. I found a letter from Dr Allen to Dr. Hepburn in which he asked that I should go at once or as early as possible. There was a steamer that left here this afternoon for Nagasaki to connect with the steamer for Korea but I could hardly get what few things I may need & be off quite so soon and still farther I deemed it advisable to make the acquaintance of the missionaries here & also the Koreans & Mr Loomis had spoken about introducing me to them this week. I therefore concluded to wait for the next steamer which will be in about 2 or three weeks

Yours Truly
Horace G. Underwood

자료 3-13 언더우드가 요코하마에서 보낸 1885년 1월 26일자 첫 편지. *Horace G. Underwood (Yokohama), Letter to Frank F. Ellinwood, (Jan. 26th, 1885)*. PHS V1-85, #18. 장로회 역사관 소장.

Horace G. Underwood (Yokohama), Letter to Frank F. Ellinwood, (Jan. 26th, 1885). PHS V1-85, #18.

Yokohama, Japan

Jan. 26th, 1885

To Dr. Ellinwood

Dear Doctor:

I arrived here yesterday morning after a rather rough passage and now stopping at Dr. Hepburn's. I found a letter from Dr. Allen to Dr. Hepburn, in which he asked that I should go at once or as early as possible. There was a steamer that left here this afternoon for Nagasaki to connect with the steamers for Korea, but I could hardly get what few things I may need & be off quite so soon, and still farther I deemed it advisable to make the acquaintance of the missionaries here & also the Koreans, & Mr. Loomis had spoken about introducing me to them this week. I therefore concluded to wait for the next steamer which will be in about 2 or three weeks.

Yours truly,

Horace G. Underwood

18850126

일본. *The Foreign Missionary* 제44권 1호, 1885년 6월, 34쪽.

요코하마, (1885년) 1월 26일.

헨리 루미스 목사,

저는 이곳에서 언더우드 목사를 만나 반가웠으며, 그는 그 (한국) 선교지에 적합한 인물인 것 같습니다; 그러나 그는 아내를 데려 왔어야 합니다.

김옥균과 그의 동료들은 기독교 강습을 받고 있으며, 진실한 탐구자인 것 같습니다. 그들은 일본인들 및 다른 예배에 저와 함께 참석했습니다.

일본의 모든 한국인 유학생은 그들 중 고상한 성격과 신뢰성 때문에 선택된 2명이 책임지고 있습니다. 이 두 관리자는 지금 발라[96] 씨가 관리하는 쓰키지 학교에 있습니다. 한 명은 양반 출신의 기독교인이며, 다른 한 명은 진실한 탐구자입니다.

Japan. *The Foreign Missionary* 44(1), 1885 June, p. 34.

Yokohama, January 26

Rev. Henry Loomis.

I am rejoiced to see Rev. Mr. Underwood here, and he seems to be the right man for that field; but he should have brought a wife.

Kim Ah Kim and his associates are receiving Christian instruction, and seem to be sincere inquirers. They have attended the Japanese and other services with me, and

96) 발라(John Craig Ballagh, 1842~1920).는 미국 북장로회가 일본으로 파송한 선교사였다. 1875년 헵번으로부터 넘겨받은 헵번학교는 이후 발라학교로 불리었다.

are reading various Christian books.

All the Korean students in Japan have been placed under the charge of two of their number, who are selected on account of their superior character and trustworthiness. Both of these overseers are now in the Tukiji school under Mr. Ballagh.[97] One is a noble Christian, and the other a sincere inquirer.

루미스

자료 3-14 루미스(Henry Loomis)

루미스(Henry Loomis, 1839~1920)는 1859년 해밀턴대학에 입학했으며, 1862년 남북전쟁에 참전했다가 1865년 7월 제대하여 학업을 계속했다. 1866년 대학을 졸업하고, 이어 어번신학교를 졸업하고 미국 북 장로회의 중국 선교사로 임명받았다. 하지만 건강이 나빠 파송이 지연되는 중에 임지가 일본으로 바뀌어 1872년 5월 파송되었다. 다시 건강이 나빠진 그는 1876년 4월 미국으로 돌아 왔다. 5년 동안 캘리포니아에서 체류하던 그는 1881년 미국성서공회 일본지부의 총리로 임명받아 1911년까지 활동했다. 그는 1883년 5월 이수정에게 성경 번역을 맡겼으며, 1883년 7월부터 1904년까지 미국성서공회 한국지부의 총무를 겸임했다.

97) John Craig Ballagh (1842~1920). was a missionary to Japan of PC USA.

18850216

요코하마의 호러스 G. 언더우드가 프랭크 F. 엘린우드에게 보낸 편지, (1885년 2월 16일).

일본, 요코하마 블러프 245.
(1885년) 2월 16일

친애하는 엘린우드 박사님:

3월 26일 이전에는 한국의 제물포 항으로 가는 증기선이 없기 때문에, 저는 그때까지 헵번 의사 댁에 머무르고 있습니다. 그 동안 저는 요코하마에 있는 몇몇 한국인 망명객들의 도움을 받았으며, 그들은 저에게 한국어를, 대신 저는 그들에게 영어를 가르치고 있습니다.[98] 한국어와 관련하여 구할 [수 있는] 책은 매우 적으며, 구한 책으로 저는 최선을 다해 [한국어] 공부를 하고 있습니다. 현재로서는 어려워 보이지 않지만, 아마도 아직 난해한 부분에 들어가지 않아서 그럴 것입니다. 제가 아는 한, 한국에서는 여성을 통하지 않고는 여성에게 접근하는 것이 완전히 불가능할 것입니다. 더욱이 현재로서는 기혼 여성과 과부에 의해서만 가능하며, 젊은 미혼 여성은 거의 소용이 없습니다. 지금은 선교사의 아내가 아니면 어떤 여자 선교사라도 한국으로 들어가는 정책을 취해서는 안 됩니다. 그러나 만일 여자 선교사를 일본으로 보낼 수 있다면, 그들은 이곳에서 한국어를 배울 수 있으며 길이 열리자마자 입국할 수 있을 것입니다. 저는 머지않아 길이 열릴 것으로 확신합니다. 박사님께서 알렌으로부터 들으셨는지 모르겠습니다만, 저는 미혼 남자의 영향력이 매우 적으며, 이 선교지(한국)의 상황이 그렇기 때문에 선교본부가 기혼이 아닌 남자는 파송하지 않는 것이 좋을 것이라는 말을 온 사방으로부터 들었습니다. 사실 알렌은 저에게 편지를 보내, 제가 일본에서 기다리는 동안 혹시 결혼할 수 있다면 기다렸다가 한국에 입국하는 것이 최선이라고 말했습니다.

98) 갑신정변 실패로 일본에 망명했던 박영효, 김옥균, 서광범, 서재필 등을 지칭한다. 이외에도 몇 명의 유학생과 이수정 등이 있었다.

저는 [푸트] 공사와 부인을 만났는데, 그들은 휴가 차 고국으로 돌아가는 길이었습니다. 그들은 참으로 유쾌했으며, 공사는 현재 제가 한국으로 들어가는 것이 지극히 안전하며, 기독교 학교를 설립하는 길이 열려 있다고 생각한다고 말했습니다. 그는 또한 현재로서는 어떠한 전도 활동도 시작하는 것을 권하지 않는다고 언급했지만, 저는 아직 한국어를 모르기 때문에 다행입니다. 그는 알렌 박사를 상당히 좋게 생각하는 것 같으며, 그를 상당히 높게 평가했습니다. 푸트 부인은 알렌 부인과 상당한 친분을 쌓은 것으로 보입니다.

정권을 잡으려는 개화파의 최근 시도(갑신정변)가 성공했더라면, 선교 사역에 큰 추진력이 가해져 선교 사역을 수행하기 위한 충분한 사람들을 구하는 일이 어려웠을 것이 여러 모로 분명합니다.

박사님이 병환에서 완전히 회복되었을 것으로 믿습니다.

호레이스 G. 언더우드 올림

Horace G. Underwood (Yokohama), Letter to Frank F. Ellinwood, (Feb. 16th, 1885). PHS V1-85, #21.

245 Bluff, Yokohama, Japan, Feb. 16th

Dear Dr. Ellinwood:

There being no steamer for Chemulpo, the port of Korea, before the 26th of March, I am stopping with Dr. Hepburn till then. In the meantime, I have secured the services of some of the refugee Koreans who are in Yokohama, and while they are teaching me Korean, I in turn am giving them lessons in English. The books to be obtained on the language are very few, and these I have got, and am doing the best I can with them. At present, it does not seem such a formidable matter, but I suppose I have not yet got to the difficulties yet. From all that I can learn, it will be an utter impossibility to get at the women of Korea except through women, and still further that at present this can only be done by married women, and widows, and that young un-married women will be almost useless. It might not be policy for any female missionaries to enter the country just now unless as missionaries wives, but if some could be sent now to Japan, they could be learning the language here and enter as soon as the way opened, which as far as I can ascertain must be before very long. I do not know whether you have yet heard it from Dr. Allen, but I hear it on every side, that the influence of an un-married man is very much lessened thereby, and that the circumstances in this field are such that it is hardly advisable for the Board to send any but Married men; and in fact Dr. Allen writes on to me that if by waiting in Japan I could go into the country married, it would be best to wait.

I have met General and Mrs. Foote who are on their way home on leave of absence. I found them very pleasant indeed and the General said that he thought it would be perfectly safe for me to go into the country now and that the way for mission schools was now open. He also stated that it would be hardly advisable to do any preaching just now but as I don't know the language, this of course is still a good way off. He seems to think a good deal of Dr. Allen and speaks of him in the highest terms, and Mrs. Foote it appears had formed quite an attachment to Mrs. Allen.

Had the late attempt of the Progressionist party to gain control been successful, there is every evidence to prove that the work of missions would have received such an impetus that it would have been difficult to find men enough to do the work that would have laid before them.

Trusting that you have now fully recovered from your sickness. I remain,

Yours sincerely,
Horace G. Underwood

18850223

서울의 호러스 N. 알렌이 프랭크 F. 엘린우드에게 보낸 편지, (1885년 2월 23일).

……

박사님께 제 병원 제안서의 공식적인 승인서를 번역해서 보냅니다. 지금 왕은 3월 3일 이사하기 위해 구궁(舊宮)을 수리하느라 바쁩니다. (구궁에서 귀신이 나온다고 합니다) 이것은 우리의 일을 지연시킬 것입니다. 그러나 지금까지 조선에서는 모든 일이 신뢰할 수 있었기 때문에 병원 설립도 신뢰할 수 있을 것입니다..

우리는 언더우드 씨가 다음 선편에 올 것으로 기대하고 있으며, 진정으로 그를 기쁘게 환영합니다. 여러 가지 이유로 그가 아내를 동반해야 합니다. 우리에게 새 의사를 보내주시기 바랍니다. 그가 아내와 함께 오도록 해 주시면, 우리는 그녀가 중국에서처럼 편안히 지낼 수 있게 할 것입니다. 사적인 편지로 감리회 의사가 이번 여름에 이곳으로 파송할 예정이란 것을 알았습니다. 저는 그와 함께 일을 하겠지만, 지난 겨울 싸워서 힘들게 확보한 우리 입지를 포기하는 것은 유감스럽습니다. 어떤 교파이건 선교사들이 내한하는 것은 큰 축복입니다. 그것은 생활비를 낮추게 될 것입니다.

……

Horace N. Allen (Seoul), Letter to Frank F. Ellinwood, (Feb. 23rd, 1885).
NYPL R1B2 Outgoing 1884~5, #9.[99)]

……

I send you the translation of the formal acceptance of my hospital proposal. Just now the King is busy fitting up the old Palace into which he moves on the 3rd of March next. (The old one is haunted they say.) This will delay our work, but the hospital seems a certainty so far as anything is certain in Corea.

We expect Mr. Underwood by the next mail, and we are eager to welcome him. He should have brought a wife for many reasons. I hope you will send us the new Doctor. Let him bring his wife and we will make her as comfortable as she could be in China. I learn by private letter that a Methodist physician is to be sent here in the coming summer. I might take him in but it seems a pity to give up our place after the fight we have had for it during the past winter. The coming of missionaries will be a great blessing - be they of whatever denomination. It will also lower the price of living.

……

99) 'NYPL R1B2'는 알렌 컬렉션이 소장되어 있는 New York Public Library에서 제작한 마이크로 필름 1번 릴(R1) 속의 2번째 박스(B2)를 뜻한다. 장로회 역사관에서는 이 편지를 다음과 같이 정리하였다. Horace N. Allen (Seoul), Letter to Frank F. Ellinwood, (Feb. 23rd, 1885). PHS V1-85, #22.

18850305

서울의 호러스 N. 알렌이 프랭크 F. 엘린우드에게 보낸 편지, (1885년 3월 5일).

……

저는 현금을 등유, 시트 천, 가죽 혹은 그 밖의 가치가 떨어지지 않을 물건들에 투자하려 했지만 충분한 양을 구할 수 없었습니다. 우리는 한 쌍의 부부를 수용할 수 있지만 어쨌건 집은 곧 마련되어야 할 것입니다. 언더우드 씨는 우리 자원을 다 사용할 것이고, 새로운 의사가 도착하면 그는 거처할 곳이 없게 될 것입니다. 그가 오지 않게 되면 저는 그 집을 어떤 선편으로 도착할 것으로 예상되는 감리회 사람들에게 유리하게 세를 놓을 수 있을 것입니다.

……

Horace N. Allen (Seoul), Letter to Frank F. Ellinwood, (Mar. 5th, 1885). PHS V1-85, #23.

……

I tried to invest the cash in kerosene, sheeting, hides or something that would not depreciate but could not get them in sufficient quantities. The house should be ready soon anyway, for though we could accommodate a man and wife. Mr. Underwood will exhaust our resources and when the new Dr. comes he would be without a place. Should he not come I can rent the place to good advantage to the Methodist people who are expected of any mail.

……

18850331

알렌의 일기 제1권(1883~1886년), (1885년 3월 31일).

4월 3일(금요일)

그저께 27통의 편지와 40개의 신문이 우리에게 도착하였습니다. 그것들은 일본 우편(선)에 의해 운반되었습니다. 우리의 정기 우편증기선과 이 배를 탄 호러스 G. 언더우드 씨가 며칠 내로 도착할 것입니다.

……

Dr. Allen's Diary No. 1 (1883~1886), (Mar. 31st, 1885).

April 3 (Friday)

Day before yesterday the mail came 27 letters and 40 papers for us. They were brought on a Japanese transport. Our regular mail steamer and Mr. Horace G. Underwood will come in the steamer in a few days.

……

18850403

서울의 호러스 N. 알렌이 프랭크 F. 엘린우드에게 보낸 편지, (1885년 4월 3일).

1885년 4월 3일

우편물이 어제 도착했고 병원이 며칠 후면 개원하게 될 것이기에 지금 제가 편지를 써 두었다가 며칠 후 증기선이 언더우드 씨를 태우고 올 때 부치려고 합니다.

......

동시에 폴크 씨는 맥클레이 박사로부터 편지를 받았는데, 조선으로 들어 갈 여러 명의 선교사가 있으며, 폴크 씨가 그들을 영접하고 병원과 선교부를 설립할 부지를 구입해 줄 것을 희망했습니다. 폴크 씨는 지금 (감리회) 선교사들이 한국에 오면 (갓 개원하려는) 병원을 죽일 것인데, 왜 그들을 (미국) 공사관에서 영접해 달라고 요청해야 하는지 이해할 수 없다고 말했습니다. 그는 (내한할) 선교사들과 아무런 관계를 가질 수 없으며, 지금 그들이 내한하여 경쟁 병원을 시작하면 이제 막 시작된 일을 망치게 될 것이라고 편지를 보낼 것입니다. 그는 언더우드 씨가 제 손님으로, 그리고 조수로 오는 것에 찬성하고, 새로운 의사는 어느 때라도 올 수 있다고 말합니다.

......

우리 [장로회] 사람들은 조금 조급합니다. 언더우드 씨는 편지를 보내 만일 제가 안전하다고 생각한다면 중국의 헌터와 리드에게 교사로서 즉시 한국으로 오도록 전보를 치라고 했습니다. 제가 그(언더우드)에게 조선정부가 미국정부에게 교사를 보내주도록 요청했다고 말했기 때문입니다. 저는 그저 그들이 올 수도 있다는 희망을 표현한 것뿐입니다. 교사들은 요청을 받은 미 국무부를 통해 확보되어야만 합니다.

......

언더우드 씨와 2명의 미국 공리회 해외선교부 소속 선교사가 어제 밤에 우리에게 왔습니다. 언더우드 씨는 사무적으로 보이며, 저는 그에게 재무의 일을 맡길 것입니다. 감리회 사람과 아픈 부인은 제물포의 일본 집에 머물고 있습니다. 우리는 방이 꽉 찼으며, 폴크 씨는 그들을 받아들이지 않을 것입니다. 하지만 저는 그 부인이 편안하게 지낼 수 있도록 하기 위해 모종의 조치를 취할 것입니다.

어제 저는 묄렌도르프와 2시간의 대화를 나누었습니다. 처음에 그는 병원을 좌절시키겠다고 말했지만 결국 그가 할 수 있는 모든 것을 동원하여 저를 돕고 심지어 일부 선교사들은 정부 학교에 고용하겠다고 약속하였습니다.

이후의 일은 언더우드 씨가 상당 부분 자신의 편지에 쓸 것입니다.

안녕히 계십시오.

에이치 N. 알렌

Horace N. Allen (Seoul), Letter to Frank F. Ellinwood, (Apr. 3rd, 1885). NYPL R1B2 Outgoing 1884~5, #11.[100]

Apr. 3/ 85

The mail arrived yesterday and as the hospital is to be opened in a few days I will write my letter now and be ready to mail it when the steamer comes in a few days with Mr. Underwood.

......

100) 장로회 역사관에서는 이 편지를 다음과 같이 정리하였다. *Horace N. Allen (Seoul), Letter to Frank F. Ellinwood, (Apr. 3rd, 1885)*. PHS V1-85, #24.

At the same time Mr. Foulk receives a letter from Dr. McClay stating that he has a batch of missionaries who are on their way for Corea and he hopes Mr. Foulk will entertain them and buy them ground for a hospital and Mission. Mr. Foulk is greatly worried. He says their coming just now will kill the hospital and he can't see why they should ask to be entertained at the Legation. He will write them that he can have nothing to do with them and that their coming now and starting a rival hospital will kill the work already begun. He consents to have Mr. Underwood come as my guest and assistant and says the new Dr. is expected and can come at any time.

……

Our own people are a little premature. A letter came from Mr. Underwood telling me to telegraph Hunter & Reid of China to come here at once as teachers if I thought it safe. It all comes from my telling him that their government had applied to our government for teachers. That is the case I expressed to him I hope we may supply them, but they must be supplied through the U. S. State Dept. as the application has gone to them.

……

Mr. Underwood and the two American Board men came to us last evening.[101)] Mr. U. seems businesslike and I shall make him treasurer in my place. The M. E. (Methodist) man with a sick wife are in a Jap (Japanese) house at Chemulpo. We are full and Mr. Foulk will not receive them. I intent to do something however, to make the lady comfortable.

I had a two hours talk with Mullendorf yesterday. He at first said he would crush the hospital but at last not only agreed to help me all he could but even promised to use some of the missionaries [in] the Government schools.

I will expect Mr. Underwood to do most of the writing hereafter.

Yours Sincerely,

H. N. Allen

---

101) American Board of Commissioners for Foreign Missions.

미국 북장로회의 한국 선교 시작 –
한국 선교를 최초로 지원한 헌터와 리드

미국 북장로회 최초의 목회 선교사 언더우드의 내한 130주년을 기념하는 이 자료집에서 꼭 다루어야 할 것이 헌터(Stephen Alexander Hunter, 1851~1923)와 리드(Gilbert Reid, 1857~1927)에 관한 내용이다.

미국 북장로회의 한국 선교는 이수정에게 세례를 준 녹스(George W. Knox, 1853~1912)의 보고에 주목한 엘린우드에 의해 진행되었다. 엘린우드는 한국 선교의 시작을 위해 일본의 녹스와 중국 산둥의 네비우스(John L. Nevius, 1829~1893)에게 현지 선교사들의 의견을 모아줄 것을 부탁했다.

이에 대해 일본에서는 여러 이유로 한국 선교의 시작이 시기상조라는 의견을 개진하면서 더 이상 논의가 진행되지 않았다. 반면 중국에서는 한 동안 이에 대한 의견이 없다가, 1883년 12월 14일 열린 산둥 및 베이징선교부의 정례 회의에서 헌터와 리드 목사가 한국행을 처음으로 지원했다. 그들은 다른 동료들이 자신들의 요청을 받아들이지 않자 12월 15일 선교본부에 자신들을 한국 선교사로 파송해 줄 것을 요청했다. 이에 대해 미국 북장로회 해외선교본부의 실행위원회는 1884년 2월 25일 열린 회의에서 헌터와 리드의 한국행을 받아들이지 않기로 결정했다. 그들이 한글을 새로 배워야 하고, 그들 대신 파송할 선교사들은 중국어를 배워야 하는 언어 문제를 이유로 들었다.

자료 3-15 헌터(Stephen Alexander Hunter)

마침 맥윌리엄스가 한국 선교 시작을 위해 5천 달러를 기부하기로 함에 따라, 헌터와 리드 대신에 4월 헤론을, 7월 언더우드를 한국 선교사로 임명했다. 그런데 1883년 중국으로 파송되어 헌터의 후임으로 임명되었던 알렌이 부인의 건강 악화 등으로 정착하지 못하고, 1884년 6월 9일자로 한국행을 지원했다. 이에 대해 미국 북장로회 해외선교본부는 7월 20일경 이를 허락하는 전보를 보냈다. 이로서 언더우드의 짝은 헤론이 아닌 알렌으로 변경되었다. 이어 9월 8일 개최된 해외선교본부 실행위원회는 알렌을 한국 선교부로 이적시킴으로써 '한국 선교부'가 탄생하였다. 이에 따라 상하이를 떠난 알렌은 부산을 거쳐 9월 20일 제물포에 도착한 이후, 가족을 데리고 한국에 정착함으로써 첫 정주(定住) 선교사가 되었다.

헌터는 1878년 제퍼슨의과대학을 졸업하고, 1879년 부인과 함께 중국으로 파송되어 산둥지부에서 주로 활동하였다. 하지만 의료 선교사로서 헌터는 교리의 관점 차이, 의료 사업에 대한 회의 등을 이유로 1882년 말 선교사 사임을 요청했다가 취소하기도 하는 등 불안정한 위치에 있었다. 이에 대해 선교본부에서는 향후 그의 역할이 의료 사업인지 전도 사업인지 의문을 제가하기도 했다. 실제 같은 지부의 머티어는 헌터의 신학적 견해가 상당히 왜곡되어 있어 장로교도의 것이 아니라고 단정했을 정도였다. 그는 1892년 선교사 직을 사임하고 미국으로 돌아갔다.

리드는 1875년 인디애나 주의 화이츠타운신학교를 졸업하고, 1879년 뉴욕 주 클린턴의 해밀턴대학을 졸업했으며, 1882년 유니언신학교를 졸업했다. 1882년 2월 27일 선교사로 임명된 그는 9월부터 중국 산동지부에서 활동을 시작했다. 그는 중국어 회화 및 작문에 상당히 능통하여 후에 독특한 경력을 쌓았다. 그는 1894년 상하이에 중국국제협회를 설립했고, '페킹 포스트'의 편집장을 역임했다. 1차 세계대전 중에는 친독일 인사라는 이유로 중국정부의 요청으로 마닐라로 강제 이송되었다가 1921년 돌아 왔다. 그는 1927년 상하이에서 사망했다.

자료 3-16 리드(Gilbert Reid,)

18850406

알렌의 일기 제1권 (1883~1886년), (1885년 4월 6일).

4월 6일 (월요일)

어제 저녁 언더우드 씨가 한국을 탐사하기 위한 2명의 미국 공리회 해외선교부 소속 선교사인 테일러 및 스커더 박사와 함께 일본으로부터 우리에게 왔다.[102] 아내가 아픈 감리회 선교사는 제물포에 채류하고 있다.[103] 나는 그들이 무슨 일을 할지 모르겠다. 그곳(인천)에는 그들이 거처할 곳이 없다.

(서울의) 우리 집은 (숙소가) 꽉 찼고, 폴크 씨는 그들을 맞이하지 않겠다고 한다. 언더우드 씨는 말쑥하고 사무적으로 보이지만 다소 거만하고 성급해 보인다. 나는 그가 문제를 일으키지 않을까 걱정된다.

나는 어제 묄렌도르프 씨와 긴 대화를 가졌다. 그는 일부 선교사에 대해 호의를 보이는 것 같지만, 그가 일본에서 목격한 일 때문에 언더우드에 대해서는 반대를 하고 있다. 처음에 묄렌도르프는 병원을 좌절시키겠다고 선언했지만, 긴 대화 끝에 그는 매우 우호적으로 되었고, 할 수 있는 모든 것을 다해 나를 돕겠으며 심지어 이 선교사들을 정부 학교에 고용하겠다고 약속했다.[104] 외아문의 독판 김윤식은 어제 오후 나를 방문했다. 그들 모두는 병원에 관심을 갖고 있는 것 같았으나, 묄렌도르프가 지금 이곳에 있기 때문에 나는 일을 서둘러서 진행하면 안 된다.

그는 거의 무제한의 힘을 갖고 있는 것 같으며, 왕의 요청으로 미국에서 올 자리에 이곳의 다른 농장주를 고용했다.

102) 테일러(Rev. W. Taylor, M. D.)는 오사카에서, 스커더(Rev. D. Scudder, M. D.)은 니가타에서 각각 활동하고 있었다.

103) 아펜젤러 부부이다.

104) 1884년 조선정부가 시작하려던 육영공원을 의미한다.

Dr. Allen's Diary No. 1 (1883~1886), (Apr. 6th, 1885).

April 6 (Monday)

Yesterday evening Mr. Underwood came to us with two men of the American Board from Japan, Drs. Taylor and Scudder who are prospecting.[105] There is a Methodist man at Chemulpo with a sick wife.[106] I don't know what they will do. There's no place there for them.

We are full and Mr. Foulk insists he will not entertain them. Mr. Underwood seems smart and businesslike but he is rather conceited and rash. I am afraid he will get us into trouble.

I had a long talk with Moellendorff yesterday. He seems favorably disposed to some of the missionaries but is down on Underwood from things he saw in Japan. Moellendorff first declared he would crush the hospital but after a long talk he became very friendly and promised to help me all he could and even put some of these missionaries in the Government Schools. The President of the Foreign Office, Kim Yun Sik called yesterday afternoon. They all seem interested in the hospital but I will have to go slowly now as Moellendorff is here.

He seems to have almost unlimited power and has bought a farmer here in place of the one sent for by the King to come from America.

---

105) Rev. W. Taylor, M. D. worked at the Osaka Station, and Rev. D. Scudder, M. D. worked at the Nigata Station.

106) Rev. and Mrs. Henry G. Appenzeller.

18850409

서울의 호러스 G. 언더우드가 프랭크 F. 엘린우드에게 보낸 편지, (1885년 4월 9일).

한국, 서울, (1885년) 4월 9일.

엘린우드 박사님께: –

저는 드디어 서울에 도착해 있습니다.[107] 여름에 비해 겨울에 증기선의 운항 횟수가 줄어들지만 않았다면 훨씬 더 일찍 도착했을 것입니다.

이곳의 정세는 조용하지만 아직도 불안정한 상태이며, 일본과 청나라의 교섭 결과가 어떻게 될 지 잘 모릅니다. 대체로 한국인들은 불확실성과 불안감을 상당히 크게 느끼고 있으며, 만일 전쟁으로 이어진다면, 이곳 사람들에게 미치는 영향은 유쾌하지 못할 것입니다. 사람들의 감정이 불안정하기에 미국 군함 오시피 호의 지휘관은 나가사키로 돌아오라는 명령을 받았음에도 (제물포에) 정박해 있기로 결정했습니다.[108] 동시에 (이곳에는) 명백한 위험은 감리회 형제들이 미국 공사관에 영접을 요청하지 않고 바로 들어왔더라면 모든 것이 좋았을 것입니다. 그러나 그렇지 않았고, 그래서 현재와 같은 시점에 선교사들이 입경(入京)하는 것이 적절한가에 대한 의문이 제기되었습니다. 결국 그들의 요청과 반대되는 결정이 내려졌고, 그들은 이제 제물포의 아주 형편없는 거처에서 머물지, 혹은 나가사키로 되돌아가든지, 혹은 이곳 미국 공사관의 충고를 무시하고 서울로 와야 합니

107) 언더우드는 4월 2일 부산을 거쳐 부활절 주일인 5일 오후 3시에 제물포항에 도착했으며, 그날 저녁 서울에 도착했다.

108) 오시피 호는 뉴햄프셔에서 건조된 1240톤 규모의 증기 범선이며, 1862년 11월 취역하였다. 이 배는 남북전쟁 중에는 멕시코 만에서 활동했으며, 1866년부터 1872년까지 태평양 함대에 소속되었다가 이후 12년 동안 서대서양 함대에 소속되었다. 1884년부터 1887년까지 극동함대에 소속되었으며, 갑신정변 직후인 1884년 12월 18일에는 서울의 미국 공사관에 해병대를 파견했고, 이후 제물포에 정박하였다. 한편 1887년 9월 알렌을 동반하여 제물포를 출발한 박정양 특명전권공사의 견미사절단이 이 배를 타고 청국 군함의 방해를 통과해서 일본으로 갔다

다.[109] 미국 시민은 누구든지 서울로 올 수 있습니다. 알렌 박사는 헤론 박사를 몹시 기다리고 있으며, 헤론 박사는 병원에 자리가 마련되었고 조선 정부도 그렇게 기대하고 있기 때문에 서울로 오는 것에는 아무런 문제가 없습니다. 알렌 박사는 일본 공사관의 의사로 임명받았는데, 연봉은 500달러이며, 그들이 약품을 제공하거나 알렌 박사가 약품대를 별도로 청구하기로 계약하였습니다. 그는 최근 이곳에서 일어난 정변(갑신정변) 때 군인들을 치료해 준 대가로 청나라로 215달러 상당의 은화와 마제은(馬蹄銀)을 받았습니다.

자료 3-17 오시피 호

(알렌) 박사는 당장 의약품을 절실히 필요로 하고 있습니다. 박사님께서 가능한 한 지체하지 않고 런던으로 주문해 주시지 않으면, 저희는 턱 없이 비싼 가격으로 일본에 주문하지 않을 수 없습니다.

에이치. G. 언더우드 올림

Horace G. Underwood (Seoul), Letter to Frank F. Ellinwood, (Apr. 9th, 1885). PHS V1-85, #26.

Seoul, Korea, April 9th.

Dear Dr. Ellinwood: -

---

109) 아펜젤러 부부가 입경하는 것에 대해 폴크 공사는 갑신정변 이후의 불안한 정세를 이유로 반대했다. 하지만 맥클레이는 1884년 여름 자신이 방한했을 때 조선 정부가 병원과 학교 사업을 약속했다며, 적극 추진하였다. 하지만 아펜젤러 부부는 4월 10알 일본으로 돌아갔다.

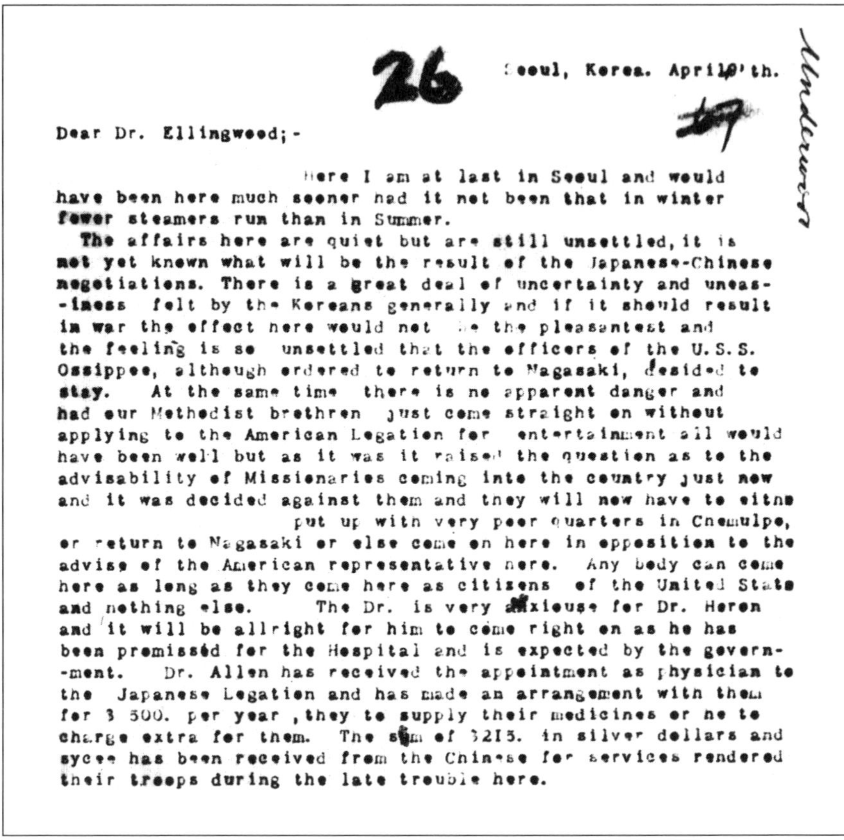

26 Seoul, Korea. April 9th.

Dear Dr. Ellingwood;-

Here I am at last in Seoul and would have been here much sooner had it not been that in winter fewer steamers run than in Summer.

The affairs here are quiet but are still unsettled, it is not yet known what will be the result of the Japanese-Chinese negotiations. There is a great deal of uncertainty and uneas--iness felt by the Koreans generally and if it should result in war the effect here would not be the pleasantest and the feeling is so unsettled that the officers of the U.S.S. Ossippee, although ordered to return to Nagasaki, decided to stay. At the same time there is no apparent danger and had our Methodist brethren just come straight on without applying to the American Legation for entertainment all would have been well but as it was it raised the question as to the advisability of Missionaries coming into the country just now and it was decided against them and they will now have to eitne put up with very poor quarters in Chemulpo, or return to Nagasaki or else come on here in opposition to the advise of the American representative here. Any body can come here as long as they come here as citizens of the United State and nothing else. The Dr. is very anxiouse for Dr. Heron and it will be allright for him to come right on as he has been promissed for the Hospital and is expected by the govern--ment. Dr. Allen has received the appointment as physician to the Japanese Legation and has made an arrangement with them for $ 300. per year, they to supply their medicines or he to charge extra for them. The sum of $215. in silver dollars and sycee has been received from the Chinese for services rendered their troops during the late trouble here.

자료 3-18 언더우드가 서울에서 보낸 1885년 4월 9일자 첫 편지. *Horace G. Underwood (Seoul), Letter to Frank F. Ellinwood, (Apr. 9th, 1885)*. PHS V1-85, #26. 장로회 역사관 소장.

Here I am at last in Seoul and would have been here much sooner had it not been that in winter fewer steamers run than in summer.

The affairs here are quiet but are still unsettled, it is not yet known what will be the result of the Japanese-Chinese negotiations. There is a great deal of uncertainty and uneasiness felt by the Koreans generally, and if it should result in war, the effect here would not be the pleasantest, and the feeling is so unsettled that the officers of the U. S. S. Ossipee, although ordered to return to Nagasaki, decided to stay. At the same time, there is no apparent danger, and had our Methodist brethren just come straight on without applying to the American Legation for entertainment, all would have been well, but as it was, it raised the question as to the advisability of Missionaries coming into the country just now, and it was decided against them, and they will now have to either put up with very poor quarters in Chemulpo, or return to Nagasaki, or else come on here in opposition to the advice of the American representative here. Any body can come here as long as they come here as citizens of the United States and nothing else. The Dr. is very anxious for Dr. Heron, and it will be allright for him to come right on, as he has been promised for the Hospital and is expected by the government. Dr. Allen has received the appointment as physician to the Japanese Legation and has made an arrangement with them for $500 per year, they to supply their medicine, or he to charge extra for them. The sum of $215 in silver dollars and sycee has been received from the Chinese for services rendered their troops during the late trouble here.

The Dr. is in great need of medicines at once, and could you not manage to forward the order to London with as little delay as possible, or we will be forced to order from Japan at most ruinous rates.

Yours sincerely,
Horace G. Underwood

19090827

Horace G. Underwood, Reminiscences. *Quarto Centennial Papers Read Before the Korea Mission of the Presbyterian Church in the U. S. A. at the Annual Meeting in Pyeng Yang, August 27, 1909,* pp. 97~100.

Reminiscences.

Dr. H. G. Underwood, D. D.

I am beginning to realize that old age brings its honors, when I am asked to give reminiscences, in the presence of this august body; and I appreciate the courage and spirit of self-sacrifice which has enabled your committee to make such a request, and I hope that you are all fully prepared to take the consequences, for it is always dangerous to start a garulous old timer on such a line.

As I look around on this gathering I cannot but feel however that it is fitting that I should receive this appointment, as my memory of “things Korean goes back further than that of any of my hearers; but it may be remembered that I am not the “father of the mission,” for of the Presbyterian trio who first

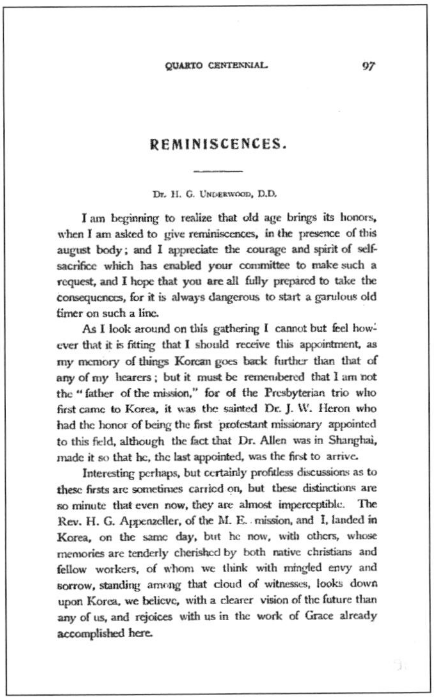

QUARTO CENTENNIAL. 97

REMINISCENCES.

Dr. H. G. Underwood, D.D.

I am beginning to realize that old age brings its honors, when I am asked to give reminiscences, in the presence of this august body; and I appreciate the courage and spirit of self-sacrifice which has enabled your committee to make such a request, and I hope that you are all fully prepared to take the consequences, for it is always dangerous to start a garulous old timer on such a line.

As I look around on this gathering I cannot but feel however that it is fitting that I should receive this appointment, as my memory of things Korean goes back further than that of any of my hearers; but it must be remembered that I am not the "father of the mission," for of the Presbyterian trio who first came to Korea, it was the sainted Dr. J. W. Heron who had the honor of being the first protestant missionary appointed to this field, although the fact that Dr. Allen was in Shanghai, made it so that he, the last appointed, was the first to arrive.

Interesting perhaps, but certainly profitless discussions as to these firsts are sometimes carried on, but these distinctions are so minute that even now, they are almost imperceptible. The Rev. H. G. Appenzeller, of the M. E. mission, and I, landed in Korea, on the same day, but he now, with others, whose memories are tenderly cherished by both native christians and fellow workers, of whom we think with mingled envy and sorrow, standing among that cloud of witnesses, looks down upon Korea, we believe, with a clearer vision of the future than any of us, and rejoices with us in the work of Grace already accomplished here.

자료 3-19 Horace G. Underwood, Reminiscences. *Quarto Centennial Papers Read Before the Korea Mission of the Presbyterian Church in the U. S. A. at the Annual Meeting in Pyeng Yang, August 27, 1909*, pp. 97~100.

came to Korea, it was the sainted Dr. J. W. Heron who had the honor of being the first protestant missionary appointed to this field, although the fact that Dr. Allen was in Shanghai, made it so that he, the last appointed, was the first to arrive.

Interesting perhaps, but certainly profitless discussions as to these firsts are sometimes carried on, but these distinctions are so minute that even now, they are almost imperceptible. The Rev. H. G. Appenzeller, of the M. E. Mission, and I, landed in Korea, on the same day, but he now, with others, whose memories are tenderly cherished by both native christians and fellow workers, of whom we think with mingled envy and sorrow, standing among that cloud of Witnesses, looks down upon Korea, we believe, with a clearer vision of the future than any of us, and rejoices with us in the work of Grace already accomplished here.

But even for us who remain, as we view this land to-day, and see all that God has done, the first overwhelming and inspiring thought is, that all this has come to pass during a part of the life time of a comparatively young man, and little though the share he has had in the real work may be, he thanks God that he has been permitted to be a witness of the marvellous miracle now in progress of the birth of a nation.

In all our reminiscences, we can but compare as it were, yesterday with to-day, and are compelled to stand in awe as we watch what He is doing, and with bated breath to exclaim "what hath God wrought."

In the winter of '82~'83. the Rev. Dr. Oltmans,[110)] now of the Meiji Gakuin of Tokyo, but then a student, gathered the volunteers at New Brunswick together, and read them a paper he had been appointed to prepare on the Hermit Kingdom at last opened by treaty to the Western World. The simple story of these twelve or thirteen million without the Gospel; of the church praying for an open door; the door, opened, thro Admiral Shufelt's treaty in 1882 and the thought of a year and more

110) 원문에 "Altmans"로 잘못 기록되어 있다. 올트만스(1854-1939)는 1954년 네덜란드에서 출생하였고, 1873년 5월 미국으로 이주하였다. 가족은 미시건 주 그랜드 래피즈에 정착하였다. 올트만스는 1883년 9월 뉴브런즈윅신학교에 입학하였고, 졸업 후 일본으로 파송되었다.

having passed without a move on the part of the church, so stirred the speaker, that he determined to set to work, and find some one to go.

자료 3-20 올트만(Albert Oltmans)

For myself, I believed I had been called to India, and in this conviction had made certain special preparations for that field, and had spent a year in medical study; but I certainly felt there must by others who would be ready to go; yet do what I would, urge as I might, a year passed, and still no one had offered, no church seemed ready to enter, and even the leaders in the foreign mission work of the churches were writing articles urging that it was too early to enter Korea. It was than that the message came home to me. "Why not go yourself?" But India, her needs, the peculiar call I believed I had had to that field, the partial special preparations, all loomed up, and seemed to bar the way.

Every door seemed closed and at first it appeared impossible to open them. Twice I applied to my own church but lack of funds compelled them to decline. Twice I had applied to the Presbyterian Board only to be told it was useless. The door seemed closing on Korea and wide open to stay at home or to follow my first intention to go to India. I had about decided upon this course and had written with much reluctance my acceptance of a call to a New York church; had sealed this letter and was about to drop it in the letter-box when it seemed almost as though I heard a voice saying "No one for Korea," "How about Korea?" I drew back the letter in my hand determined to make another effort Korea ward and turned my face once again toward 23 Center Street (the old Presbyterian Board rooms). This time the secretary that I had previously seen was out and I saw a new face, that of Dr. F. F. Ellinwood[111], who assured me of his interest and in a few days I was notified that at the next meeting of the Board I should be appointed.

자료 3-21 엘린우드 (Frank F. Ellinwood)

Just prior to my appointment, a somewhat lengthy discussion had been in progress, as to opening Korea, some of our secretaries being ardently in favor of it, others believing they must wait some years. It was just at this time, that the senior secretary of the American Board published a lengthy article urging delay in entering this country.

Mr. D. W. McWilliams[112], a christian layman and a member of the Presbyterian Board of Foreign Missions, reading the article took it to Dr. Ellinwood and enquired whether he felt able to answer it The doctor agreed, and at luncheon soon showed to the satisfaction of Mr. McWilliams that Korea should be entered at once but he acknowledged that his colleagues and the Board did not agree with him.

Mr. McWilliams then enquired as to the cost of their opening a new mission and then drew his check for $6,000.00 to be used for opening a mission to Korea if that

---

111) 엘린우드(1826~1908)는 다년간 미국 북장로회 해외선교본부 총무로 활동하면서 한국 선교의 시작을 결정하였다. 그는 재임기간 중 한 번도 한국을 방문한 적이 없었지만, 누구보다 한국 실정을 정확히 파악해 선교 사업을 지휘했다. 그는 해밀턴대학을 졸업하고, 어번과 프린스턴신학교를 졸업했다. 1853년 그는 뉴저지 주 벨비디어의 제2장로교회에서 시무하였고, 1854년부터 1865년까지 뉴욕 주 로체스터의 중앙장로교회에서 시무했다. 그는 1866년부터 1871년까지 장로회의 교회건립 위원회 및 기념기금 위원회에서 활동하다가, 1871년 해외선교본부의 교신총무로 임명되었다. 그는 스피어(Robert E. Speer) 및 브라운(Arthur Judson Brown) 등과 함께 19세기 말에서 20세기 초까지 미국 북장로회의 해외선교를 주도했다. 이외에 그는 1886년부터 1903년까지 뉴욕대학교에서 비교종교학을 강의하였다.

112) David W. McWilliams (1838~1919).

mission were begun at once.

I cannot proceed, without just stopping a moment to recall, that in the work of the last year and a half in America, in behalf of Korea, we have had both in the Board, and in the church, the warm and hearty sympathy and co-operation of this devoted christian brother. His was one of the last faces that I saw as with deep regret that he could not come out at this time, he sent his fatherly and saintly benedictions to the missionaries here.

It was almost immediately after my appointment, that I met for the first time Dr. Heron, and together we talked with the Board over our plans for Korea.

The only steamship available for the port of Chemulpo was the old Tserio Maru,[113] a sailing vessel converted into a S. S. of a few hundred tons burden.

Chemulpo at that time consisted of a very few Chinese and Japanese newly erected huts, and here we put up at either[114] Daibutsu or Harry's hotel, both called first class. Daibutsu's beds consisted of a blanket, laid over plain boards in a bedstead, and at Harry's one had to tip the one only basin to prevent the water running out of a hole on the other side. We had been directed to put ourselves in care of Mr. Cooper, who would secure ponies and start us on our way. I wish I had time to picture to you old Mr. Cooper, who carne to our hotel and told us that he would make all arrangements and particularly warned us that we must be sure and leave not a minute later than eight, because otherwise we should risk being locked out at the closing of the city

113) 아펜젤러는 이 배의 이름을 'Seirio'로 표기했으며, 현재의 발음은 'Seiryu – 세이류(青龍)"이다. 이 배는 1867년 스코틀랜드에서 'Coquette'라는 이름으로 건조되었으며, 그해 구루메(久留米)번에게 팔리면서 치토세마루(千蔵丸, Chitose Maru)로 이름이 변경되었다. 1873년에 다시 한 번 명칭이 변경되는데, 이때 붙여진 이름이 세이류마루(青龍丸, Seiryu Maru)이다. 木津重俊 편, 日本郵船船舶 100年史, (도쿄: 海人社, 1984년), 47쪽.

114) 한국 최초의 호텔은 제물포 일본조계 입구(현 인천시 중구 중앙동)의 대불(大佛)호텔로 알려져 있다. 이 호텔은 1884년 일본인 호리 리키타로(堀力太郎)가 자신을 저택을 개조해 만든 것이었다. 이후 1888년 집 옆에 유리창이 있는 3층짜리 그리스풍의 벽돌 건물을 지었다.

자료 3-22 구한말의 인천항. 별표(*)를 한 건물이 대불호텔이며, 오른쪽 뒤로 멀리 월미도가 보인다.

gates. Dr. Allen had already been settled some six months in Seoul and had passed thro the experiences in connection with the emeute of 1884 and had been appointed physician to the emperor as well as to several of the legations then resident in Korea.

19180000

Lillias H. Underwood, *Underwood of Korea*. Fleming H. Revell Company, New York, 1918, pp. 30~38.[115]

Chapter I
Ancestry And Training

As a little boy of four, young Underwood had made a child's resolution to become a missionary, after hearing an address by a man from India, and this became his settled decision when he began to study for the ministry. His plan was to study medicine as well, so as to go out fully equipped for work in interior stations, if need be, where medical aid could not be had. In getting his education, he was of course considerably straitened as to means, but even so, his open-handed freedom in the use of money left him too often with an empty pocket, not knowing at all from whence his next meal was to come. However, his absolute faith in God was such that he never felt a moment's anxiety; he never knew the meaning of the word worry. Often have I marveled, when remittances were delayed, or when we seemed face to face with some critical emergency and could see no way out, he was perfectly cheerful and calm ; not in appearance only but in reality. "It will be all right," he averred, and so it always was. For example, on two different occasions several years apart, our supply of. hard coal, very rare in the Bast, failed during a bitter winter, and none could be had either from dealers in Seoul or from the mines or from the ports. More and more ghastly the vacancy in the coal bin yawned, while lower sank the thermometer, until at last there was only one scuttleful of the precious commodity left, but still he was as confident that the Lord would provide as though the coal were there; and before the last scuttle

115) 호러스 언더우드의 선교사 지원과 임명에 관련한 내용을 부인 릴리어스의 저서인 *Underwood of Korea*에서 뽑아 실었다.

was empty the coal came on both occasions from utterly unexpected sources. The first time word came from the palace that his majesty had heard of our need and had sent from the royal stores more than enough; and the second time, some years later, a dealer at the port sent word he had some to spare and feeling sure we should be glad of it, had sent it up just in time.

On one of those needy days in college, a Monday, after having on the previous evening at church emptied his pockets at some specially persuasive call, there came a sudden knock at his door and one of his good old professors, refusing to come in, simply grasped his hand, leaving in it sufficient money to carry him on for some time. He often earned a little filling empty pulpits and in the summer of '82, he undertook a book-selling tour through the country which turned out to be remarkably successful, not only in the profits gathered, but in the friends he made. It was a veritable triumphal march and was often recalled with great glee in later days. Years after, when one of those who had been a witness of this book-selling: itinerary heard of the wonderful avidity with which Korean crowds bought books and tracts from him she remarked that she was not at all surprised from what she had seen of his early successes in that line among New Jersey farmers.

During the summer of '83 and part of his last year in the seminary he had charge of a church in Pompton, N. J. His relations with this church as a whole, and with every individual in it, seem to have been the happiest. They were more like one family than a church organization, and everyone, whether young or old, seems to have looked upon him as his very particular friend. One old lady, hearing of his intention to go to a heathen land, replied to the objection that they are hard to reach: "Oh, they won't be hard for him to win. He will love them all right into the Kingdom." He pressed the cause of missions so often and insistently upon these people that the consistory warned him if they gave so much to the foreign field, they could never afford to pay his salary. His reply was characteristic: "Never mind; if that turns out to be the case I will gladly go without my salary." As a matter of fact the usual amount given for missions was very greatly increased (I believe quadrupled) and at the end of his pastorate they offered to double his salary. Aside from this objection to his strong missionary bias, purely on economical considerations, I have never heard of any other criticisms or complaints against the young pastor, except that of an unconverted pew-holder who declared that he "couldn't sit and listen to that dominie who preached so he couldn't sleep nights, thinking."

During that summer a remarkable revival took place in a somewhat remote country district in the hills, the exact locality of which, although I have been told, I have been unable to remember. It was a settlement of very rough and lawless people; many of them real outlaws whose hands seemed to be turned against every man. Their huts were only approached by ladders which they drew up on the approach of strangers. When they sent for young Underwood, he found the whole ragged, disreputable community, men, women and children, gathered in a hastily prepared make-shift meeting place, waiting, for the first time in many of their lives, to hear a message from God. Most deeply he felt the terrible responsibility. Agonizing in prayer, he had sought how best to preach the truth to these people but no light came. He took his place before them not knowing what he was to say but relying in faith on Christ's promise to show in that hour, how and what he should speak. The prayer was offered; the Bible was opened at the 103d psalm ; the preacher had read as far as the words, "Like as a father pitieth his children," when a woman threw up her arms screaming, "God be merciful to me a sinner," and fell forward sobbing on the floor. She was followed at once by one and another until nearly the whole roomful were sobbing, mourning their sins, or lying unconscious on the floor. Mr. Underwood labored with them for hours and on many subsequent days, and a marvelous change took ,place in the whole community in character, manner of living, dress, appearance, every possible way, so that the change was the wonder of all the surrounding country. They were new-bom men. Many were the interesting stories of work at and near Pompton, but we must hasten on to the main life story.

As I have said, Mr. Underwood had decided to be a missionary and to go to India, and was taking his first year's study of medicine preparatory thereto at this time. He received, for so young a man, a flattering call to the pastorate of one of the collegiate Reformed Churches of New York, which offered him fifteen hundred dollars a year and asked only one sermon on Sundays, and the charge of the midweek prayer meeting, in order to give time for his medical studies. He had graduated from the seminary in the spring of '84, and received from New York University the degree of A. M. He was licensed to preach by the Classis of Bergen shortly after; in November of '84 he was ordained by the Classis of New Brunswick. He had been led to think very seriously of Korea and her needs although his decision had been given for India.

Let me quote his own words in the Quarto Centennial to the Board. "In the winter of '82 and '83 the Rev. Dr. Altman, now of Meiji Gakuin,* of Tokio, but then a student, gathered the volunteers of New Brunswick together and read them a paper he had been appointed to prepare on the Hermit Kingdom, at last opened by treaty to the western world. The simple story of these twelve or thirteen millions without the Gospel, of the church pra3ring for an open door, the door opened by Admiral Shu felt's treaty in- '82 and the thought of a year or more having passed without a move on the part of the church so stirred me that I determined to set to work and find someone to go. For myself, I believed I had been called to India and in this conviction had made certain special preparations for that field and had spent a year in medical study; but I certainly felt there must be others who would be ready to go; yet do what I would, urge as I might, a year passed and no one had offered. No church seemed ready to enter, and even the leaders in the foreign mission work of the churches were writing articles saying it was too early to enter Korea. It was then that the message came home to me - why not go yourself? But India, her needs, the peculiar call I believed I had had to that field, and the partial special preparation all loomed up and seemed to bar the way. I applied twice to the Reformed Board but they had no funds to start a new work. I also applied twice to the Presbyterians and was told it was useless. The doors seemed to be closing on Korea but wide open to stay at home or go to India. So I wrote a letter accepting the call to the Reformed Church and was about to drop it into the letter box when it seemed as though I heard a voice saying, 'No one for Korea.' "

* Theological Seminary.

He drew back and decided to make one more attempt with the Presbyterian Board. Here, as he went up the steps, he passed a postman coming down and as he entered Dr. Ellinwood's office, the latter remarked that a letter had just then been received notifying the Board that one whom they had expected to send could not go, and therefore that Mr. Underwood would be gladly accepted and would receive his appointment in a few days. Mr. McWilliams of the Lafayette Avenue Presbyterian Church, Brooklyn, after reading an article written by a member of the American Board of Missions against opening Korea as yet, asked Dr. Ellinwood if he could show that it was yet time to enter Korea. Dr. Ellinwood said that he could do so, and at a luncheon with Mr. McWilliams was able to prove that the time was ripe for sending missionaries there. Mr. McWilliams then drew a check for six thousand dollars to begin the work. Only a year before the arrival of Dr. Allen in Korea, the Korean government had demanded the death of a Christian Chinese soldier who had dared to sell the Scriptures in Seoul. He had been arrested but was not killed, owing to the intervention of powerful friends. The Orient was still very much terra incognita. Japan had come somewhat more into the light but China was a terrible, dark unknown, and as for Korea, even among the people of education and intelligence, not one in a hundred had more than heard of it, or had the faintest gleam of an idea where it was. Those who had heard anything had heard no good. It was the Cocee, an island somewhere near China where Jesuit priests who many years before had secretly effected an entrance had been caught, tortured and killed. The people, too, were supposed to be a wild sort of semi-savage, semi-barbarian race.

Mr. Underwood's brothers decided that if he must go to those dark regions perhaps never to return, he should at least take a trip to England and bid a long goodby to all his kin on the other side. So in the summer of '84, he crossed the Atlantic and paid a brief visit to the uncles, aunts and cousins. None of them had had much expectation of ever seeing him again, but English people are used to roving up and down in the earth and going to and fro in it. He had two cousins in India, one in Africa, one in Australia and then, or a little later, one in Brazil, so they took it all rather as a matter of course.

One of Mr. Underwood's uncles, the Rev. Edward Jones, who happened to be one of the secretaries of the London Missionary Society, invited him around to the office and introduced him to the others, one of whom remarked when he heard his destination, "Korea, Korea; let me see, I believe we sent a man out there some twenty years ago and he was never heard from again." This was often rehearsed with amusement by the prospective sharer of such a cheerful fate. The man referred to was the unfortunate Mr. Thomas, who was sent out on the American steamer General Sherman in 1866 and was doubtless killed with all on board. But that Horace was not discouraged, or likely to be, by any number of dark tales and prognostications, goes without saying. Many a man with nothing but commerce in view has taken equal risks with equal *sang froid*. So he returned to America, joined the Presbytery of New Jersey by certificate in December and started on his long journey. He had taken out his papers as an American citizen after coming of age and entered Korea on an American citizen's passport. On one of his trips back to America he voted at the Presidential Election for the only time in his life. John T. Underwood, his older brother, went with him as far as Chicago. The brothers were always very deeply attached to each other, and even when Horace was a man of fifty, John still seemed to think of him as his little brother who must be looked after, advised, reproved on occasion, and always loved and cared for.

Horace supposed he was starting out with plenty of money, but extra baggage took most of his spare cash, even though he went personally loaded with a large Camera, a typewriter (not an Underwood yet), and a suit case. San Francisco hotel bills took about all that was left and, arriving at Yokohama, our young man tells us he went ashore in an expensive hotel launch rather than the ordinary missionary sampan, because he could get trusted on the former and had no change for the latter.

The Hepbums, who had then been in Japan a long time, met him and took him at once to their warm hearts and comfortable home. In the Orient, wherever one missionary meets another, he meets a brother; his house, his purse, his time, everything is at his friend's disposal. So far as money is concerned, almost anybody, if you have missionary credentials, will give you credit to almost any extent. Why? Because first of all, you are the representative of a great Board in America that pays its indebtedness, and second because missionaries, according to age-old eastern tradition, have an established reputation for honesty which nothing can shake. So Mr. Underwood had no more trouble about funds. Steamers were not going over often to such an out of the way place as Korea, so while he waited he held special evangelistic services on the ships and in the sailors' homes: met Rijuite, the Korean, who had sent out the call to Korea, and began with him the study of the language.

제4부

기타 자료

Part 4.
Miscellaneous Materials

1.
화란개혁교회와 한국 선교
(Dutch Reformed Church and Korea Mission)

미국 북장로회에서 한국으로 파견한 최초의 목회 선교사 언더우드는 이수정의 호소를 읽고 1884년 2월 자신이 다니던 개혁교회에 자신을 한국 선교사로 임명하여 파송해 줄 것을 요청했다. 하지만 교세가 그리 크지 않았던 개혁교회는 중국과 일본의 선교부를 위한 경비 부담으로 새로운 선교부 설치를 거절하였다. 1891년 1월에도 뉴욕의 한 단체가 한국에 선교부 설치를 조건으로 5천 달러를 기부하겠다고 제의했지만 이미 한국에서 여러 교회가 활발히 선교 활동을 하고 있고, 또 재정 부담 등의 이유로 역시 거절하였다.

18840000

임명 지원. 1884년 4월 30일 끝나는 연도의 미국 개혁교회, 해외선교본부 제52차 연례보고서. 뉴욕, 1884년, 13쪽.

임명 지원.

현재 일본에 체류 중인 개종한 한국 양반 이수정이 보낸 '미국 교회가 한국에 선교사를 파송해 달라'는 호소에 반응하여, 우리 선교본부는 (1884년) 2월에 뉴브런즈윅신학교의 학생이 자신을 임명해 개혁교회의 선교사로 한국으로 파송해 달라는 지원을 받았다. (하지만) 그 자리 (마련이) 너무 촉박했고, 이미 진행 중인 사역지에서의 요구 때문에 선교본부는 그 제의를 거절할 수 밖에 없었고, '은자의 나라'에 구원의 복음을 소개하는 영광과 사역을 다른 교파에게 넘겼다.

Applications for Appointment. *The Fifty-Second Annual Report of the Board of Foreign Missions, of the Reformed Church in America for the Year ending April 30th, 1884.* New York, 1884, p. 13.

Applications for Appointment.

In response to the appeal of Rijutei, the converted Corean nobleman now resident in Japan, for Missionaries to be sent to his countrymen from the American Churches, the Board received an application in February, from a student in the Theological Seminary at New Brunswick, to be appointed and sent as a Missionary of the Reformed Church to Corea. Owing to the exigencies of its position, and the demands of the work already in hand, the Board felt compelled to decline the proffered service, and leave to others the honor and labor of introducing into the "Hermit Kingdom" the gospel of salvation.

18850000

재정. 1885년 4월 30일 끝나는 연도의 미국 개혁교회, 해외선교본부 제53차 연례보고서. 뉴욕, 1885년, 16쪽.

재정

재정에 관해서는 최대한 경제적으로 절약하고, 심지어 자제함으로써 지출을 줄였다고 하는 것이 적절할 것이다. 여러 측면을 고려할 때 되풀이되는 요청 때문에 총액이 수백, 수천 달러 증가하였다. 언더우드 씨가 우리 교회의 이름으로 한국에 복음을 처음으로 소개하겠다는 사역을 교회의 이름으로 거부하는 것이나, 다른 선교본부와 교회의 후원으로 축복 받은 사명을 위해 그가 출발하는 것을 목격하는 것은 쉽지 않았다.

Finances. *The Fifty-Third Annual Report of the Board of Foreign Missions, of the Reformed Church in America for the Year ending April 30th, 1885.* New York, 1885, p. 16.

Finances.

It is proper to say here that the expenditures have only been kept down by the most careful economy and even self-denial. Repeated occasions have offered when every consideration but that of prudence urged to an addition of hundreds and even thousands of dollars to the sums expended. It was not easy to decline, in the name of the Church, the offered service of Mr. Underwood, to be among the first to introduce, in our behalf, the Gospel into Corea, or witness his departure on that blessed errand under the auspices of another Board and Church.

18850000

유니언대학. 1885년 4월 30일 끝나는 연도의 미국 개혁교회, 해외선교본부 제53차 연례보고서. 뉴욕, 1885년, 81쪽.

유니언대학. – 와이코프[116] 부인은 지난 1년 동안 4명의 한국인 학생을 가르쳤는데, 이중 2명은 유니언대학의 예비과에 입학했으며, 2명은 고향으로 돌아갔다.

The Union College. *The Fifty-Third Annual Report of the Board of Foreign Missions, of the Reformed Church in America for the Year ending April 30th, 1885.* New York, 1885, p. 81.

The Union College. - Mrs.[117] Wyckoff has been teaching, during the year, four Corean students, two of whom have since entered the Preparatory department of the Union College, and two have returned home.

116) 당시 도쿄에서 활동하던 와이코프 교수(Prof. M. F. Wyckoff)의 부인이다. 당시 미국 개혁교회는 도쿄, 요코하마 및 나가사키에 선교사를 파견하고 있었다.

117) Prof. M. F. Wyckoff

18900000

전도 사역. 1890년 4월 30일 끝나는 연도의 미국 개혁교회, 해외선교본부 제58차 연례보고서. 뉴욕, 1890년, 83쪽.

전도 사역

요코스카. - 요코스카의 교회는 재정적으로 자립 상태이지만, 성찬식의 집행에 있어 선교부의 도움을 받고 있다. 교회는 증가한 것도 있고, 감소한 것도 있다. 감소한 것은 (일본) 정부가 새로운 해군기지를 일본 남부에 건설했기 때문이며, 따라서 많은 장교와 사람들이 일본 제국의 유일한 해군 기지였던 이곳에서 철수했다. 여러 척의 군함도 한국으로 파견되었다. 해군의 많은 장교와 사람들은 진실한 기독교 신자이며, 그들이 이동한 곳에서 그리스도를 증언할 것이다. 한국 장로회 선교회의 에이치 G. 언더우드 목사는 한 때 인천항에 정박 중이던 모든 일본 배에 기독교 신자가 승선하고 있었고, 여러 사람들이 한국인을 대상으로 한 기독교(전도)의 진전에 대해 물어 보았다고 말했다.

Evangelistic Work. *The Fifty-Eighth Annual Report of the Board of Foreign Missions, of the Reformed Church in America for the Year ending April 30th, 1890*. New York, 1890, p. 83.

Evangelistic Work.

Yokosuka. - The church at Yokosuka continues to be self-supporting financially, but depends on the Mission for aid in the administration of the ordinances. The church has had many additions and many losses. The latter are owing to the opening, by the government, of new naval stations in Southern Japan, and the consequent withdrawal of many officers and men from this place, which was before the only naval station in the Empire. Several ships have also been sent to Korea. A number of officers and men in the Navy are earnest Christians, and seem to be witnessing for Christ in the places to which they have been removed. Rev. H. G. Underwood, of the Presbyterian Mission in Korea, says, that at one time all the Japanese ships in Chemulpo harbor had Christian men on board, and that several inquired after the progress of Christianity among the Koreans.

18900000

새로운 선교부의 설치 제안. 1891년 4월 30일 끝나는 연도의 미국 개혁교회, 해외선교본부 제59차 연례보고서. 뉴욕, 1891년, 17쪽.

새로운 선교부의 설치 제안.

지난(1891년) 1월 관대한 것으로 알려진 뉴욕시의 믿을 만한 단체가 한국에 개혁교회의 선교부를 설치하는 것을 조건으로 5천 달러를 기부하겠다고 제안했다. 이미 진행하고 있는 (해외) 선교지에서 사역에 일들이 많고, 새로 설치한 선교부의 향후 유지에 대한 약속이 없었기 때문에 선교본부는 부득이 너그러운 제안을 사절할 수밖에 없었다. 그래서 두 번째로 그 흥미로운 나라(한국)에 복음을 전해주는 기회가 주어졌지만, 다시 사절하였다.

Proposed New Missions. *The Fifty-Ninth Annual Report of the Board of Foreign Missions, of the Reformed Church in America for the Year ending April 30th, 1891*. New York, 1891, p. 17.

Proposed New Missions.

In January last the Board received a proposition from responsible parties of known liberality in New York city, agreeing to furnish the generous sum of $5,000 on condition and for the purpose of establishing a Mission of the Reformed Church in Korea. In view of the great needs of the work already in hand, and the fact that the offer was accompanied by no pledges for the future maintenance of such a Mission when, once established, the Board felt itself reluctantly compelled to decline the generous proposition. Thus, for a second time, has the opportunity presented itself of helping to carry the Gospel to that interesting country and been declined.

19000000

헨리 N. 콥, 미국 개혁교회의 선교 100년 1796~1896년. 해외선교본부: 뉴욕, 1900년 경, 16쪽.

한국, 1884년. 1884년, 최근 한국의 개국(開國)으로 그 나라 국민들의 복음 전도를 위하고 이를 시도하려는 사람들 눈에 '은자의 왕국'이 끌렸다. 그중의 한 사람인, 우리 교파의 뉴브런즈윅신학교의 졸업생 호러스 G. 언더우드 목사가 그해 2월 선교본부에 선교사로 파송해 줄 것을 지원했다. 그러나 당시 비록 1명의 선교사의 임명으로 새로운 선교부의 설립 가능성이 적절하지 않은 것으로 생각되었다. 따라서 이 지원은 마지못해 거절되었으며, 더우드 씨는 한국에 선교부 개설을 고려하고 있는 것으로 알려져 있던 장로회 선교본부로 진심으로 추천되었다. 개혁교회는 비록 그를 파송할 수 없었지만 선교지에서 그가 수행했던 사역을 즐거워할 이유를 갖고 있다.

한국 다시 1891년. 같은 주제가 1891년 1월 다시 선교본부에 제기되었다. 그 달에 관대한 것으로 알려진 뉴욕시의 믿을 만한 단체가 "한국에 개혁교회의 선교부를 설치하는 것을 조건"으로 5천 달러를 기부하겠다고 제안했다. 그러나 다른 교회들이 이미 그 나라에 설치한 선교부가 활발한 사실은 젖혀 두고라도, (우리 선교본부가) 관할하고 있는 선교부에서의 요구가 너무 컸기에 이 새로운 선교부 설치를 할 수 없었다. 따라서 제안은 어쩔 수 없이 거절하였다.

Henry N. Cobb, *A Century of Missions in the Reformed Church in America 1796~1896*. Board of Foreign Missions: New York, ca. 1900, p. 16.

Korea, 1884. In 1884, the recent opening of Korea was drawing to the "Hermit Kingdom" the eyes of those who desired the evangelization of its people and longed to attempt it. One such, a graduate of our Theological Seminary at New Brunswick, (the Rev. Horace G. Underwood,) made application to the Board, in February of that year, to be sent thither as a missionary of the Board. But it was not deemed either expedient or even possible to establish a new Mission at that time, even by the appointment of a single missionary. The application was, therefore, reluctantly declined, and Mr. Underwood cordially recommended to the Presbyterian Board, which was known to be considering the establishment of such a Mission. The Reformed Church has reason to rejoice in the work he has been permitted to do in that field, though unable' to send him forth to it herself.

Korea again 1891. The same subject was brought before the Board again in January, 1891. In that month a proposition was received from a gentleman of known liberality in the city of New York to furnish the sum of $5,000, "on condition and for the purpose of establishing a Mission of the Reformed Church in Korea." But, aside from the fact that other churches already had flourishing missions in that country, the claims of its existing missions were too great, and were too scantily met, to admit of its undertaking this new responsibility. The proposition was therefore necessarily though reluctantly declined.

2.
미국 장로회 역사관 소장 자료
(Presbyterian Historical Society, Philadelphia, Pennsylvania)

미국 장로회 역사관에 소장되어 있는 자료의 상당 부분은 언더우드 전집에 수록되어 있다.[118] 하지만 이 책이 다루는 언더우드의 내한 이전과 관련된 자료는 이 전집에 수록되어 있지 않으며, 이중에는 언더우드에 관한 개인 폴더가 있다. 이곳에는 이 개인 폴더의 자료 중에 일부를 실었고, 마지막으로 언더우드의 여권 신청서를 담아 미국 귀화 등 다른 자료에서 볼 수 없는 내용을 소개하였다.

118) 이만열, 옥성득 편역, 언더우드 자료집 Ⅰ~Ⅴ, 연세대학교 출판부, 2005~2010.

00000000

선교사. 언더우드, 신학박사, 법학박사, – 목사 호러스 G. PHS RG 360.

1884년

선 교 사

이 름 언더우드, 신학박사, 법학박사, – 호러스 G. 목사 선교지부 서울

선교부 조선

미 국 선교지 서울, 조선(한국)

주 소 주 소

출 생: 1859년 7월 19일.

결 혼: 1889년 3월 13일 사역의 종류 새문안교회의

릴리어스 S. 호튼 박사와 책임자

지원 및 임명 전도 및 교육

항 해

안식년 종류 H. A. 시작일 항해일 교 육

안식년 – 1912년 5월 4일. 1912년 7월 27일.

" 의료. – 1916년 5월 5일.

선교본부 혹은 선교부 결정 비 고

1912~13년: 1912년 4월 1일이후 5개월 동안 자비로 안식년.

16년 6월 5일: 선교본부는 진단서에 의해 미국으로의 귀환을 승인하고, 투표를 함

Died October 12, 1916년 10월 12일 뉴저지 주 애틀랜틱시티에서 사망.

친척 및 자녀는 뒷면에

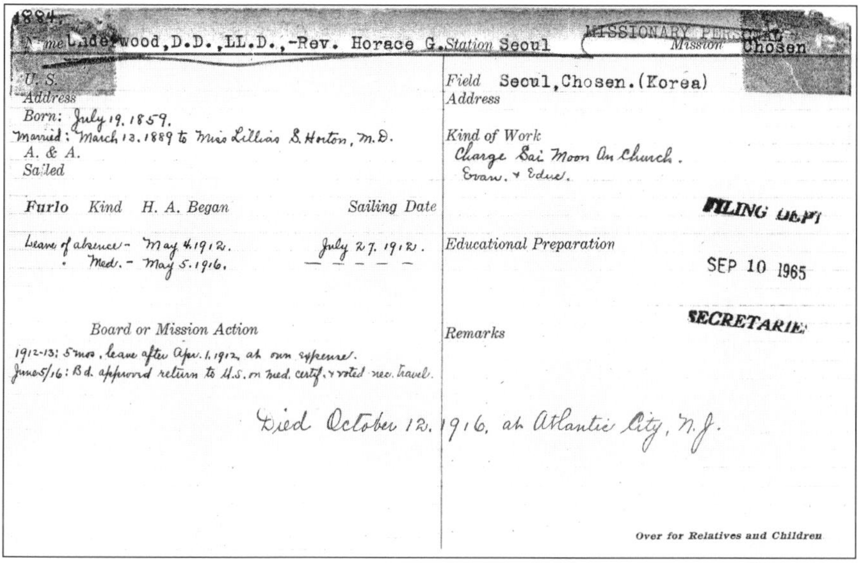

1884.
Name Underwood, D.D., LL.D., -Rev. Horace G. Station Seoul MISSIONARY PERSONAL Mission Chosen

U. S. Address
Born: July 19. 1859.
married: March 13. 1889 to Miss Lillias S. Horton, M.D.
A. & A.
Sailed

Field Seoul, Chosen. (Korea) Address
Kind of Work Charge Sai Moon An Church. Evan. & Educ.

Furlo	Kind	H. A. Began	Sailing Date
	Leave of absence -	May 4. 1912.	July 27. 1912.
	Med. -	May 5. 1916.	- - - - -

FILING DEPT
Educational Preparation
SEP 10 1965
SECRETARIES

Board or Mission Action
1912-13: 5 mos. leave after Apr. 1. 1912, at own expense.
June 5/16: Bd. approved return to U.S. on med. certif. & voted nec. travel.

Remarks

Died October 12. 1916. at Atlantic City, N.J.

Over for Relatives and Children

자료 4-1 *Missionary Personal. Underwood, D. D., LL. D., – Rev. Horace G*. PHS RG 360. 장로회 역사관.

Missionary Personal. Underwood, D. D., LL. D., - Rev. Horace G. PHS RG 360.

1884

Missionary Personal

Name Underwood, D.D., LL.D., - Rev. Horace G. Station Seoul

Mission Chosen

U. S. Field Seoul, Chosen. (Korea)

Address Address

Born: July 19, 1859.

married: March 13, 1889 to Miss Lillias S. Horton, M. D.

Kind of Work Charge Sai Moon An Church

A. & A. Evan. & Educ.

Sailed

Furlo	Kind	H. A. Began	Sailing Date	Educational Preparation
	Leave of absence - May 4, 1912.		July 27, 1912.	
	" Med. - May 5, 1916.			

Board or Mission Action	Remarks
1912-13: 5 mo. leave after Apr. 1, 1912 at own expense.	
June 5/ 16: Bd. approved return to U.S. on med. certif. & voted nec. travel.	

Died October 12, 1916, at Atlantic City, N. J.

Over for Relatives and Children

00000000

언더우드, 목사. 호러스 그랜트, 신학박사, 한국. PHS RG 360.

언더우드, 목사 호러스 그랜트, 신학박사 한 국

출 생… 1859년 7월 19일
출생지… 영국 런던

교 육… 콕스공립학교, 런던
디에학교, 프랑스
해스브룩학원, 저지 시티, 뉴저지 주
뉴욕대학교, 1881년
뉴브런즈윅(뉴저지 주) 신학교, 1884년.
학 위… 신학박사, 법학박사

결 혼… 1889년 3월 13일 릴리어스 스털링 호튼 박사와
선교지… 한국

임 명… 1884년 7월 28일
선교지 도착… 1885년 4월 5일
은 퇴…
사 망… 1916년 10월 12일

버겐 노회로부터 강도사 자격을 받고; 1884년 11월 뉴브런즈윅 노회로부터 목사로 안수되다. 저지 시티 장로회 노회로 전출됨.

한 국

창립 이래 조선성교서회의 교신 총무.

한국어 성서번역위원회의 회장.

언더우드 박사의 영어 저술.

Call of Korea

The Theisms of China, Japan and Korea As Compared with the Theism of the Old and New Testament.

Religions of Eastern Asia

Underwood, Rev. Horace Grant. D. D. Korea. PHS RG 360.

Underwood, Rev. Horace Grant D. D. Korea

Birth ...	July 19, 1859
Birth-Place ...	London, England
Education ...	Cox's Collegiate Institute, London
	Ecole Die, France
	Hasbronk Institute, Jersey City, N. J.
	University of the City of New York, 1881.
	New Brunswick (N. J.) Seminary, 1884.
Degree ...	D. D., :LL. D.
Marriage ...	March 13, 1889 to Lillias Sterling Horton, M. D.
Field ...	Korea
Appointed ...	July 28, 1884
Arrival on Field ...	April 5, 1885
Retired ...	

Death ...   Oct. 12, 1916

Licensed by the Classis of Bergen; ordained by Classis of New Brunswick, Nov. 1884. Dismissed to Presbytery of Jersey City.

Korean

Corresponding Secretary of the Religious Tract Society from its organization. Chairman of the Board of Translators of the Bible into the Korean Language.

Books in English by Dr. Underwood.

Call of Korea

The Theisms of China, Japan and Korea As Compared with the Theism of the Old and New Testament.

Religions of Eastern Asia

18941123

신상기록, 호러스 그랜트 언더우드, (1894년 11월 23일). PHS RG 360.

1916년 10월 12일 사망

신상기록

1. 이 름 호러스 그랜트 언더우드.
2. 임명 당시 미국내 주소 뉴저지 주 뉴더햄
3. 부모 이름 아버지 존 언더우드

어머니 엘리자베스 메어

4. 기혼이라면, 부인 혹은 남편의 이름과 결혼일 릴리어스 스털링 호튼

(18)89년 3월 13일

5 현재 활동지 한국 서울

6. 임명일 혹은 미국 출발일 1884년 8월 28일
7. 임명 당시 소속 노회 저지 시티
8. 귀하 혹은 가족에게 배정된 수소에 거주하고 있습니까? 예

그렇다면, 집은 소유주는 누구입니까? 선교본부

9. 하숙을 하고 있거나 배정된 집이 없다면 그 이유를 적으시오.

임명 이후 안식년 기록.

선교지 출발일	미국 도착	미국 출발	선교지 도착
1891년 4월	1891년 5월 20일경	1893년 2월 1일	1893년 5월

자녀에 대한 기록

이 름	출생일	현재 체류지
호러스 호튼 언더우드	(18)90년 9월 6일	한국, 서울

만일 원하면 뒷면에 중요한 날자와 행사를 간단하게 첨가하시오.

날 자, (18)94년 11월 24일 189

다 기재했으면 뉴욕 시 5번가 53번지, 재무 윌리엄 덜레스, 주니어에게 보내 주세요.

뒷면을 볼 것

응급 시 접촉할 미국 내 친구 및 친척.

이 름	주 소
제이 T. 언더우드	뉴욕시 비지 가 30번지.
제이 M. 호튼	일리노이 주 시카고, 레이크 가, 172 E.

선교부에 알렸음.

영국 런던 출생,	1859년 7월 19일
미국 뉴욕 도착	1872년 3월
졸업, 뉴욕대학교	1881년 6월
" 뉴저지 주 뉴브런즈윅신학교	1884년
임 명,	1884년 7월 28일

Biographical Record, Horace Grant Underwood, (Nov. 23rd, 1894). PHS RG 360.

Died Oct. 12, 1916

Died Oct. 12, 1916

Underwood

TREASURER'S O...
JAN 12 1895
RECEIVED

Biographical Record.

1. Name Horace Grant Underwood.
2. Home address when appointed New Durham N. Jersey
3. Parents' Names. Father John Underwood

   Mother Elizabeth Maire
4. If married, name of wife or husband, and date of wedding Lillias Stirling Horton. 13/3/89
5. Present location Seoul. Korea
6. Date of appointment or first sailing from U. S. July 28 1884.
7. Presbytery with which connected when appointed Jersey City.
8. Are you residing in dwelling assigned for your own use or for your family? Yes.

   If so, who owns the house? The Board.
9. If boarding, or not in special house, state facts

RECORD OF FURLOUGHS SINCE APPOINTMENT.

Dates of leaving field.	Reaching U. S.	Leaving U. S.	Reaching field.
April 1891	about May 20th 1891	Feb 1st 1893	May 1893

RECORD OF CHILDREN.

Name.	Date of Birth.	Present Location.
Horace Horton Underwood.	Sept 6th/90	Seoul Korea

Please add, on back of this sheet if willing, brief statement of important dates and events in life.

Dated, Nov 23rd/94 189

When filled, please send to WILLIAM DULLES, JR., Treasurer, 53 Fifth Avenue, New York.

see next sheet (over)

자료 4-2 *Biographical Record, Horace Grant Underwood, (Nov. 23rd, 1894)*. PHS RG 360. 장로회 역사관 소장.

Friends and relatives in U.S. to be addressed in case of emergency.

NAME.	ADDRESS.
J. T. Underwood.	30 Vesey Street N.Y. City.
J. M. Harton.	172 E. Lake Street Chicago Ill.

Noted Events.

Born in London England. July 19th 1859
arrived in New York U.S.A. March 1872
Graduated University of the City of N.Y. June 1881
" Theolog. Sem. New Brunswick N.J. 1884

appointed, July 28, 1884

Biographical Record

1. Name Horace Grant Underwood
2. Home address when appointed New Durham in Jersey
3. Parents' Name Father John Underwood
   Mother Elizabeth Marie
4. If married, name of wife or husband, and date of wedding Lillias Sterling Horton, 13/ 3/ 89
5 Present location Seoul, Korea
6. Date of appointment or first sailing from U. S. July 28, 1884
7. Presbytery with which connected when appointed Jersey City
8. Are you residing in dwelling assigned for your own use or for your family? Yes
If so, who owns the house? The Board
9. If boarding, or not in special house, state facts.

Record of Furloughs Since Appointment

Dates of leaving field	Reaching U. S.	Leaving U. S.	Reaching field
April 1891	about May 20th 1891	Feb. 1st, 1893	May 1893

Record of Children

Name	Date of Birth	Present Location
Horace Horton Underwood	Sept. 6th/ 90	Seoul Korea

Please add, on back of this sheet if willing, brief statement of important dates and events in life.

Dated, Nov. 24rd, 94 189

When filled, please sent to William Dulles, Jr., Treasurer, 53 Fifth Avenue, New York

see next sheet (over)

Friend and relatives in U. S. to be addressed in case of emergency.

Name	Address
J. T. Underwood	30 Vesey Street, N. Y. City.
J. M. Horton	172 E. Lake Street, Chicago, Ill.

	Noted Society.
Born in London England,	July 19th, 1859
Arrived in New York, U. S. A.	March 1872
Graduated, University of the City of N. Y.	June 1881
" Theology Sem. New Brunswick, N. J.	1884
Appointed,	July 28, 1884

19140315

언더우드 박사 부부의 은혼, (1914년 3월 15일). PHS RG 360.

언더우드 박사 부부의 은혼

1914년 3월 15일.

금요일 오후 남대문 근처의 자택에서 열린 은혼 축하 파티에 수 많은 외국인, 일본인 및 한국인이 참석함으로써 언더우드 박사 부부에 대한 대단한 존경과 인기가 명백하게 확인되었다. 영사단을 포함한 거의 대부분의 저명 외국인 신사 숙녀, 많은 저명한 일본인 관리 부부, 약간의 한국인 귀족, 많은 유명한 한국인들이 그들 부부를 촉하하기 위해 방문했으며, 방들은 완전히 그들로 가득 찼다. 많은 손님들은 주인 부부에게 그들의 축하를 담은 귀중한 선물을 증정하였다. 서울의 장로회 학교의 학생 전체는 교사의 인도로 학교에 두드러진 공헌을 한 언더우드 박사 부부를 축하하기 위해 방문했다.

언더우드 박사 부부는 그들의 특징적인 친절과 예의로 하객들을 맞이했다. 자신의 진정한 축하를 표현한 고 선교사는 필자에게 자신이 끼고 있는 큰 진주가 달린 금반지를 보여주면서, 이것은 자신이 결혼할 때 전 황제가 자신에 주었던 선물이라고 말했다.[119] 이 설명에 따라 필자는 언더우드 박사 부부가 한국인들의 영적 향상을 위해 최소한 4반세기를 조선에서 활동한 것으로 결론지었다. 필자는 그날 오후 각계를 대표하는 사람들이 보여준 그나 큰 존경과 사랑을 확인한 것이 놀랍지 않았다. 사실 언더우드 부부의 이름은 조선에서 집에서 흔히 쓰는 단어이며, 모든 한국 기독교신자가 존경과 호의로 이야기한다. 그것은 다년간 자기희생과 고상한 사역을 했던 열매이며, 그들은 현재 자신들이 차지하고 있는 영광스런 자리를 받을 만하다. 우리는 진정으로 그들 모두가 행복하며, 금혼 축하 때까지 살기를 희망한다.

119) 고종을 의미한다.

Silver Wedding of Dr. and Mrs. Underwood, (March 15, 1914). PHS RG 360.

Silver Wedding of Dr. and Mrs. Underwood
March 15, 1914.

The great esteem and popularity, in which a great many foreign residents, Japanese and Koreans hold Dr. H. G. Underwood and Mrs. Underwood were unmistakably demonstrated on Friday afternoon when they celebrated their silver wedding by givings an "at home" at their residence near the South Gate. Almost all the notable foreign ladies and gentlemen, including members of the Consular corps, many prominent Japanese officials and their wives, some Koreans peers and many distinguished Koreans called on them to offer their congratulations and the rooms were literally packed with them. Many of the visitors presented the host and, hostess with valuable articles in token of their congratulations. The entire body of students of the Presbyterian Academy in Seoul, led by their teachers also came to express their felicitations to Dr. and Mrs. Underwood, who have rendered distinguished service to the school.

Dr. and. Mrs. Underwood received their guests with their characteristic hospitality and courtesy. To the writer, who offered his sincere congratulations, the veteran missionary showed a gold ring set with a big pearl which he was wearing, saying that it was the gift of the Ex-emperor of Korea on the occasion of his marriage. From this statement, the writer concluded that Dr. and Mrs. Underwood had spent at least a quarter of a century in Chosen working for the spiritual uplifting of the Korean people. The writer has not surprised to see the great esteem and love shown them by representative people that afternoon. In fact the names of Dr. and Mrs. Underwood are household words in Chosen and are spoken by all Christian Koreans with respect and affection. It is the fruit of many years of self-sacrificing and humane work and they well deserve the honoured position they occupy today. We sincerely wish them all happiness and hope that they will live to celebrate their golden wedding.

19141103

호러스 그랜트 언더우드의 개인 기록, (1914년 11월 3일). PHS RG 360.

The Board of Foreign Missions
of the
Presbyterian Church In the U.S.A.
156 Fifth Avenue

기입한 후 보낼 것

1916년 10월 12일 사망

개인기록 호러스 그랜트 언더우드

출생지 및 날자 영국 런던, 1859년 7월 19일 부모의 이름 존 언더우드

임명 당시 미국내 주소 뉴저지 주 뉴더햄 " " 엘리자베스 메어

결혼전 이름, 릴리어스 스털링 호튼

부인 결혼일, 1889년 3월 13일

출생지 및 날자, 1851년 6월 21일

임명 당시 미국내 주소, 일리노이 주 시카고

자녀 - 이름 및 출생일, 호러스 호튼, 서울 1890년 9월 6일

선교부, 한국

임명일, 1884년 7월 28일

선교지 도착

~~미국~~ 출발일, 1885년 4월 5일

부인의 임명일, 1887년 4월 4일

부인의 미국 출발일, 1888년 1월

교육 - 교육을 받은 가관의 이름과 졸업일,

콕스공립학교, 런던

디에학교, 불로뉴 쉬르 메르, 프랑스

해스부룩학원, 저지 시티

뉴욕대학교, 뉴욕

뉴브런즈윅신학교, 뉴저지 주

이전 직업 (있다면),

미국의 소속 교회, 화란개혁 및 장로교회

임명 당시 소속 노회, 저지 시티 노회

미국 내 가까운 친척의 이름과 주소.

존 T. 언더우드	비지 가 30번지
조지 P. 코나드	블루클린 워싱턴 가 361번지
클래런스 스티븐스 부인	핏츠필드, 매사추세츠
찰스 이건 주니어 부인	테러스 뷰에나파크,

미국 내 찬헌 친구 2~3명의 이름과 주소

날자 11월 3일 19 14년

서명 호러스 G. 언더우드

양식 1750

Personal Record of Horace Grant Underwood, (Nov. 3rd, 1914). PHS RG 360.

The Board of Foreign Missions
of the
Presbyterian Church In the U.S.A.
156 Fifth Avenue

To be Filled out and Returned

Died, Oct. 12, 1916

Personal Record of Horace Grant Underwood

Place and date of birth London, Eng.
July 19, 1859

Parents' full names John Underwood
" " " Elizabeth Marie

Home in the U. S. when appointed, New Durham, N. J.

Maiden Name, Lillias Sterling Horton

Wife: Date of marriage, March 13, 1889

Place and date of birth, June 21, 1851

Home in the U. S. when appointed, Chicago, Ill.

Children - Names and dates of birth, Horace Horton. Seoul, Sept 6th, 1890

Mission, Korea

Date of Appointment, July 28, 1884

Arrival on Field

~~Date of Departure from U. S.~~, April 5, 1885

Date of Appointment of wife, April 4, 1887

Date of Departure of wife from U. S., January 1888

Education - Names of Institutions where you have studied, and dated of graduation,

Cox's Collegiate Inst., London

Ecole Die, Bonlongue Sur Mer, France

Hasbrouk Institute, Jersey City

N. Y. University

New Brunswick Theol. Sem., N. J.

Former occupation (if any),

Church connection in U.S., Dutch Reformed & Presbyterian

Presbyterial connection when appointed, Presbytery of Jersey City

Names and addresses of nearest relatives in U. S.,

John T. Underwood	30 Vesay Street
Geo. P. Conard	361 Washington Ave., Brooklyn
Mrs. Clarence Stphens	Pittsfield Mass.
Mrs. Cha. Ragan, Junior	Ferrace Buena Park,

Names and addresses of two or three intimate friends in the U. S.

Date Nov. 3rd 19 14

Signature, in full Horace G. Underwood

Form 1750

3.
기타

18930227

미국 여권 신청서, 1795~1925, (호러스 G. 언더우드, 1893년 2월 27일).

[1889년 양식.]

여권 수수료, ... $1.00
신청서를 2매 작성하는 수수료, ... .50
선서를 2매 발급하는 수수료, ... .50

귀화인

-----=-----

번호 868호 발행, 2월 27일, 1893

나, 호러스 G. 언더우드 는 귀화한 충실한 미국 시민으로서, 런던 에 있는 미국공사관에 본인과, 아내 릴리어스 H., 그리고 18 90년 9월 6 일 한국 서울에서 출생한, 어린 애인 호러스 H. 와 함께 여권을 신청하는 바입니다.

나는 1859년 7월 19일 영국 런던 에서 출생했으며; 1873년 2월 런던 에서 덴마크호 에 승선하여 미국으로 이주했으며; 1873 년부터 1884 년 까지 계속 11 년 동안 뉴저지 주 뉴더햄 에서 거주했으며; 첨부한 귀화 증명서에서 보듯 1882년 10월 26일 뉴저지 주 뉴브런즈윅 소재의 민사 법원에서 미국 시민으로 귀화했으며; 나는 18__년 __월 __일 발행된 여권 번호 ______의 소지인으로서 이제 반납하며; 나는 그 증명서 ~~및 여권~~에 기술된 동일인이며; 나는 미국에 거주하는데, 주소는 뉴욕 주 브루클린 에서 거주하고 목회 의 직업에 종사하고 있으며; 최근 나는 1893년 2월 1일 브리태니커 호 에 승선하여 미국을 떠나 1893년 2월 10일 리버풀 에 도착했으며; 나는 1893년 2월 11일부터 런던 에 거주하고 있으며; 나는 잠시 웨스트릭 29번지, 런던, 웨스트 에 거주하고 있으며; 7년 내에 미국으로 돌아 와 거주하고 시민으로서 의무를 다 할 예정임을 엄숙히 선서합니다.

나는 미국 장로회 선교부의 선교사로서 동양을 여행하기 위해 여권의 발급을 희망합니다.

충성의 서약

더욱이, 나는 해외 및 국내의 모든 적에 대해 미국의 헌법을 유지하고 방어하며; 진실된 믿음과 충성을 지니고; 주저하지 않고 회피의 목적이 없이 자유의사로 이러한 의무를 받아들인다는 것을 맹세코 엄숙하게 선서합니다. 그러니 신이여 나를 도우소서

호러스 G. 언더우드

런던 의 미국 공사관

1893년 2월 27일 내 앞에서 선서함

오디사

신청자의 인상착의

나이	: 33 세	입	: 콧수염
신장	: 5 피트, 8 인치,	턱	: 턱수염
이마	: 높음	모발	: 갈색
눈	: 갈색	피부색	: 건강함
코	: 보통	얼굴	: 타원형

신원 증명

________, 18__

나는 위 __________ 를 개인적으로 알고 있으며, 귀화 증명서에 기술된 범위 안에서 동일인임을 알고 있고 진술서에 언급된 사실들이 내가 알고 믿는 한 틀림없다고 맹세합니다.

(위의 선교부의 재무, 더블유 W. 덜레스, 주니어의 편지)

Is ____________

(증인의 주소) ____________

주의. – 이 양식은 두 장을 작성하며, 하나는 공사관에 보관되며, 다른 하나는 사분기 마다 미국 국무부로 보낸다. 지원자가 작성하는 경우 수수료를 부과하지 않는다.

U. S. Passport Application, 1795~1925, (Horace G. Underwood, Feb. 27, 1893).

[Edition of 1889.]

Naturalized.

Fee for Passport,	$1.00
Fee for filling out application in duplicate,	.50
Fee for administering oath in duplicate,	.50

No. 868 Issued, February 27 , 18 93

I, Horace G. Underwood a naturalized and loyal citizen of the United States, hereby apply to the Legation of the United Stated at London for a passport for myself, accompanied by my wife Lilias H. and, minor children, as follows, Horace H. , born at Seoul, Korea don the 6 day of September 18 90 , and a nursery governess

I solemnly swear that I was born at London, England on or about the 19 day of July , 1859; that I emigrated to the United States, sailing on board the Denmark from London , on or about the month day of February , 1873; that I resided 11 years, uninterruptedly, in the United States, from 1873 to 1884 at New Durham, N. J. ; that I was naturalized as a citizen of the United States before the Common Pleas Court of New Jersey at New Brunswick on the 26 day of the October 1882 as shown by the accompanying Certificate of Naturalization; ~~that I am the bearer of Passport No. , issued by on the day of 18 , which is returned herewith~~; that I am the identical person referred to in said certificate ~~and passport~~; that I am domiciled in the United States, my permanent residence being at Brooklyn , in the State of New York where I follow the occupation of clergyman ; that I last left the United States on the 1 day of February , 1893, on the board the Britannica arriving in Liverpool the 10 day of February , 1893; that I am now temporarily residing at 29 Westurick London, W. , and that I intend to return to the United States within seven years with a purpose of residing and performing the duties of citizenship therein.

I desire the passport for the purpose of travelling in the East, as a Missionary for the Presbyterian Board of Missions of the United States.

Oath of Allegiance.

Further, I do solemnly swear that I will support and defend the Constitution of the United States against all enemies, foreign and domestic; that I will bear true faith and allegiance to the same; and that I take this obligation freely, without any mental reservation or purpose of evasion: So help me God,

Horace G. Underwood

Legation of the United States at London

Sworn to before me, this 27th day of February , 1893

Audersa

Description of Applicant

Age: 33 years

Stature: 5 feet, 8 inched, Eng.

Forehead: high

Eyes: brown

Nose: regular

Mouth; moustache

Chin: bearded

Hair: brown

Complexion: frcsh

Face: oval

Identification

__________, 18_

I hereby certify hat I know the above named _________ personally, and know h__ to be the identical person referred to in the within-described Certificate of Naturalization, and that the facts stated in h__ affldavit are true to the best of my knowledge and belief.

(Letter from W. W. Dulles, Jr. Treasurer of the above named Board of Missions.)

____

Address of witness, __________

Note. - This form is to be filled out in duplication, one copy being retained on the files of the Legation and the other forwarded with the quarterly returns to the Department of State. It may be so filled out by the applicant, in which case no fee therefor is chargeable.

[EDITION OF 1889.]

NATURALIZED.

Fee for Passport, - - - $1.00
Fee for filling out application in duplicate, - - .50
Fee for administering oath in duplicate, - - .50

No. 868 ISSUED, February 27, 1893

I, Horace G. Underwood a naturalized and loyal citizen of the United States, hereby apply to the Legation of the United States at London for a passport for myself, accompanied by my wife Lilias H., and minor child, as follows: Horace H., born at Seoul, Korea on the 6 day of September, 1890 and a nursery governess

I solemnly swear that I was born at London, England on or about the 19 day of July, 1859; that I emigrated to the United States, sailing on board the "Denmark", from London, on or about the month of February, 1873; that I resided 11 years, uninterruptedly, in the United States, from 1873 to 1884, at New Durham, N. J.; that I was naturalized as a citizen of the United States before the Common Pleas Court of New Jersey at New Brunswick, on the 26 day of October, 1882 as shown by the accompanying Certificate of Naturalization; ~~that I am the bearer of Passport No. ......, issued by ...... on the ...... day of ......, 18......, which is returned herewith~~; that I am the identical person referred to in said certificate ~~and passport~~; that I am domiciled in the United States, my permanent residence therein being at Brooklyn, in the State of New York, where I follow the occupation of clergyman; that I last left the United States on the 1 day of February, 1893 on board the Britannic arriving in Liverpool the 10 day of February, 1893; that I have resided in London since the 11 day of February, 1893; that I am now temporarily residing at 29 Westwick Gdns, London, W. and that I intend to return to the United States within seven years with a purpose of residing and performing the duties of citizenship therein.

I desire the passport for the purpose of travelling in the East, as a Missionary for the Presbyterian Board of Missions of the United States.

OATH OF ALLEGIANCE.

Further, I do solemnly swear that I will support and defend the Constitution of the United States against all enemies, foreign and domestic; that I will bear true faith and allegiance to the same; and that I take this obligation freely, without any mental reservation or purpose of evasion: So HELP ME GOD.

H. G. Underwood

LEGATION OF THE UNITED STATES AT London

Sworn to before me, this 27 day of February, 1893.

[illegible] Anderson

DESCRIPTION OF APPLICANT.

Age: 33 years.	Mouth: moustache
Stature: 5 feet, 8 inches, Eng.	Chin: bearded
Forehead: high	Hair: brown
Eyes: brown	Complexion: fresh
Nose: regular	Face: oval

IDENTIFICATION.

......, 18......

I hereby certify that I know the above-named ...... personally, and know h...... to be the identical person referred to in the within-described Certificate of Naturalization, and that the facts stated in h...... affidavit are true to the best of my knowledge and belief.

(Letter from W. W. Dulles, Jr., Treasurer of the above-named Board of Missions.) [ADDRESS OF WITNESS.]

NOTE.—This form is to be filled out in duplicate, one copy being retained on the files of the Legation and the other forwarded with the quarterly returns to the Department of State. It may be so filled out by the applicant, in which case no fee therefor is chargeable.

자료 4-3 *U. S. Passport Application, 1795~1925*, (Horace G. Underwood, Feb. 27, 1893).

언더우드 내한 관련 연표

1859. 7. 19.	존 언더우드와 엘리자베스 그랜트 매리 사이의 3남, 넷째로 런던에서 출생
1865. 2사분기	모친, 영국 런던 판크라스에서 사망
–	부친, 이후 캐롤라인과 재혼
–	런던 집 근처의 콕스공립학교에서 초등 교육을 받음
1869.	프랑스 불로뉴 쉬르 메르에 있는 천주교 남학교(Ecole Die)에 입학
1872	부친, 아버지 미국으로 이주하여 뉴더햄에 정착
1873. 2.	계모 캐롤라인, 존 T., 프레데릭, 호러스 및 헬렌이 런던 출발
1873. 3. 3.	계모 캐롤라인 등이 뉴욕 도착
1874. 3. 20.	계모 캐롤라인 사망
–	뉴저지 주 저지 시티의 해스브룩학원에 다님
1874. 12. 5.	뉴저지 주 노스 버겐의 그로브 개혁교회에 출석
1875. 5. 23.	누나 헬렌, 뉴욕에 도착
1877. 1. 1.	그로브교회의 메이본 목사로부터 희랍어를 배움
1877. 6. 12.	뉴욕대학교 입학 허가
1877. 9. 19.	뉴욕대학교 입학
1879. 1.	뉴욕대학교 필로머시언 소사이어티의 편집인으로 활동
1879. 7.	뉴욕대학교 필로머시언 소사이어티의 제2부회장으로 선임
1880. 3. 26.	3학년 웅변대회에서 웹스터 상을 수여 받음
1880. 7.	뉴욕대학교에서 발행하는 *The University Quarterly*의 편집인으로 활동
1881. 6. 7.	부친 사망. 그로브 교회 묘지에 안장
1881. 6. 23.	뉴욕대학교 졸업
1881. 9. 20.	뉴브런즈윅신학교 입학
	럿거스대학 대학원 입학

1882.	형 존이 브루클린에서 사업을 시작한 것으로 추정됨
1883. 여름	목사가 없던 뉴저지 주 폼프턴 교회에서 활동
1882. 10. 26	미국 시민권을 받음
1883. 9.	규정 변경으로 럿거스대학 대학원에서 뉴욕대학교 대학원으로 전학함
1884. 5.	뉴브런즈윅신학교 졸업
1884. 2.	개혁교회 선교본부에 한국 선교사로 보내줄 것을 지원했으나 거절됨
1884. 6. 19.	뉴욕대학교에서 문학석사 학위 받음
1884. 7. 3.	뉴욕대학교 헨리 M. 베어드의 추천서가 보내짐
	뉴욕의 헨리 N. 콥이 미국 북장로회 해외선교본부로 편지를 보냄
	뉴저지 주 뉴브런즈윅의 윌리엄 V. V. 메이본이 미국 북장로회 해외선교본부로 편지를 보냄
1884. 7. 5.	새뮤얼 M. 우드브리지 학장이 장로교회 해외선교본부로 편지를 보냄
	뉴저지 주 뉴브런즈윅의 토머스 C. 이스턴이 장로교회 해외선교본부로 편지를 보냄
1884. 7. 7.	조지 W. 코클리의 증명서가 보내짐
1884. 7. 10.	미국 북장로회 해외선교본부에 한국의 선교사 자원 편지를 보냄
	하워드 크로스비의 추천서가 보내짐
	제임스 A. 블레이크의 건강 증명서가 보내짐
1884. 7. 14.	언더우드의 지원이 미국 북장로회 해외선교본부로의 회의에 제출됨 (2주 동안 공람)
1884. 7. 28.	미국 북장로회 해외선교본부로부터 한국의 첫 목회 선교사로 임명됨
여름	영국 방문
1884. 11. 11.	뉴브런즈윅 노회로부터 목사 안수를 받음

	저지 시티 장로회 노회로 이적됨
1884. 12. 1.	형 존이 미국 시민권을 받음
1884. 12. 2.	저지 시티 장로회 노회에 참석하여 자신의 자질과 동기를 설명함
1884. 12. 22.	시카고에서 샌프란시스코를 향해가는 기차 속에서 동생 헬렌에게 편지 보냄
1885. 1. 25.	일본 요코하마에 도착
1885. 1. 26.	엘린우드에게 첫 편지를 보냄
1885. 3. 26	요코하마를 출발함
1885. 4. 2.	부산 도착
1885. 4. 5.	제물포에 도착
	서울에 들어옴
1885. 4. 9.	한국에서 엘린우드에게 첫 편지를 보냄

• 참고자료

A General Catalogue of the University of the City of New York, Departments of Arts and Science. New York: D. O Crawford & Co., No. 62 Fulton Street, 1882.

Alexander McLean, *History of Jersey City, N. J.: A Record of its Early Settlement and Corporate Progress.* Press of the Jersey City Printing Company, 1895.

Biographical Catalogue of the Chancellors, Professors and Graduates of the Department of Arts and Science of the University of the City of New York. The Alumni Association, New York, 1894.

Bookseller, *Pigot and Co's Commercial Directory of London*, 1825~6.

Burial Record, Grove Church Cemetery, North Bergen, N. J.

Catalogue of the Officers and Students of Rutgers College, New Brunswick, N. J., 1881-'82, 1882~'83, 1884~'5.

Catalogue of the Officers and Students of the Theological Seminary of the Reformed (Dutch) Church in America, New Brunswick, N. J., 1881~'82, 1882~'83, 1883~'84.

Catalogue of the University of the City of New York, 1876~77, 1877~78, 1878~79, 1879~80, 1880~1.

Church Members, Grove Reformed Church, North Bergen, N. J.

Class Merit Book, July 1835~June 1888, New York University.

Commencement Week, 1881, University of the City of New-York.

Critchett & Woods, *The Post-Office Annual Directory for 1812, 1814, 1816, 1817, 1819, 1820, 1829.*

England & Wales, FreeBMD Birth Index, 1837~1915.

England & Wales, FreeBMD Death Index, 1837~1915.

England & Wales, Non-Conformist and Non-Parochial Registers, 1567~1970.

England Census, 1851, 1861, 1871

England, Select Births and Christenings, 1538~1975.

England, Select Marriages, 1538~1973.

Fifty-first Commencement, 1884, University of the City of New York.

Find A Grave Index, 1600s~Current.

Henry N. Cobb, *A Century of Missions in the Reformed Church in America 1796~1896.* Board of Foreign Missions: New York, ca. 1900.

Holden's Annual London and Country Directory, of the United Kingdoms, and Wales, in Three Volumes, for the Year 1811. First Volume, London Part, London, 1811.

Horace G. Underwood, Letter to Helen M. Underwood, (Dec. 22nd, 1884).
Horace G. Underwood, Reminiscences. *Quarto Centennial Papers Read Before the Korea.*
Mission of the Presbyterian Church in the U. S. A. at the Annual Meeting in Pyeng Yang, August 27, 1909.
Horace Newton Allen papers, New York Public Library.
Howard J. Banker, *The Underwood Families of America. In Two Volumes, Volume 2, 1913.*
Lain's Brooklyn Directory for the Year Ending May 1, 1886, 1894.
Lillias H. Underwood, *Underwood of Korea.* Fleming H. Revell Company, New York, 1918.
London, England, Marriages and Banns, 1754~1921.
Matriculation Book, 1853~1893, Vol. 2, New York University.
Minutes of the Particular Synod of New Brunswick, Convened at New Brunswick, 1883, 1884, 1885.
Minutes Volume 4~5, Presbyterian Historical Society.
New Jersey, Deaths and Burials Index, 1798~1971.
New York Herald.
New York Tribune.
New York University, Eightieth Commencement, June 5th, 1912.
New York, Marriage Index, 1866~1937.
New York, Passenger Lists, 1820~1957.
New York, State Census, 1892, 1905.
Presbyterian Church in the U. S. A. Board of Foreign Missions. Departments of Missionary Personnel Records, Secretaries' files, 1832~1952.
Presbyterian Church in the U. S. A. Board of Foreign Missions. Missions Correspondence and Reports 1833~1911.
Presbyterian Church in the U. S. A. Board of Foreign Missions. Secretaries' files, 1829~95.
Sixtieth Commencement, 1892. University of the City of New York, June 9th, 1892.
The Foreign Missionary.
The New York City Directory for the Year 1892.
The New York Times.
The Report of the Board of Foreign Missions, of the Reformed Church in America, 1884, 1885, 1890, 1891.
The University Quarterly, New York University, 2(2), Jan. 1879, 2(4), July 1879, 3(4), July 1880.
Theodore Francis Jones, *New York University, 1832:* 1932, The New York University Press, 1933.

Trow's New York City Directory, 1883, 1885, 1886, 1887, 1888, 1890, 1892, 1894

Truth.

U. S. Passport Application, 1795~1925.

United States Federal Census, 1880, 1900, 1910, 1930.

University of the City of New York, Catalogue and Announcements 1884~1885. Printed for the University, May, 1885, p. 65.

Web: RootsWeb Death Index, 1796~2010.

찾아보기

D

E

F

G

H

W